ALSO BY RACHEL HARRIS

Children Learn What They Live
(with Dorothy Law Nolte)

20-Minute Retreats

20-MINUTE RETREATS

Revive Your Spirits
in Just Minutes a Day with
Simple Self-Led Exercises

RACHEL HARRIS, PH.D.
PRODUCED BY THE PHILIP LIEF GROUP, INC.

An Owl Book   ◆   Henry Holt and Company   ◆   New York

Henry Holt and Company, LLC
Publishers since 1866
115 West 18th Street
New York, New York 10011

Henry Holt ® is a registered trademark of Henry Holt and Company, LLC.
Copyright © 2000 by The Philip Lief Group and Rachel Harris, Ph.D.
All rights reserved.
Published in Canada by Fitzhenry & Whiteside Ltd.,
195 Allstate Parkway, Markham, Ontario L3R 4T8.

Library of Congress Cataloging-in-Publication Data
Harris, Rachel.
    20-minute retreats: revive your spirits in just minutes a day with simple self-led
  exercises / Rachel Harris. — 1st ed.
      p. cm.
  "An Owl book."
  Includes bibliographical references.
  ISBN 0-8050-6451-6 (pbk.)
    1. Retreats.   I. Title: Twenty minute retreats.   II. Title.
  BL628 .H37   2000
  158.1'2—dc21   99-049067

Henry Holt books are available for special promotions and premiums.
For details contact: Director, Special Markets.

First Edition 2000

Designed by Kate Nichols

Illustration on page 261 by Matthew Young Design

Printed in the United States of America

10 9 8 7 6 5 4 3 2 1

This book is dedicated to all the people who have trusted me to witness and participate in the unfolding of their lives during the past thirty years in my private practice in Miami, Florida, and Princeton, New Jersey, and in my workshops, especially at the Omega Institute in Rhinebeck, New York, and at the Esalen Institute in Big Sur, California.

Contents

Contents

Acknowledgments

I am deeply indebted to Judy Linden and Fiona Hinton of The Philip Lief Group, Inc., without whom this book would simply not exist. I would also like to thank Amelia Sheldon and the team at Henry Holt and Company for their belief in and commitment to *20-Minute Retreats*.

20-Minute Retreats

Introduction

There is only one journey. Going inside yourself.
—Rainer Maria Rilke

I retreat to learn how to be in the world in a different way. I retreat to remember how to experience the world of the spirit during my daily life. I retreat to reconnect with the divine that permeates all of existence. I retreat simply because I am called by the silence.

Some of us seem to be born with this inner yearning, a "great homesickness," as Rabbi Seymour Siegel calls it. Our search is to quench this thirst, to return to the experience of union, which is our spiritual home. Our life becomes a journey, a process of transformation.

I almost can't remember when I didn't see my life as a spiritual journey. Extended retreats have been a part of my life since adolescence, and it seemed natural to me to seek experiences from a variety of religious traditions. My mother had been an active member—simultaneously, not sequentially—of the Jewish center, the Quaker meeting, and the Unitarian Church. These religious organizations were part of her spiritual path, but her personal journey was unique to her.

As an adult, looking back, I can now say she was seeking to develop a nonjudgmental acceptance of her life, to learn how to be happy with what is. Growing up, I knew only that she was different from the cookie-baking moms. Although I yearned for those cookies, I was nurtured by an early awareness of life as a spiritual process.

The other "religion" to which my mother subscribed, actually with more zeal and belief than her traditional faiths, was psychotherapy. This was back in the 1950s, when psychotherapy was mentioned, if at all, only in hushed tones. While other girls my age accompanied their mothers to Daughters of the American Revolution meetings, I went with my mom to the state psychiatric hospital to visit with patients on the locked wards.

The retreats in this book reflect my life and my mother's influence. They are transtraditional, representing a variety of the world's religions, and they are also psychological, drawing from a range of therapeutic approaches. I make no distinction between the spiritual and psychological retreats, since the purpose of both is personal transformation. Retreats—both long and short, with companions and alone—transform us as we journey by opening us to those subtle spiritual realms that we instinctively crave.

This transformation process involves shedding layers of personality, beliefs, and acculturations, which form the veils separating us from the world of the spirit. The very way we perceive the world is an example of one of these layers. Just as a fish doesn't perceive the water it's in, we are likewise unaware of the veils separating us from the ultimate reality. We can peel away these layers, lifting the veils so we cleanse our "doors of perception." The world remains the same, it is we who are changed.

We undergo an inner shift so we can perceive the eternal shining through everyday life. Abraham Heschel, the twentieth-century Jewish philosopher, refers to this transformation as an "education in sensing the ineffable." This is what I personally seek from a retreat—a quiet timelessness to enter my own inner stillness. This is what nurtures my own inner transformation, allowing me to see the world through new eyes.

Retreats

Everybody has their own idea of what a retreat is. I once sent a dear friend to an introductory Buddhist retreat that sounded wonderful to me. Lawrence, a very eligible bachelor, thought he'd be spending the weekend with a group of sensitive women clad in Lycra and adept at unusual yoga positions. With this vision in mind, he was really looking forward to his first retreat experience, but what he got was quite different. Lawrence called me soon after his return. He'd spent the weekend in total silence with a group of women in sweatpants, meditating eight hours a day. He said it was an interesting experience but not what he'd hoped for.

Every retreat I've been to has been held in a beautiful location, from mountain valleys in California to orange groves in Florida. These settings often have a magical quality to them, as a world apart. The atmosphere is rarefied; the silence, exquisitely still. The people at these retreats are always compassionate and respectful. We pass each other silently on garden pathways, perhaps with a gentle smile and a slight bow. We understand our shared spiritual search and silently encourage one another along our journey. The retreat experience is so gentle and supportive, I begin to feel a certain kind of spiritual confidence, as if I've attained a new equilibrium. Surely I will feel nothing but peace and loving-kindness toward everyone. Surely this newfound equanimity will tame my hormonal roller coaster for good.

Then I return home. After I leave the retreat center, cars seem to whiz by at forty miles an hour, drivers passing with angry stares and familiar nonverbal gestures. I'm shocked, my sensibilities offended. But I tell myself to maintain my retreat frame of mind. Breathe in peace; breathe out calm. Dare I try a quick stop at the supermarket? I wisely decide against that but then realize I need gas. The attendant wipes my windshield. I observe the movement of the squeegee with mindful attention. He misses a spot, a rather obvious, in-the-middle-of-my-vision spot. Should I accept the spot without judgment? Should I say something to the attendant? Should I get out of the car and wipe it off myself? Within thirty minutes of leaving the retreat center, I am mired in the quicksand of my own mind. How could this have happened, and so soon? And I haven't even reached home yet to face the challenges that await me there—the usual relationship problems, work stress, and, last but not least, my own unique ways of overreacting—all of which try me at the heart of where I live. I'm still at the gas station, having thoughts of returning immediately to the retreat center.

Each person has their own unique retreat experience, but everyone I talk to has a similar reentry experience. Our ability to maintain equanimity is seriously challenged by our everyday lives. I know I need daily spiritual practice to renew and deepen my retreat experience. The retreats in this book meet this need for me, as I hope they will for others seeking to integrate their spiritual process into their daily lives.

A spiritual friend told me this story, attributed to Hari Das, an Indian yogi who has remained silent for about thirty years. Using a small chalkboard, Hari Das told my friend, a serious yoga student, "Every day we toss our consciousness up into the air, just like tossing a ball. Then one day, our consciousness stays up there."

Daily retreat time is a way to toss our consciousness up, to attain a higher perspective. It helps us develop our equanimity and not be swept away by our reactions, our feelings, or the circumstances of our stressful days. It helps us to stay centered no matter what is going on. The retreats I've collected here nurture and strengthen our ability to do that, to take a breath before we speak words we regret, to choose our actions with clear intention and awareness.

The purpose of a daily retreat, then, is to create a sacred time and space in which we can reconnect with the Spirit, experience the Divine. We take a break from our everyday lives so that we can once again remember who we really are, breathe the breath of God, hear the song of the Sacred, and respond.

Twenty-Minute Retreats

I have used these short retreats personally and have taught them professionally for the past thirty years. As a psychotherapist, I work within the context of people's spiritual journey, in my private practice and in workshops at the Esalen Institute in Big Sur, California, and the Omega Institute in Rhinebeck, New York. It's my belief that we're all in the process of learning from life, and sometimes therapy can help us do this more gracefully and with less suffering. But life itself remains the great teacher, and how we live each day is the true reflection of our spiritual journey.

Our individual quest and the challenges we face are unique. Some of the retreats here will appeal to you more than others. Embrace and use your favorites. My favorite retreats are the ones that use emotional drawings. I have no formal art training, so I feel particularly free to scribble and smear the oil pastels with abandon. I have no critical judgments and no expectations about how the drawings I create should look. I'm interested only in how I feel drawing them and looking at them. The amazing thing I have found with my drawings is that, as I continued doing them, patterns spontaneously emerged.

One rainy afternoon, I pushed the living room furniture out of the way and laid out a year's worth of drawings on the carpet. There were more than fifty drawings, arranged in the order in which they had been made. Then I stood on a chair to get a higher perspective. To my surprise, I saw a pattern. Drawings done at different times were clearly related, one leading into the other. A spot of black in one drawing grew into a shadowy tornado a few drawings later. Angry red spikes gradually turned into yellow-orange rays of sun. I felt I was looking at the movements of my unconscious, that this was a glimpse into the workings of my inner self. Likewise, these spiritual exercises can open new passages into and visions of our inner landscape. We can use them to nurture and heal ourselves in new and unexpected ways as part of our spiritual unfolding.

How to Use This Book

I hope you will use this book to further your personal spiritual journey, and since our paths unfold in such unique ways, I trust that you will adapt the material here to suit you personally. There is often mystery involved in the unfolding of our spiritual lives, and that is as it should be, for we cannot control the movement of the spirit.

The specific examples of how different people use the retreats are all taken from my workshops or private practice. Names have been changed to protect privacy, and some examples are combined from more than one person. It has been a privilege for me to witness and nurture the personal development and spiritual lives of the people described in this book. They have served as teachers for me, often walking into my office just when I needed the specific lesson illustrated by their life stories. I am profoundly grateful to have shared in their lives. I have chosen to alter the telling of these life examples so they read not as therapy but rather as real people using the retreats from this book. In this way, they serve as models for how you, the reader, can actually use these retreats in your own life.

The retreats are organized into themes that touch on different aspects of our spiritual journey: faith, forgiveness, gratitude, healing, intuition, joy, love, patience, peace, relaxation, self-acceptance, and self-care. I've devoted a chapter to each of these themes, exploring how they may emerge in our lives. Even though I present each of them individually, they are, in fact, inseparable. Gratitude can lead into joy and love, just as love can lead into gratitude or joy. Relaxation is as much a part of peace as peace plays a role in relaxation. And, of course, faith and healing are intertwined. Our journey is not linear; we curve and backtrack, and sometimes get lost. However, I can assure you that no matter where you are on your personal path, these themes will always be relevant.

Please feel free to use the themes and the variety of retreats within each chapter in the order that best meets your personal needs. All of us will be drawn to different retreats at different times in our lives. The way to know which ones to pursue is to simply trust your immediate response to the chapter themes or individual retreats as you make your selection. Trust what feels right to you as you read the instructions, for you can always alter the details to meet your personal needs. At best, this book may function as a signpost, illuminating the direction you choose as you follow your own path. However, the real wisdom and guidance exist within you.

This book contains a wide assortment of self-led retreats. Most take twenty minutes, others five, and some just one minute. Also included are real-life examples that illustrate how you can use retreats creatively to help you as you face a variety of life situations. These personal stories demonstrate how one retreat can naturally lead to the practice of another retreat as the circumstances change or you develop.

Chapter 1, "Retreats for the Spiritual Journey," lays the foundation for understanding how retreats help us along our spiritual path. The retreats here offer us the silence and solitude we need to experience what is holy within each of us and, in so doing, nurture and guide our spiritual unfolding.

Chapter 2, "Everything You Need to Know to Retreat," will give you all the practical information you need to actually start using retreats in your everyday life. In it, I detail how to create a sacred space for your retreats and what retreat tools and materials you will need for the chapters ahead. Here I describe the various wisdom traditions inspiring the retreats as well as definitions of specific techniques you will encounter in these pages. Last, chapter 2 explains how using daily retreats will help you become more adept at shifting back and forth between your quiet, inner world and your outer life.

Chapters 3 through 14 are each dedicated to one of the twelve retreat themes mentioned earlier. These themes represent common human concerns that weave and overlap through our spiritual lives as we develop and mature. Each represents a process, not a final destination; it is not our goal to be finished with them. In fact, we revisit these themes many times as our spiritual lives unfold over the years, and as we mature spiritually, our experience of specific retreats also changes and evolves.

The final chapter, "In the World," provides guidelines for adapting the retreat instructions to use when you're at work, traveling, or making a retreat with a group of kindred spirits. It also provides tips on how to retreat even when you're emotionally upset or seriously stressed, which are, of course, the times when you most need to retreat.

I've enjoyed creating these retreat practices during my years as both a participant and leader of retreats and workshops. They have all been a part of my personal journey at different times in my life. It gives me great pleasure to share them with you. It is my hope that they will enliven your inner life, help you to feel more whole, and awaken your spirit.

O moon above the mountains' rim,
please shine a little further on my path.

—Izumi Shikibu, poet

1

Retreats for
the Spiritual Journey

*The Spiritual Path is an infinite journey across
a shoreless ocean.*

— Llewellyn Vaughan-Lee,
Jungian psychologist and Sufi

The concept of a sacred journey is ancient. The Lakota Indians described it as "hearing with the ear of the heart, returning home like the flight of the jay." It is a journey guided by poetic images rather than maps, landmarks, or directions. During our journey we turn inward into the silence. The silence calls to us, beckoning us to cross a threshold and enter the spiritual dimension. This is the spiritual life—the choice of the inward journey as a sacred path. It is the search for the soul, and we are transformed as we travel.

Retreats are an important part of our spiritual journey. They give us time to turn our attention away from mundane concerns so we can attend to that "still small voice inside us," as the Quakers say. Retreats give us an opportunity for undiluted concentration in which we can attune our subtle awareness to our experience of the spirit. Then, when we return to the world, we can continue to perceive this presence in the midst of our daily lives, within us, within others, and in the very fabric of the world.

In our fast-paced lives, we desperately need retreats to regain our perspective, help us balance our inner and outer lives. Otherwise we are at risk for being carried away by the powerful tides and undertow of our mass media, electronic communications, and consumer culture, not to mention office meetings or our children's soccer games and dance recitals. The structure of a retreat gives us a chance to just say no to incessant stress and time pressure, so we can balance the busyness of our outer lives with the quiet calmness of our inner center.

Some of us need regular brief retreats to quench our spiritual yearning. We need the quiet time to commune with the sacred as much as we need to eat or sleep. No other activity, achievement, or excitement will satisfy. Steve, a forty-year-old computer programmer, was this kind of person. He knew what stress was and had seen plenty of colleagues burn out. He knew what he needed for his own sanity and spiritual peace of mind. Without his twenty minutes of quiet reflection every morning, his fast-paced work-day seemed empty, bordering on the absurd, and he felt uncomfortably pressured. Steve generally preferred retreats that focused on breathing with awareness, helping him to enter a wonderful inner world of silence. After that, he was ready for anything.

Karen, on the other hand, liked to practice her daily retreats in the evening. She was a thirty-two-year-old graphic designer who worked with a group of people who were unusually warm and supportive. At the end of the day, she needed quiet time for herself. She enjoyed the variety of the retreat activities and the psychological nature of the journaling exercises. Karen would often sit in bed to write in her journal just before going to sleep.

Some people, like Steven and Karen, know they yearn for a retreat and are restless when they don't heed that call. But if you have never retreated, how do you know it's what you crave? Here are some clues.

SIGNS THAT YOU NEED TO RETREAT

1. You can hardly remember the last time you had a moment to yourself.
2. You feel an unquenchable inner yearning.
3. You don't laugh as much as you used to.
4. All you do is take care of others' needs, neglecting your own.
5. Your heart feels closed.

6. You rush everywhere.
7. You don't remember your dreams.
8. You feel disconnected, without an inner center.
9. You know there's more to life, but you don't know what it is or what to do about it.
10. You comment to friends that you feel like you're running on empty.
11. With no energy to do anything else, you spend evenings and weekends zoned out in front of the TV.
12. You want to experience more love in your life.

Most of us can identify with at least some of these signs, but if more than half of them are true for you, it is clear you need to turn your attention to your spiritual life. Taking twenty minutes a day to retreat will give you the silence, solitude, and sacred time to remember the divine in yourself and in your life.

There is no enlightenment outside of daily life.

—Thich Nhat Hanh, Vietnamese Buddhist monk

Twenty-Minute Retreats

A retreat can be anything that allows us to intentionally enter another world where time slows to nonexistence, silence prevails, and a certain tranquillity permeates the atmosphere. Here, in this sacred space, we can replenish our souls, restoring our connection to the eternal.

A daily retreat nurtures our inner life and encourages our progress along our unique spiritual journey. I have provided a variety of retreats in this book so that you can explore and find your favorite entries into the quiet, nurturing space of calm within you. The instructions for each retreat are listed step-by-step so they can easily be understood and practiced. They provide a structure, allowing us to be actively involved and engaged in the spiritual exercises. Organized by theme, each chapter focuses on retreats for expressing one aspect of the spiritual journey: faith, forgiveness, gratitude, healing, intuition, joy, love, patience, peace, relaxation, self-acceptance, and self-care. We will each encounter these themes as we move through life, and the retreats within them give us the opportunity to become more aware of how they are currently manifesting in our lives. Practicing regular retreats will make a difference in how we deal with these themes as they arise, thus changing the course of our lives. It's my experience that even twenty minutes a day can enhance the clarity with which we approach life and its daily choices.

One example can be drawn from the experience of Fred, a thirty-five-year-old manager, who was stuck in an ongoing personality conflict with his boss. Every day was miserable, and Fred saw no way out. However, he began practicing specific retreats on forgiveness and relaxation, which enabled him to change how he perceived and felt about his boss, and perhaps most important, how he behaved in the office. Fred no longer seemed to have a chip on his shoulder. Needless to say, his boss noticed this positive change and began asking Fred for his opinion more frequently, even giving Fred more responsibility and decision-making power. Fred's work with forgiveness and relaxation helped him to create a positive outcome from a difficult situation.

I've selected retreats for each chapter to cultivate the various themes, infusing them with energy and consciousness so that they deepen and expand in our daily lives. The term *cultivate* comes from horticulture and encompasses the whole process of preparing the soil, planting the seed, nurturing the plant, and yes, even weeding the environment. This metaphor describes our relationship to our spiritual life. Just as we cannot hurry a plant in its growth cycle, we cannot force our own inner development. We can only prepare, seed, nurture, and weed. Daily retreats help us tend our inner garden and, with this steady attention, we often find ourselves growing and blossoming in ways we couldn't have imagined or foreseen.

The retreats described here are inspired by a variety of cultures and religions, from native peoples, Judaism, Christianity, Islam, Hinduism, and Buddhism. This multicultural, transtraditional approach reflects the current blossoming of the spiritual revolution, evidenced by the fact that never before have we had such access to sacred texts or spiritual teachers of all the world's great wisdom traditions. Our daily retreat practice can be enriched by this wide range of techniques and philosophies, giving us the opportunity to select the ones that suit us the best.

Daily Retreat Time

I realize that setting aside twenty minutes a day is not always easy. We are experts at coming up with reasons why we can't find the time. The five-minute retreat entitled "No Time to Retreat" will help you honestly clarify your daily commitment to your spiritual life. Devoting twenty minutes a day requires discipline as well as a re-prioritizing of our lives. Concretely put, we have to be willing to say, "My spiritual life is as important to me as brushing my teeth, reading the paper, or talking on the phone." For the truth is that we need daily spiritual practice to sustain our journey, and nothing can compensate for the lack of it.

This book includes dozens of self-led twenty-minute retreats, as well as one-minute and five-minute retreats that serve as reminders of our inner life while we are in the midst of our busyness. The idea for the shorter retreats emerged spontaneously from my writers' group. They are all high-powered career women who enthusiastically embraced the idea of a retreat book, yet immediately asked if they couldn't do the retreats while they were ironing or stuck in traffic. I was horrified. My heart's desire was to do a four-month retreat, and they wanted sixty seconds!

A synchronous event helped me to hear their request on a deeper level and broaden my understanding of the role of retreats in daily life. I was invited to attend the yearly Princeton lecture of two Tibetan brothers, both highly respected teachers. The younger brother translated for the older, yet the contrast between their orange-red robes and our western culture still seemed unbreachable. The lamas had grown up in monasteries and spent their entire lives devoted to spiritual practice. How could we, a small group of suburbanites, begin to think we could follow such a path?

FIVE-MINUTE RETREAT—NO TIME TO RETREAT

Lama Surya Das, a Tibetan Buddhist, writes that "Even the Dalai Lama says he doesn't have sufficient time for quiet meditation and reflection." So how can we poor mortals come up with twenty minutes a day?

The Dalai Lama is probably wishing not for twenty minutes of quiet time but perhaps twenty hours. We, on the other hand, probably watch twenty minutes of TV commercials a day. So let's get very honest with ourselves.

We're too busy—For many of us, this statement is a reflection of our attachment or addiction to our daily lives. For the rest of us, it's that we imagine the world would fall apart if we didn't do everything ourselves.

We're fearful of the unknown—Retreats invite us into a different state of consciousness, expanding our awareness by shining light on what was previously unconscious. This can be uncomfortable until we learn to navigate our inner world.

What inner life?—Some of us may be so out of balance that we think our daily activities are all there is to life. The development of a spiritually nourishing inner life requires both solitude and silence.

I have no discipline—That may be true. We live in a self-indulgent culture. We seek comfort and ease, having forgotten how to say no to ourselves.

For the next few minutes, simply consider these questions: What reason or excuse do you give yourself for not having twenty minutes a day to nurture your soul? Is your rationalization for not having the time significantly different from the reasons listed above? If you're really honest with yourself, can you find the time?

The older brother spoke passionately in Tibetan, giving us long explanations along with his shining face and beaming smile. I was mesmerized by the strange sounds and rhythms in his speech and the liquid sunshine radiating from his being. Then the younger brother translated, "You can do one-minute meditations, during your day. Just stop and pause and breathe."

I couldn't believe it. Permission to do retreats while ironing, while waiting in traffic. One-minute retreats sanctioned by high-ranking Tibetan lamas. My corporate writing friends were right. In my own life, these brief retreats help me to wake up during the day, to renew the sacred experience from my regular twenty-minute retreats. By pausing to connect with our inner life, even for a moment, we shift our perspective to remember the eternal and that whatever we are doing in the outer world is transient.

The Experience of God

I must confess, I have tried to write this entire book without making a reference to God. I wanted to avoid having to define the ineffable and, instead, use every sacred euphemism known to spiritual literature. But the purpose of retreats is to connect with our personal experience of the Ultimate, which many call God, and there are chapter themes in which God is implicit. For instance, how could I write about faith without considering faith in God? So please, trust your own experience of the Infinite and your own way of expressing it.

> *Kabir says· Student, tell me what is God?*
> *He is the breath inside the breath.*
>
> —*The Kabir Book*, Robert Bly's translation of
> a fifteenth-century Indian mystic

Inner Guidance

As we travel on our spiritual journey, we realize that there are few guideposts, and sometimes the ones we see are confusing. How do we really know which retreat to start with, how long to do it, and which one to do next? Of course we could always rely on serendipity by opening the book at random and trusting that wherever our hand falls is the retreat best suited to us at this moment.

This approach actually will work, because the retreats here can be practiced in any order or combination, for any length of time. You can repeat a retreat and make it part of your ongoing practice, skip it entirely, or adapt it to meet your needs. However, if you feel drawn to a theme or specific retreat, follow your energy. If you feel anxious or insecure about some of the retreats, please don't push yourself through them. Learning to trust your own sense of what feels right to you is part of your inner development.

As you work with the retreats, you will naturally become more sensitive and attuned to the subtle effects they produce within you and to the ways they influence your daily life. Gradually you'll gain confidence in knowing which retreats to select and how to use them to guide your own spiritual unfolding.

All of us journey in unexpected ways, often with detours and disappointments. This is to be expected. The key is to use our retreat time to listen to the silence deep within us, that wellspring of inner guidance.

The next chapter will provide you with all the practical information you need to begin using the twenty-minute retreats as part of your spiritual journey.

By practicing God's remembrance your inner being will be illumined little by little.

—Jalal al-Din Rumi, thirteenth-century Sufi

2

Everything You Need to Know to Retreat

Teach us and show us the Way.

Chinook blessing litany

We are called to retreat by the yearning of our inner lives for silence and solitude. Yet many of us need practical advice on how to put our own desire for retreat into practice. We need to know how to create a sacred space in which we can explore our spiritual lives. We need user-friendly techniques so we know what to do to respond to our inner yearning. This chapter meets these realistic needs by answering the question, "What do I do now?"

The most important thing for you to know is that you can retreat anywhere, at any time, just by turning your attention inward. A retreat is an inner condition independent of the external situation. Your inner life is always present within you, flowing through you like an underground river. Even in the midst of your busiest day, you can retreat to reconnect with your experience of the sacred.

Having said that, I want to acknowledge that the setting for a retreat can help immensely. Think of churches, synagogues, mosques, or monasteries that you've visited. These are all sacred spaces, aesthetically designed to invite you to enter your inner spiritual realm as you cross the physical threshold. High vaulted ceilings inspire you to open up to your own inner spaciousness. Stained glass windows and candles emphasize the significance of light as a symbol of the source. In contrast, the unadorned Quaker meeting house creates its own sacred space, which modestly focuses you inward in silence and simplicity.

Remember your feelings upon entering such sacred spaces. There's an impulse to whisper even if you're visiting when no service is going on. The quiet atmosphere evokes this response. You may have experienced a similar feeling in especially beautiful places in nature or at sites of ancient ruins. The response is one of awe and wonder. And silence. These sacred spaces all have their own quality of subtle energy, which you can sense and which speaks to your soul.

Creating Your Sacred Space to Retreat

How can we create the grandeur of such sacred spaces in our own homes? Not many of us have enormous vaulted ceilings in the house or ancient ruins in our backyards. The answer is simple: we can create a sacred space wherever we live simply by intentionally dedicating a small area for spiritual purposes.

I am blessed to be friends with a wonderful couple who are both artists. When I stay with them, I always like to see what new art pieces, their own and other artists', they have added to their collection, which fills every corner and available space in their modest home. But the room I like best is their meditation room, an almost totally empty space except for some pillows, crystals, and candles. The energy in this room is both refreshing and purifying, even though the rest of the house is overflowing with creative chaos as well as a young teenager. The subtle energy in the small meditation room makes it seem spacious, quiet, and still. They use it only for sacred practices.

This is an ideal situation, to have a whole separate room reserved solely for retreats. Although most of us don't have that luxury, we can still create a sacred space for ourselves by using just a corner of a room and reserving that small space for our retreats. Or we can create a sacred space for the moment by intentionally preparing it. The preparation may be as

DEDICATING YOUR RETREAT SPACE

Once your retreat space is arranged, you may want to perform this ritual. It uses the basic elements of fire, light, and water to purify the subtle atmosphere of the space you are intentionally reserving for spiritual purposes. As you practice your retreats here, you will gradually create a more refined spiritual atmosphere, which will support your continued practice. Just entering your sacred space will signal your psyche that you are entering into retreat, allowing time and silence for the spirit.

Step 1: *Entering into Retreat:* For the first five minutes simply sit in your space and breathe. Sense the atmosphere you have created. Look around at the objects in your space, seeing them as they are. Notice any thoughts that enter your mind. Acknowledge them, then let them go, returning your attention to your breathing.

Step 2: During the next ten minutes, perform one or two of the following rituals meditatively, moving slowly with concentration. Choose whichever rituals appeal to you. Light a candle. Fill a bowl with water. Ring the meditation bells. Use lighted incense or a sage stick to bring smoke and scent into the four corners of your retreat space.

Step 3: *Returning to the World:* Use the last five minutes to simply sit again in your retreat space. Notice the atmosphere as if for the first time. Say silently, deep within you, "This is sacred space for spiritual retreats." Repeat this statement out loud. Again look around at the space, noticing the objects. Breathe, and let any thoughts float by. Complete this retreat by extinguishing candles, incense, or sage. Empty the water from the bowl.

simple as placing a beautiful cloth on a small table or dresser top, lighting a candle or incense, and filling a crystal bowl with water. This intentional preparation of the sacred space is actually the beginning of the retreat and will attune your energy for spiritual purposes.

The most basic furniture needed for a sacred space is merely a table for journaling or drawing and a cushion or chair for meditation. It would be nice to add a beautiful rug to stretch out on for relaxation, and a sound system for music or meditation tapes, but, if necessary, you can always use a dresser top and a dining room chair. So look around your house and see if you can find even a small space just for your spiritual practice.

Once you have decided on your sacred space, you can choose to keep it simple and empty or bring in objects of beauty and inspiration. A plant or flowers always adds life to the sacred space. Some people use aromatherapy atomizers to create a scented atmosphere, while others like to burn incense or sage sticks, which are dried sage leaves tied into a bundle with string and used in Native American rituals.

You might like to create an altar by arranging a collection of carefully selected objects from nature or art. Each object should carry a story or a memory. You could collect pine cones, stones, or seashells that speak to you from a sacred time spent in nature. Art pieces, cherished objects, and family heirlooms that evoke your inner sense of beauty and personal history can be inspiring. You may also want to include a favorite photograph, candle holder, crystal, or religious symbols like a cross, statue of Buddha, or a chalice. When you create your altar, make sure you select each piece for its special significance and meaning to your spiritual life. Remember, you are creating your retreat space to express your individual spiritual aesthetics and also to call you into sacred time. Carefully choose the objects that fill this space with this in mind.

Retreat Tools

The equipment you'll need to practice all the retreats in this book is actually quite minimal. Here's what you should have on hand before you begin.

Journal: You can use a blank book, either one of the beautifully bound ones from a bookstore or, more simply, a student's notebook. Keep pens and pencils handy.

Art supplies: Now you have an excuse to buy yourself a large new box of crayons. Also get a pack of oil pastels that costs less than $5.00, not the more expensive artists' quality. I personally prefer oil pastels to crayons, because they're softer and so much more expressive of feelings transmitted by hand pressure. The pastel colors can also be easily blended on the paper using fingertips and palms, almost like finger painting. Drawing paper can be newsprint tablets of whatever size you like. Most people use eleven-by-fourteen-inch paper, but I did work with one woman who created large murals on her retreats using three-foot-wide rolls of paper. Also treat yourself to various colors of finger paints and the appropriate paper. Look for some Fimo or other easy-to-use modeling clay that comes in a variety of wonderful colors.

Clock: I prefer relying on a clock because it's easier to see than a wrist watch, and you can set an alarm when needed. Be sure to use one that does not make a ticking sound.

Bells: You can use any type of bell to ring at the beginning and end of a retreat. The sound and vibrations clear the air, distinguishing the retreat as time separate from everyday activity. Different styles of bells from a variety of cultures can be ordered from Mystic Trader (800-634-9057). One type consists of two small saucers of metal, struck together to create the sound, while another is a metal bowl that is held in an open palm and struck with a small wooden stick. Always allow the sound of the bell to disappear before ringing it again. For meditative purposes, you can let your awareness follow the bell's vibration until it recedes into the distance.

Candles: Lighting a candle is one of the most universal rituals in all the world's religions. The choice of using an aromatherapy candle is up to you. I like to use those scented with sandalwood or lavender.

Incense: For those who like incense, a retreat wouldn't be the same without it. The safest way to handle incense is to have a bowl filled with sand into which you can place the stick of incense and let it burn.

Crystals: A crystal bowl filled with water is wonderful because the water absorbs negative energy, and the crystal reflects light into the retreat space. You could also include a quartz crystal which, with its clear, pure color and vibration, is the one most frequently recommended for spiritual purposes.

Divination tools: The term *divination* refers to seeing into the future to predict outer world events or inner spiritual development. The "Faith" and "Gratitude" chapters include retreats using tarot cards, a deck of seventy-eight cards with beautiful full-color drawings. If you choose to include tarot cards in your space, I recommend the classic deck developed by Arthur Edward Waite, a student of magic and mysticism, along with his *Pictorial Key to the Tarot*, which explains in complete detail how to use and interpret the cards. Tarot cards can be found in bookstores.

Meditation cushions *(zafu)*: For those who don't need the back support of a chair, a variety of very firm cushions have been designed for the sole purpose of meditation. They are made in bold, bright colors and can be ordered from Carolina Morning Designs (828-675-0490).

Retreat Techniques

The twenty-minute retreats in this book are inspired by the great wisdom traditions of the world's religions as well as by practices and beliefs of the original tribal cultures that are more closely linked to the natural rhythms of the earth and its seasons. This section gives a brief description of the many techniques used in the retreats in the following chapters. The techniques can be divided into the general categories of awareness practices, rituals, creative expression, psychotherapy, body work, and subtle energy sensing. You should keep in mind that this is an artificial delineation of techniques, since many retreats fit into more than one category. However, this section can serve as a reference guide to which you may frequently return as a source of background information for greater understanding of the retreat practices.

Awareness Practices

Centering Prayer is a contemplative practice purportedly based on the fourteenth-century classic *The Cloud of Unknowing*. It's been taught since 1975, primarily within the Catholic Church, a sign of the recent blossoming of mystical interest among laypeople. It's described as an encounter with the presence of God and is seen as an opportunity for deep spiritual healing. The instructions for centering prayer use the silent internal repetition of a word or phrase of your own choosing, which you use as a focus point. As in mindfulness meditation, when you notice your attention drifting, simply return your attention to the repetition of your word or phrase.

The **Gurdjieff work** is named after its originator, George Ivanovitch Gurdjieff, a turn-of-the-century spiritual seeker and teacher. He integrated techniques from many esoteric spiritual groups and remained a mythical and mystical figure up to his death in 1946. Gurdjieff taught that most people are asleep, meaning that they live their lives in an automatic, semiconscious state. He used techniques in self-observation to make his students wake up to the fact that they are asleep most of the time. One such exercise involved the attempt to be consciously aware of ourselves throughout the day. Most of us can't sustain this level of attention for even a few minutes.

Mindfulness is one of the central practices in Theravada Buddhism, probably taught by the Buddha himself to his own monks. It's a quality of awareness practiced during meditation as well as throughout your daily activities. Mindfulness is the process of being aware of your experience, including your breathing, right here, right now. As your thoughts move through your mind, you simply notice them without clinging, analyzing, or judging. Mindfulness is pure observation practiced with compassion and equanimity. When you're using it during a retreat, notice as soon as your thoughts begin to drift to everyday concerns such as work responsibilities or the dirty laundry. Simply notice, and then gently return your attention to your breathing.

> **W**e are drawn to a spiritual path out of
> a desire for tranquil abiding.
>
> —Elizabeth Lesser, cofounder, Omega Institute

The Relaxation Response is a term coined by Herbert Benson, a Harvard medical researcher, to describe an approach to stress reduction through physical relaxation, the use of a mantra, and an open, accepting attitude. The relaxation response is widely taught in body-mind clinics and has been found to be effective with a wide range of medical diagnoses, from heart disease to anxiety.

Shamanism is a nonlogical view of the universe that has survived in tribal cultures all over the world. The shaman is the person in the native village who can travel into different realities—the medicine man or woman, the trance medium, the visionary, the sorcerer or sorceress. The shamanistic belief in the reality of the dream world is at the heart of many of the retreats dealing with dreams. From this point of view, you don't remember your dreams; you journey to the time and space of your dream world to reenter your dream.

Sufism is the mystical strand of Islam. The Sufis emphasize following an internal path of immersion into Allah through an ecstatic union with the Divine. The Sufi Order of the West is organized in the United States by Pir Vilayat Khan, son of Hazrat Inayat Khan, a musician and mystic who came to the West from India in the early part of the twentieth century. The Four Elemental Breaths is a healing and purification practice taught in this Sufi order. It uses the imagery of earth, air, fire, and water to purify and revivify the subtle energy in the body. The Sufi practices form the inspiration behind most of the retreat methods that involve opening your heart. Heightened sensitivity and awareness in the heart center are an important part of the path of love.

Rituals

Ritual magic, the practice of sacred acts, can be found in all cultures and their religions. The ritual, performed with clear intention and emotional concentration, magically creates a change in both your inner and outer world. One well-known type of ritual magic is the burning of a letter you never intend to send. Burning objects helps you to let go of hurtful people, old wounds, negative behaviors, and angry resentment. Watching the object burn and dissolve into ashes magically symbolizes the inner process of transforming your emotion. During this ritual, the process taking place in the outer world stimulates and inspires a parallel process in the inner world, allowing you to truly discard the pain and anger you are ready to release.

Creative Expression

Emotional drawing: The instructions that I give for emotional drawing are: "Make a nonrepresentational drawing that illustrates your feelings, dream, poem, situation, or anything from within your psyche that needs to be called out into the world. Please don't try to draw people or real scenes. Just play with colors, shapes, movement, and the intensity of your hand across the paper. Trust what feels right or looks right to you." Your choice of color, speed and intensity of movement, symbolic shape, and use of space will reflect your feelings. The creative expression of an inner psychic state into the outer world is enormously clarifying, healing, and empowering. Using the drawings as objects of meditation intensifies this therapeutic process of healing. In *Pictures of a Childhood*, the Swiss psychiatrist Alice Miller shares her personal process of psychotherapy using her own emotional drawings.

Journaling: Journaling is far more than writing in a diary or keeping a record of daily events. It's a progressively deepening process of writing, according to Ira Progoff, the founder of the Intensive Journal Process. He says that this process reconnects you to the "contents and continuity of [your] life, the inner thread of movement by which [your] life has been unfolding." I remember one woman I met at a writers' conference who had been keeping a journal, of sorts, since she was five years old. Her forty years of journals were precious, giving her a rare glimpse into her childhood and the whole story of her life. Retreats in many of the chapters use journaling techniques, such as writing a letter which is never mailed, tracing significant turning points in your life, and, of course, writing down your dreams. Journaling accelerates your progress; it enables you to express inner feelings concretely in the outer world, giving you a chance to literally see things differently on paper.

Writing poetry: More than any other style of creative expression, writing poetry opens the heart and speaks to the soul. I've asked thousands of people to write a poem based on one of their dreams, and with very easy instructions and a totally accepting attitude, no one has ever said, "I can't write a poem." Poetry carries the feelings, moving them from a felt inner sense to an outward expression that can be seen, heard, and shared. This very process is healing.

Psychotherapeutic Techniques

Altered states of consciousness can include hypnosis, trance, dreams, ecstasy, or those transitions we experience when entering sleep (hypnagogic) or gradually waking up (hypnopompic). Altered states allow us to be more open to learning and creative expression. Some of the retreats use those few seconds or minutes just before sleep or after waking up to focus your intention or expand your awareness. As a child, I used to play a game with myself to not move when I woke up in the morning, so I could see what position I slept in. I would program myself before I went to sleep to try to remember not to move as soon as I woke up. Like many children in all the world's cultures, I was playing with the transition from one state of consciousness to another.

Cognitive therapy focuses on those repetitive messages we all have playing inside our heads. The inner critic, the best-known example, can be so loud and judgmental that it interferes with the quality of our lives. This therapeutic approach teaches us how to change the volume and content of these inner "tapes." The retreats often combine cognitive therapy with journaling, because once you write down all the things you say to yourself, you begin to gain some conscious control over the messages. *Feeling Good*, by David Burns, teaches you how to use cognitive therapy yourself, and it's the book most widely recommended by therapists for their clients.

Visualization techniques include the Jungian process of **active imagination** as well as **guided imagery,** or **fantasy.** The technique underlying these slightly different approaches is the ability to create an inner image with enough detail so that it feels real. For instance, if you imagine walking through a forest, you would involve all of your senses. You would hear the birds, feel the cushioned path covered with moss, smell the woodsy fragrance, see the sunlight filtered through the leaves, and touch the bark on the ancient trees. Carl Jung, a disciple of Sigmund Freud who broke away to develop Jungian analysis, saw the technique of active imagination as a bridge between the unconscious and the conscious, allowing images from the unconscious to be expressed through writing and artwork.

Body Work

Dance therapy uses movement for creative expression and self-exploration. Young children dance for pure pleasure and joy, but we adults tend to be self-conscious and limited in our ability to dance freely. Any retreat instructing you to move spontaneously has its roots in dance therapy.

Feldenkrais movement: Moshe Feldenkrais, an Israeli physicist and martial artist, devised thousands of exercises to expand one's habitual range of movement patterns, to keep the neurological system young and flexible. The quickest example of his approach is in the "One-Minute Neurological Wake-Up" retreat, which instructs you to lace your hands together in your habitual way, and then again in the other way. The amazing thing is that you can feel this small exercise affecting your entire body.

The **Pilates method** of body conditioning is often used by professional dancers to prevent injury. It focuses on body balance, ease, and economy of movement. Both Pilates and Structural Awareness (see below) emphasize the important function of the psoas muscle, which lies deep within the body, originating along the upper lumbar spine and attaching at the lesser trochanter of the femur (thigh bone). You use the psoas muscle when I ask you to press your lower back against the floor, and working with it will give you an inner sense of strength and support.

Polarity therapy, Shiatsu, and **Jin Shin Jyutsu** are all based on traditional Oriental medicine and the acupuncture meridians, or pathways through which energy flows. Each discipline uses pressure at specific points along the acupuncture meridians to affect internal organs. One of the most useful self-help techniques is used to relieve headaches: apply pressure with the thumb of one hand at a point on the other hand between the thumb and forefinger. If you feel into the webbed part of this hand, you'll feel an indentation where your thumb easily fits. This is the point where you apply pressure.

Reichian therapy originated with Wilhelm Reich, who broke away from Sigmund Freud's teachings in order to work directly with his patients' bodies. His ideas were later integrated by John Pierrakos, a medical doctor who developed **Core energetics,** which works deeply with the energy blocks in the body to release held energy. Reich believed that one of the ways we block energy is with our eyes. You will notice that a number of retreats focus on soothing the eyes or intentionally softening your vision.

Sensory Awareness, often called the Zen of body work, is still being taught by Charlotte Selver at ninety-something years of age. Selver originally learned this discipline in Germany and then introduced it in the United States. It has often been included at meditation retreats because it uses a meditative focus on small, subtle movements of the body. Retreats that suggest a slow letting go from deep within the body are inspired by this practice.

Structural Integration is also called **rolfing®** after its founder, Ida P. Rolf. It's a system of ten sessions of deep massage by a trained **rolfer,** intended to align and balance the body. **Structural Awareness** is a series of movement lessons based on rolfing and is also designed to improve posture. One of the techniques used in Structural Awareness is the retreat instruction to breathe up through the top of your head. Of course, you can't literally do this, but just imagining it lengthens your neck so you rise to your full height.

Subtle Energy Sensing

According to Tantric Buddhist or Hindu theory, the **chakras** are seven centers of psychic energy situated along the spinal column. **Kundalini** energy rises from the base of the spine up through the chakras to the crown of the head (also called the thousand-petal lotus). Many of the retreats included here focus on the heart center, also known as the fourth chakra. Ajit Mookerjee's book *Kundalini* shows many examples of traditional art depicting the flow of energy through the chakras. Studying the photographs in this book imprints your psyche with an ancient model of how energy moves through the body.

Therapeutic Touch and Barbara Brennan's **Energy Healing** are based on the ancient practice of laying on of hands and focusing on the subtle energy flowing through the body. Psychically sensitive people can see or sense this energy as an aura surrounding the body. Retreats that use laying on of hands or smoothing the energy field are inspired by both these systems.

$\mathcal{R}$eturning to the World

Each twenty-minute retreat ends with a few minutes to make the transition from the sacred world of the retreat to your everyday life. Some of you will want to take a little more time for this shift, while others will jump up, ready to continue your day. This is a very individual preference, and either style is appropriate.

There are a few standard techniques to facilitate this transition, and you can use whichever one or two work best for you. They are all intended to help you reconnect with the physical world and prepare for everyday activity.

- Return your attention to your breathing. Feel the physical movement as you inhale and exhale.
- Look around the room. Notice the colors of objects in the room.
- Feel the floor (or chair) underneath you.
- Think of what you intend to accomplish today and what schedule you need to follow.
- Listen for sounds in your environment.
- Sense the whole outline of your body from head to toe.
- Stretch and begin to move gently and slowly.
- Blow out the candle or incense and ring a meditation bell to mark the end of the retreat.
- Think of what part of your retreat experience you'd like to carry over into your life today. Feel it in your body.

As we return to the world, we want to carry with us some of our retreat experience, such as greater awareness, personal insights, or feelings of calmness. This is part of our purpose in doing the twenty-minute retreats: we want the retreats to help us live our daily lives in a more spiritual way.

The one-minute and five-minute retreats found throughout the chapters are also designed to help us to do this. They re-create for us some of the inner quiet of the twenty-minute retreats and can easily be practiced in the middle of a busy day. They renew our spiritual perspective by helping us to perceive our immediate situation in the light of the eternal. This kind of shift in our sense of reality enables us to see things with a more spiritual perspective and behave accordingly.

The twenty-minute retreats are a practice in the true sense of the word. The more we do them, the easier it becomes to integrate them into our lives and to draw on our spiritual resources during the stressful times of our daily life. We gradually deepen and expand our connection to the Sacred so we can sustain it for longer periods of time and in more challenging circumstances. And the way we know we are learning how to do this is that we are able to behave with awareness and loving-kindness.

As spiritual maturity develops,
it brings kindness to the heart.

—Jack Kornfield, psychologist
and Buddhist meditation teacher

3

Faith

Faith is the belief in the heart in that knowledge which comes from the unseen.

—Muhammad ben Kafif, eighth-century Sufi poet

There are times of trial in our lives when all we have is our faith to carry us through, whether it's faith in ourselves, faith in others, faith in our process, or faith in God. All the joy of life has disappeared from view. These are the dark times, and there's no way to avoid them, for they are an integral part of life. It's at these times that we need to find courage and hope from deep within, even when there seems to be no rational justification for such optimism.

Well-meaning friends may be pained to watch us struggling through these times and may not know what to say. Advice like "Think positive" or "Snap out of it" is not what we want to hear. For no matter what the crisis, from divorce, to illness, to job loss, there is always an implicit opportunity for transformation. But to get to that point, we need to go through the entire process.

In the first session with a new psychotherapy client, I often ask them what they're looking for, what they want to get out of therapy. If they answer, "I just want to be happy," my internal warning system goes off. I interpret this as a request, "I want you to stop this pain. Make me happy." Life doesn't work that way and neither does therapy.

We need to have faith that we can learn and grow from the tough times. This is what I mean by faith in our process. We need to accept our feelings of doubt and discouragement during these times as part of the process. We have to search inside for the strength we didn't know we had and for the faith that will carry us beyond what we think we can do.

Faith in the Face of Loss

Nicholas was in exactly this kind of crisis. His hardware store had gone out of business, and he found himself in debt with no job prospects. He was suffering deep shame for failing to support his family, and his faith in himself was seriously shaken. He wanted to give up or run away, thinking his family would be better off without him.

Since he felt he had nothing to lose, Nicholas tried the "Enhancing Faith" retreat (page 39). Reflecting on other times in his life when things looked bleak, Nicholas remembered in great detail what he did that made a difference, how other people helped, and how circumstances changed, allowing him to find a solution. He began to see that, as bad as things were now, there had actually been times in his life that were worse. He had not only survived but had grown stronger as a result of working through them. This retreat renewed Nicholas's faith in himself, giving him the inner certainty that he would find a way through this difficult time.

This story reminds me of a small invitational conference for self-made millionaires, back when being a millionaire meant something. The fifteen or so people met for a weekend to share experiences. The pattern that emerged as they discussed how each had developed their businesses was that they had all failed at least once. And some of the failures were total wipeouts of all financial resources, personal as well as business investments. Yet they never lost faith in themselves, they just started over. Also, when asked what they would do if they lost everything again, they didn't hesitate. They'd been successful once, they could do it again. The participants in this group were from all over the country, of all different ages, and with a variety of cultural backgrounds. They had made their fortunes in many different businesses. What they had in common was this unshakable faith in themselves that persisted even in the worst of situations.

*T*ests of Faith

We learn how to have faith during our first years of life, as we grow to trust those around us. Babies learn that Mom will come back even if she's out of sight; toddlers know when to expect Daddy home for dinner. As we grow up, and our trust is fulfilled, our faith naturally develops. Our world is as it should be, and we have the full expectation that it will continue to be so. However, if something catastrophic happens, something totally unexpected, our faith is tested, and we are at risk for spiritual disillusionment.

Probably no other experience tests our faith as much as illness and death, our own or that of a loved one. The threat of our own death makes us question our faith that our lives hold meaning: What does it all mean? Did my life make a difference? Similarly, the possibility of losing a loved one often leads us to question, "Can I go on? Is it worth it?" We never really know how we would handle such a situation until we are actually faced with it. We may even have marveled at others: "I don't know how they do it. I couldn't imagine."

Michael was a thirty-two-year-old widower. His wife was diagnosed with cancer and treated aggressively but died anyway, all within six months. He was left with a six-year-old daughter, Emily, who alternately clung to him or sat limply on the sofa clutching her blankie and watching cartoons. Michael was overwhelmed with the devastation in his life, in shock that everything had happened so fast.

Almost a year after his wife's death, Michael was no longer just bereaved; he was very bitter about life, blaming God for his loss. It wasn't fair that his wife died. This wasn't how it was supposed to be. And oh, how he resented the fact that she had suffered, and for no good reason.

It would no doubt surprise you to know how many people are angry at God. Even people who don't exactly believe in God have anger toward

God. These feelings are very buried, and they admittedly don't always make rational sense. But anger toward God is one of the most common hindrances to faith, and faith not just in God but in life itself.

Michael began using the "Anger at God" retreat, found later in this chapter, and discovered that he could fill page after page with feelings of anger, disappointment, regret, and cynicism. His faith in everything around him had crumbled. After a few weeks of intense writing, Michael realized he was beginning to feel better, that he was able to enjoy himself again with his daughter.

Gradually Michael's letters to God became less angry and more in search of guidance. He began to ask how to balance work and parenting, for example, or what to tell Emily about heaven. Writing the letters had given Michael a way to express his anger, making room for other feelings to emerge spontaneously. Writing to God, no matter what is said, helps to build a personal relationship that can only deepen the experience of faith.

Sometimes bitterness creeps up on us and overtakes us. We may not know how much of our faith and hope we've lost until we reflect on the state of our inner lives and our outer choices. Then we may realize that it's time to cultivate faith. Here is a simple list of clues that will help you determine if you should focus on faith.

SIGNS THAT YOU NEED A FAITH RETREAT

1. You feel demoralized, disillusioned.
2. You no longer experience wonder in your life.
3. You have come to the conclusion that life is about looking after number one.
4. You try to control everything in your life and the lives of loved ones.
5. You feel like a failure who can't do anything right.
6. You feel pessimistic about the future.
7. A cynical coldness has descended over your heart.
8. You feel paranoid more often than is warranted.
9. You don't trust your ability to make important decisions.
10. Nothing seems worth the effort.

11. You don't trust anyone, expecting the worst.
12. You've lost confidence in yourself.

Janice's Story

It's an old lesson: be careful what you wish for, because you might get it. This was certainly true for Janice. She and her husband had tried for years to have a baby, and miraculously, at the age of forty-two, she had a beautiful, healthy daughter.

For the first few months, Janice thought she was just overtired. She had decided not to return to work so she could devote herself to the baby, and now she just didn't feel like doing anything. Her existence seemed to be reduced to child care and grocery shopping.

Janice blamed herself, assuming she was depressed or selfish or both. She tried telling herself that she should be grateful for finally having a child, but that only made her feel worse. After all, feeling empty when a dream comes true leaves a person sad in the present and bereft of dreams for the future.

Janice was not depressed; she was disconnected from her spiritual life. All her energy was spent taking care of the baby, and she no longer had time to meditate, take long walks, or garden. It was as if an inner light had gone out.

Faith grows out of our connection to our spiritual lives. When we are disconnected, we feel empty and believe that life is meaningless. If our faith is not renewed by a living sense of the divine, it begins to crumble and dry up.

Janice turned to her past to reconnect with her memory of the flow of the divine in her life. She started journaling her "Faith Map" (see page 41), a timeline highlighting the spiritual landmarks and existential "aha's" in one's life story. This retreat extends over at least four days, with deepening and expanding journal exercises. Retracing her past spiritual journey brought Janice back in touch with her inner light.

She worked with the faith map retreats for weeks, filling two blank books with notes, drawings, and poems. Janice had had a lifelong yearning

FIVE-MINUTE RETREAT—HARMONY

This retreat uses deceptively simple instructions. Simply see that everything is as it should be, right here, right now. However, this involves seeing the world through different eyes, through the eyes of a mystic. To do this we have to let go of our expectations, judgments, and desires in the faith that harmony will prevail. In the middle of a busy day, try deciding to see that this very moment is perfect, just as it is, in perfect harmony. Even just a split second of this perspective, a flash so to speak, is enough to open us to the possibility of harmony as a reality.

for the sacred that enriched her map with experiences and characters filled with wonder, humor, and synchronicity. She really enjoyed seeing the chronology of her spiritual journey, how one experience led to another, and how people magically seemed to enter her life at just the right time.

Janice felt reaffirmed at a very deep level, even though her current life was still consumed with child care busyness. She was sure her spirit was continuing to unfold. She trusted that the inner movement of her soul described in her faith map was still happening.

In fact, Janice's faith that all things were happening exactly as they should be actually strengthened. She believed that whatever she was experiencing was part of her spiritual unfolding, even if she didn't understand it at this time. She began to practice the five-minute "Harmony" retreat during the day at random times. This retreat helped Janice to shift from resisting her feelings of being tired and empty to accepting her inner experience and her current life. She would look around her, no matter where she was at the time, and trust that harmony prevailed.

The most beautiful music of all
is the music of what happens.

—Irish proverb

$\mathcal{R}$etreats to Cultivate Faith

Enhancing Faith

Our greatest need for faith comes when we are severely stressed, yet this is also the time our faith is most likely to waver. Recalling past moments of crisis and reflecting on how things worked out for the best can give us the faith we need to face our present situation. We can see things in the past that we are blind to in the present. This retreat uses a cognitive therapy approach to enhance the faith we already have and apply it to a new situation.

Step 1: *Entering into Retreat:* Choose a time in your life that was every bit as difficult as the current challenge you are facing. For the first five minutes, remember that situation in as much detail as you can possibly summon. How did you feel? What did you do? What did others do to help or hinder you?

Step 2: For the next five minutes, focus on how that situation from your past was resolved. Was there a sudden breakthrough or a gradual process? What did you do that made a difference? What were the specific steps that occurred?

Step 3: For the next five minutes, reflect on what you learned from this past experience. How did you change? How have you behaved differently since then? How did this experience influence other decisions in your life? Looking back, how did things work out for the best?

Step 4: *Returning to the World:* For the last five minutes, consider what you can apply from this previous situation to your current life challenge. Is there something you learned that could be helpful to you now? Are the two situations at all similar? Is there a pattern here? How could things possibly work out for the best now?

Anger at God

Susan Jorgensen, a spiritual director who guides people's spiritual development, says that anger toward God interferes with faith more than any other emotion. Journaling is suggested here to help you heal your relationship

FIVE-MINUTE RETREAT—SKY GAZING

This retreat is adapted from Lama Surya Das's Tibetan Buddhist meditation on "dissolving into the infinite by becoming one with the open sky." It's also about letting go, allowing whatever is to be, and having faith that things are okay even if you're not controlling them. It would be wonderful to do this retreat lying on your back on the grass on a beautiful summer day. Wear sunglasses if the sky is very bright. Simply lie back, relax, and observe the spaciousness of the sky. Allow your eyes to be in soft focus. Notice clouds floating by. Let your focus drift as the clouds drift. Changes come and go. Let them. Breathe. Allow your inside space to be as vast as the sky. Allow yourself to dissolve into the sky.

with God so faith can be restored. Please give yourself full permission to have these feelings. Criticizing or judging yourself harshly only adds to the negativity you're experiencing. It's far better to explore your feelings than judge them or try to change them, for they are a legitimate part of your relationship with God and your spiritual unfolding. And know that not only can you work through them, you will grow as a result, just as Michael did when he used this retreat to help renew his faith in God after his wife died. Repeat this retreat as long as you still feel angry. As your anger resolves, you will be more open to communication with God, and you may find value in continuing to write about other aspects of your spiritual life.

Step 1: *Entering into Retreat:* Gather a pen or pencil and your journal, and make yourself comfortable for writing. Use a full five minutes to give yourself permission to, first of all, have your feelings, and secondly, to express them. Trust that God will understand and accept all. Write down a statement of permission if you want one, such as, "You are granted full permission to be in touch with your whole range of feelings. I am open to hearing them and will accept them completely."

Step 2: For the next twelve minutes, write a letter to God giving full vent to all your anger, resentment, and disappointment. List details, specific events, and how you've been hurt. Write quickly without rereading.

Don't worry if you don't get it all out in this letter. You can continue tomorrow.

Step 3: *Returning to the World:* In the last three minutes, repeat to yourself the permission statement. Reaffirm your belief that you will grow spiritually and deepen your experience of faith by expressing yourself, and congratulate yourself for doing so.

Faith Map

These four retreats yield a faith map describing how your faith has developed and deepened over your lifetime. We rarely grow spiritually without the help and grace of others. The faith map reflects how events and people in our outer world have nourished the development of our inner world.

Throughout our lives, our faith has developed and deepened, often as a result of spiritual experiences we've had or significant people we've met. The "Faith Map" retreat gives you a way to trace the development of your faith in terms of the main influences in your life. The idea that your spiritual faith develops as you mature psychologically is based on theologian Jim Fowler's book *Stages of Faith*.

The faith map retreats should be worked with as a unit in the order they're presented. These retreats use creative expression techniques, including journaling, emotional drawing, and poetry writing. Each retreat builds on the previous in creating a picture of your faith developing

---

ONE-MINUTE RETREAT—FAITH IN YOURSELF

The fastest, most effective way to give yourself a confidence boost at any point during the day is to use this technique from Structural Awareness (see page 30). You can do this sitting, standing, or even walking. Simply imagine that when you inhale, the breath goes straight up through your torso and out through the top of your head. As you inhale, feel your rib cage expand and lift. This slight shift in posture will give you the confidence you need to have faith in yourself.

throughout the story of your life. Each day's retreat can be done seated comfortably at a table with journal materials at hand. Day 2 requires art materials as well (see page 22). Please note that you may need more than one day to complete some stages of this retreat process. Extend your journaling over as many days as you need.

DAY 1

Step 1: *Entering into Retreat:* Spend the first three minutes reflecting back over your life, sorting through for those times when you had the most meaningful spiritual moments or experiences of the divine. Search back for your earliest memory of the numinous.

Step 2: For the next fifteen minutes, list these experiences, starting with your first memory. Leave plenty of space between experiences, as you will be adding to these pages on day 3. Describe your experience, the situation, your age, how you understood your experience at the time, what it meant to you, and how it changed you.

Step 3: *Returning to the World:* Don't reread your writing at this time. Instead, use these last two minutes to be aware of the flow of your spiritual path as it is interwoven throughout your life.

DAY 2

Step 1: *Entering into Retreat:* Use the first five minutes to reread your journaling from day 1. Choose one experience to illustrate with an emotional drawing (see page 27).

Step 2: Take twelve minutes for this step. Using oil pastels and paper of whatever size you prefer, do a nonrepresentational drawing of your inner feelings during one of the spiritual experiences described in your journal. In other words, don't try to draw the scene; use the colors and shapes to reflect your spiritual experience. Trust yourself to be spontaneous with your drawing and to recognize what looks right, what accurately reflects your memory of your feelings.

Step 3: *Returning to the World:* During your last three minutes, simply bring together your journal entry and your emotional drawing. Look at them both together, feeling once again what you felt during your spiritual experience. This experience is a part of who you are.

DAY 3

Step 1: *Entering into Retreat:* For the first five minutes, read again your journal describing your experiences of the divine.

Step 2: Spend the next twelve minutes writing in the space after each spiritual experience a description of one person who played an important role during that time in your life. This person could be anyone—for example, a grandparent, a neighbor, or a teacher. Be sure to mention that person's special gifts and qualities, what you admired in them, and what you learned from them.

Step 3: *Returning to the World:* For the remaining three minutes, simply feel the presence of one or more of these people with you right now. People who have made a significant impact on our spiritual journey continue to live on within us.

DAY 4

Step 1: *Entering into Retreat:* For the first five minutes, read over your journaling about the people in your life who have been important in your spiritual development. Choose one person and underline the words in your description of him or her that stand out for you. Copy the underlined words into a new section of your journal.

Step 2: During the next twelve minutes, write a poem about this person using this list of words from your description. Your poem can be open and free-flowing; it doesn't need to rhyme or be in any specific form. It's an expression of your feelings from this relationship.

Step 3: *Returning to the World:* In the remaining three minutes, read over your poem and invoke the presence of this person. Realize the

ONE-MINUTE RETREAT—LET THERE BE LIGHT

The symbolism of light is present in all the great religious faiths, and is perhaps one of the most powerful images for invoking the divine. Simply repeat the phrase "Let there be light" at any time during your day and feel the light within you. See the light surrounding others, and allow the light to illuminate the task at hand.

difference he or she made in your spiritual path and consider ways you can practice or pass on what they've given you.

Trusting and Letting Go

When we don't have enough spiritual faith, we try to control things—ourselves, others, events, situations. Letting go of this control means trusting a higher reality, greater than ourselves. Using a subtle technique from Structural Awareness (see page 30), we can practice letting go by releasing some of our physical tension. Most of us exert unnecessary energy and tension in the vain attempt to hold ourselves together physically. This retreat is about letting go of those tensions and having the faith that we will not fall apart.

Step 1: *Entering into Retreat:* Lie down on a firm bed or cushioned mat so you can stretch out and relax. Use the first five minutes to simply breathe and let go. As you exhale, let out a long sigh. Repeat this a few times, letting the sigh get louder until it becomes a sound. Exhale and let out this sound. Feel the sound moving through your inside space, up through your chest and throat, and out your mouth.

Step 2: For the next five minutes, focus on how your legs attach to your pelvis. Concentrate your attention inside your body at your hip joints. Imagine you can untie the strings that attach your legs to your torso. See how much you can let go, trusting that you won't fall apart. With every exhale, let go of your legs even more.

Step 3: Focus on how your arms attach to your shoulders for the next five minutes. Concentrate your attention inside your body at your shoulders. Imagine you can untie the strings that attach your arms to your shoulders. See how much you can let go, with the faith that you won't fall apart. With every exhale, let go of your arms even more.

Step 4: *Returning to the World:* For the remaining five minutes, shift your focus to your whole body, including hips and shoulders. With every exhale, just let go of your arms and legs. Stop holding yourself together. Let go and have faith that you won't fall apart.

Abundance

Many of us grew up with feelings that we didn't receive enough of something, whether it was love, attention, material things, opportunities, or money. The concept of abundance affirms that we have enough; all we need is available, and we have enough to share. My dear friend Sonya Milton, a Unity minister, embodies this teaching by somehow always having the time and energy to give to others while maintaining faith that her needs will be met by the Ultimate Source.

Step 1: *Entering into Retreat:* You can do this retreat either lying down or sitting up, as long as you're positioned so your hands can be palm up. (Holding the hands palm up to receive a spiritual blessing is a tradition in the Islamic faith.) Just settle into your body and attend to your breathing for the first three minutes. Sense the wholeness of your body from head to toe, front to back, and side to side.

Step 2: For the next twelve minutes, imagine that you can receive positive energy from the universe with every inhale, that this energy can stream in through the palms of your hands, the soles of your feet, the crown of your skull, even directly into your heart center. Allow your body to open up in full receptivity to this positive life force that is abundantly available to you. Experience this unlimited flow, which may be sensed as pure energy, radiant light, warmth, or love. However you experience this abundance, allow it to descend upon you, surround you, and fill you.

Step 3: *Returning to the World:* For the final five minutes, simply soak up this feeling of abundance. Allow it to permeate your physical and spiritual being, filling you up to overflowing. As you prepare to move, remember that you can have faith that this abundant energy is always available to you.

Inspirational Reading

Probably the most frequently used technique to renew faith is reading inspirational literature. Some of us may prefer the sacred texts from our personal religion, while others will use New Age writing, poetry, or inspirational stories. Choose a short selection of any material that you find inspirational.

Step 1: *Entering into Retreat:* For the first three minutes, sit quietly in silence with your reading material close at hand. Breathe quietly. Steps 2 through 5 will take four minutes each.

Step 2: Read the piece slowly. This is a different kind of reading, not for speed or content, rather for absorption. Simply take your time.

Step 3: Reflect on the reading, using both your intellect and your imagination to fully receive the message. For instance, you can rephrase the reading in your own words, or you can imagine what it was like for the author to write this passage.

Step 4: Allow the words to touch your heart, their meaning to sink in and deepen your understanding.

Step 5: Enter into silence with the meaning of the reading.

Step 6: *Returning to the World:* For the remaining minute, consider how this reading can make a difference in your life today.

Changes

Life is constantly changing, unfolding in mysterious ways that we can neither control nor predict. The *Tao Te Ching,* by Lao-Tzu, a Chinese master thought to have lived around the time of Confucius, says, "If you realize all things change, there is nothing you will try to hold on to." We can attempt to control, pretend to control, but in the end we are forced to realize how little control we actually have. This is where faith comes in.

FIVE-MINUTE RETREAT—ROOTS OF FAITH

This retreat, inspired by a meditation of Thich Nhat Hanh's for children, combines visualization with subtle energy sensing to give you a grounded, physical experience of faith. Anchoring an abstract concept like faith with a concrete sensation will deepen your experience of it now and during challenging times ahead.

Sit on a firm chair or on a meditation cushion on the floor. Make sure you're seated firmly on your sitting bones. As you exhale, send energy down through the center of your body directly through the chair, through the floor, and into the earth. Really extend your energy so you feel connected with the ground. Now, imagine that you are like a mountain with a solid base. You rise up out of the earth, and yet you are a part of the earth. You have existed for centuries and will continue to exist for centuries. The weather may change all around you, yet you remain solid and consistent. Take this feeling of groundedness into your day and repeat this retreat any time you feel unsure or imbalanced.

We can choose to trust that there is a higher order at play, and that everything will turn out as it should.

Step 1: *Entering into Retreat:* Sit in a meditative position and just pay attention to the changes in your breathing pattern. For the first four minutes, simply notice the shifts as they occur, from inhale to pause, pause to exhale, exhale to pause, pause to inhale.

Step 2: For the next six minutes, think back to your experiences in childhood of the weather shifting: the changing of the seasons, the time right before a summer storm, the first inkling of spring, the last leaves falling.

Step 3: For the next six minutes, think through the transformations in your life: growing up, buying a new car or house, becoming a parent, learning a new skill, changing physically.

Step 4: *Returning to the World:* For the final four minutes, choose to have faith that changes beyond your control can happen for the best. Notice what this experience of trust feels like in your heart center. Compare this feeling with how you experience your attempts to control what is essentially not controllable.

Light a Candle

The traditional ritual of lighting a candle to honor a loved one, to celebrate an occasion, or to wish for something, is an example of living faith. As we perform this sacred act, we clarify and focus our intention, believing that it will be fulfilled.

Step 1: *Entering into Retreat:* Spend the first five minutes quieting yourself and concentrating totally on your intention. Become very clear about what you want to have happen, whether honoring the memory of a family member or wishing for world peace. Focus your concentration like a laser beam.

Step 2: Light the candle. You might want to light an extravaganza of candles, filling your retreat space with glowing light, color, and scent. Sit for ten minutes in the light of the candle. Continue to focus your awareness on your intention with the full faith that it will be so.

ONE-MINUTE RETREAT—DO SOMETHING

 I'm personally prone to empathy fatigue, feeling overwhelmed by all the sad stories and outright tragedies in the world. Watching the nightly news or reading the front page of the newspaper can leave me feeling helplessly pessimistic. The only thing that works to restore my faith in humankind and civilization is the "Do Something" retreat.

During my regular day, whenever I see an opportunity to do something that brings peace or kindness into the world, I just do it. Try approaching your day with the same outlook. You can do anything: Smile at a baby. Hold a door open for someone. Thank a salesperson. It usually means a little extra time and energy, but it's worth it. Also, the more you practice this retreat, the more opportunities you'll see. And I have faith that if we all did this, the world would be a much better place.

Step 3: *Returning to the World:* For the last five minutes, imagine that what you have intended has already come true. Your faith has been fulfilled. Carefully extinguish the candle.

Faith in Serendipity

If we believe that all things happen as they should, trusting that there's a higher order to seemingly random events, then we can perceive meaning in the serendipitous drawing of a tarot card. Tarot cards are particularly perfect for this retreat because they are ripe with vibrant color yet depict ambiguous scenes that you can interpret for personal meaning.

Preparation for Retreat: For this retreat, you'll need a tarot deck and a book that interprets the meaning of each card. Either Arthur Edward Waite's book or Eden Gray's is fine.

Step 1: *Entering into Retreat:* Use the first five minutes to concentrate your attention on your inner question, your request for guidance. Have faith that the card you draw will provide direction, clarification, or insight in response to your present request.

Step 2: Draw one card from the deck. For the next ten minutes, study this card, noticing all the rich detail in the picture. Imagine what action led up to the scene in this card. What is happening to the people in the scene? What are they doing? What will happen after this scene is over? How do you feel as you look at this card? What is your emotional response to it? Finally, look the card up in your tarot book and read the author's interpretation. Remember, your response to the card is as valid as the author's description.

Step 3: *Returning to the World:* Use the last five minutes to contemplate how the messages you received from this tarot card can be applied to your inner question or request for guidance. Have faith that you drew by chance the precise card you needed to see at just this moment in time.

Be Still

As described earlier, illness and death challenge our faith more than any other life experience. Our faith in ourselves, others, and even God is naturally shaken during these times. This is why hospitals hire full-time chaplains to visit with patients. Louise L. Kingston, an Episcopal priest, works as a hospital chaplain, helping patients and their families to maintain their faith even under dire circumstances. She has found that this "Be Still" retreat brings comfort to people dealing with serious medical crises. Because the technique relies on the repetition of a simple, well-known sentence from Psalm 46, most people find it easy to maintain their concentration even under difficult physical circumstances.

Step 1: *Entering into Retreat:* Use the first three minutes to simply find a comfortable position, either sitting or lying. Focus your attention in the center of your heart space inside your chest.

Step 2: For the next sixteen minutes of this retreat, simply repeat the following phrases to yourself silently. Allow the words to float on your breath. Repeat the sequence as many times as you can in the time given.

> Be still and know that I am God.
> Be still and know that I am.
> Be still and know that I.
> Be still and know that.
> Be still and know.
> Be still.
> Be.

Step 3: *Returning to the World:* In the last minute of this retreat, open your eyes and look around while you continue to repeat the phrase. The inner feeling created with this retreat will reaffirm the faith you need to deal with whatever crisis you may face.

You see, the whole world is praying all the time.

—Schlomo Carlbach, Jewish Renewal rabbi

Still, Small Voice

The Quakers value silence and patience. They believe that wisdom will emerge from quietly listening to the voice that speaks to us out of the silence inside our hearts. The gradual emergence of this inner voice is part of the "continuing revelation" that guides us along the spiritual path of our faith. This retreat is inspired by this Quaker tradition.

Step 1: *Entering into Retreat:* Sit with your eyes closed and, for the first five minutes, turn your attention inward. The Quakers use the phrase "centering down." Enter the silence there.

Step 2: For the next twelve minutes, patiently listen for your inner voice. Everyone "hears" differently. The still, small voice may not literally be a voice for you. It may be a sensation, an image, or a thought. Just be receptive and notice what message comes up for you from this place deep inside.

Step 3: *Returning to the World:* Use the last three minutes to raise your awareness back up to your surroundings. Find words to express any inner messages you have received. Consider how this experience can influence what you do today in your everyday life.

*F*or the Great Spirit is everywhere;
he hears whatever is in our minds and hearts,
and it is not necessary to speak to Him in a loud voice.

—Black Elk, holy man of the Teton Sioux

4

Forgiveness

There are a number of people in my life I would like to forgive but can't. I know I *should* forgive them; it would be *better* for me if I could forgive them; I actually *intend* to forgive them . . . someday. I even have to forgive myself for not forgiving them. Yet I hold on to the anger, blame, and resentment. I cannot force myself to forgive.

Most of us are stuck with similar negative feelings toward someone in our lives or toward ourselves. Often we are toughest on ourselves. "I'll never forgive myself" is a too familiar phrase. Unfortunately, we cannot just simply decide to forgive ourselves.

The cost of not forgiving others or ourselves is high. Chronic anger and resentment can darken our hearts, leading us to an emotionally bitter relationship with life. Yet we continue to blame, reciting an internal litany of complaints and justifications that stokes our anger and keeps our resentments alive.

On the other hand, there is great danger in forgiving too soon. Denying the anger we really feel to try to appear forgiving is actually harmful to us and our relationships. Please don't accept the mistaken belief that it is more spiritual to forgive. What is spiritual is the journey toward forgiveness, and for that we need to be in touch with *all* our feelings. Retreats in this chapter use anger and resentment to energize the process of moving toward forgiveness. It's far better in the long run to work through the process of forgiveness by embracing our negative feelings than by trying to cover them over.

Forgiveness for ourselves or others is a process that has its own mysterious timetable. I cannot use willpower to make my negative feelings miraculously disappear. But I can accept where I am in my process of moving toward forgiveness and nurture my progress along the way using an assortment of twenty-minute retreats. The process of forgiving is about being personally transformed so we can see things differently, release negativity, and let go of old pain. We undergo an inner shift in the way we remember the past and arrive at a new understanding of ourselves and others. This kind of personal transformation includes a spontaneous opening of the heart and leads to a greater capacity for compassion and love.

How to forgive is something we have to learn,
not as a duty or an obligation
but as an experience akin to the experience of love;
it must come into being spontaneously.

—Rev. Theodore C. Speers

Forgiving Others

Learning how to forgive others is part of all our relationships, but the most difficult situation to forgive is a betrayal. Such a breach of trust is often felt as an assault and is extremely difficult to get over. Without forgiveness, the person betrayed is harmed doubly, first by the betrayal itself and second by the effects of carrying the anger that comes from being betrayed.

In the book *Sunflowers*, by famed Nazi hunter Simon Wiesenthal, Rabbi Harold S. Kushner offers this piece of advice to a divorced woman: "I'm not asking you to forgive him because what he did was acceptable. It wasn't; it was mean and selfish. I'm asking you to forgive because he doesn't deserve the power to live in your head and turn you into a bitter, angry woman. I'd like to see him out of your life emotionally as completely as he is out of it physically, but you keep holding on to him. You're not hurting him by holding on to that resentment, but you're hurting yourself."

This advice was perfect for Suzanne, a client of mine, but first she had to deal with her anger before she could let go of her resentment. Suzanne began her process of forgiveness at the very beginning—enraged. She was totally unwilling to forgive her ex-husband, Mark, or the "other woman," Anne, whom she blamed for ruining her marriage. Suzanne was drawn to the "Being with Your Anger" retreat in this chapter because it reflected her current experience. She wanted to respect her authentic anger, yet not become embittered by it. Using the guided meditation exercises in this retreat, Suzanne was able to allow her rage to rise up from the depths of her being. She acknowledged, and even welcomed, these negative feelings. In Jungian terms, Suzanne became conscious of her shadow—those aspects of her personality that are considered to be socially unacceptable. Suzanne was truly furious and didn't want to deny her feelings or act them out through destructive fighting with Mark. Following the directions for the retreat, Suzanne visualized her anger as the inside of a volcano with molten lava churning, dark smoke swirling, and noxious fumes erupting. The first few times Suzanne practiced this retreat she felt affirmed and empowered, delighting in the catastrophic power of her volcano image. But over time, Suzanne began to be bored with her anger and even started to worry about the volcanic fumes and ashes poisoning her psyche and spirit. This was the signal that she was ready to move on in her process of forgiveness.

Suzanne had honored her angry feelings enough so that letting go of them would be a true release and not a repressive denial of her emotions. Her acceptance of the full range of her feelings was precisely what allowed her forgiveness process to unfold. Suzanne also knew that she could forgive Mark as a fellow human being with all the standard frailties and still not forget or condone his behavior. In fact, she could forgive Mark and still choose not to have anything to do with him. The process of forgiveness empowered Suzanne to rise above the victim role, accept all her feelings, and choose to do what's best for her.

Never spend time with people who don't respect you.

—Maori proverb

When We Can't Forgive

We cannot push or rush forgiveness. We have to begin with where we are with our true feelings, and then trust that we will gradually progress toward forgiving. However, it is true that our resistance can keep us stuck. We may hold on to our anger as an illusion of power or control, mistakenly thinking that it will protect us from further pain. Sometimes we even become too comfortable with being a victim, since it allows us to blame others and avoid taking responsibility for our own experience. These are possibly the most common ways we interfere with our naturally unfolding process of forgiveness and transformation.

FIVE-MINUTE RETREAT—RESISTANCE

Use this quick exercise when you feel stuck in your process, when you continue to hold on to your anger or blame others. Ask yourself, "What would have to change if I forgave ———?" Keep repeating this question to yourself, then list several responses, one after the other, so you uncover layer upon layer of resistance. Seeing your answers on paper will help you to identify your barriers to forgiveness, view them objectively, and move on.

*F*orgiving Ourselves

Oftentimes forgiving ourselves is even more difficult than forgiving others. Even though it sounds irrational, emotionally we need to forgive ourselves for not being perfect. We need to let go of the ways in which we "should" ourselves or sacrifice ourselves to live up to the expectations of others. Perhaps the most difficult time to forgive ourselves is when we feel we have disappointed or hurt someone we love and they have passed out of our lives, removing the possibility of redeeming ourselves through apology or reparation.

I can pardon everyone's mistakes but my own.

—Marcus Porcius Cato, 234–149 B.C.

William had stayed at his father's bedside in the hospital day and night. His father passed in and out of consciousness, so William never knew when he would have a precious last visit. After days of this painful vigil, William had to leave the hospital for a few hours to tend to some business. During this time, his father awoke, asked for his son, and then died quietly. Upon learning of his father's final moments, William became inconsolable. He felt that he had abandoned his father during his final hour of need, that his father would never forgive him, and that he could never forgive himself. Nothing anybody said helped to lighten his guilt.

William still needed one last chance to communicate with his father. He began to use the twenty-minute retreat, "Communing with a Loved One" (page 66), to imagine that he was with his father once again. He could sense his father's presence and silently talk to him inside himself. This retreat proved to be a balm to William's disturbed spirit. He felt he was completing what had been unsaid between them. In fact, William realized that he was able to be freer in his communication with his father during these retreats than when his father had been alive. Gradually William's feelings of guilt lifted. He was able to forgive himself for not being there at the crucial moment.

William's experience during the retreat allowed him to shift the way he saw things. He no longer focused on the time he wasn't at the hospital, but remembered all the days and nights he was there with his father. He understood the reality of his needing to leave the hospital and that there was no way he could have known what would happen. Forgiving himself emerged as the natural next step.

Most of us are well aware when we need a forgiveness retreat. The burden of carrying resentment and anger is great. However, the following list will clearly indicate the personal cost of not forgiving and the need to focus on forgiveness.

SIGNS THAT YOU NEED A FORGIVENESS RETREAT

1. You experience temper outbursts over insignificant situations.
2. You're consumed with revenge fantasies.
3. You blame others and avoid taking responsibility for your own behavior.
4. In your mind, you obsessively replay your own and others' mistakes.
5. You don't trust others.
6. You have not laughed in a long time.
7. You feel like a victim.
8. You spend an enormous amount of time being negative in both your thoughts and your actions.
9. Sometimes you may feel a subtle sense of deadness behind your eyes or a cold, frozen quality in your heart.
10. You feel tired and depressed more than you should.
11. You feel that something is "eating you up inside."
12. You suffer with excessive guilt.

Christina's Story

Although a beautiful and happily married young woman in her late twenties, Christina was just as angry with her mother as she had been during her adolescence. Christina had never forgiven her mother for what she felt was serious neglect during her childhood. But once she had a little girl of her own, Christina didn't want to let her rage continue to separate her from her mother. She wanted her daughter to have a good relationship with her grandmother, and she now understood how difficult it was to be a mother.

Every night after the baby fell asleep, Christina took time to practice the "Visualization of Ancestors" retreat (page 59) based on the Confucian tradition of respect for one's ancestors. Christina would sit quietly and visualize the maternal link from grandmother to mother to granddaughter. As her visualization grew stronger, Christina began to see that the flow of love went in all directions, linking these three women in every possible combination. It was healing for Christina to visualize her mother embracing her daughter and her daughter blossoming with that attention. Christina began to feel more open toward her mother as she sat in her quiet retreat every night, seeing the love flow between the generations.

Christina encouraged her newly discovered compassion to flow when her mother came to visit. She very discreetly added a one-minute retreat during these visits: "Breathing through Your Heart" (page 68), a technique used by the Sufi Order of the West. When she was in her mother's presence, she would imagine that she could breathe in and out through the center of her chest, her heart space. Christina eventually began to feel that her heart was opening in her mother's direction when her mother was present.

Of course, Christina's mother was unaware of these happenings and didn't notice anything different. She just kept on being a doting grandmother, for she had learned a lot since Christina's childhood and was determined to be more loving with her granddaughter than she had known how to be with her daughter. And Christina was equally unaware of her mother's realizations, but did notice the difference in her behavior as a grandmother. Christina never spoke to her mom about her own process of forgiving. Her internal transformation was all that was necessary. As time

FIVE-MINUTE RETREAT—VISUALIZATION OF ANCESTORS

This brief retreat, based on the Confucian tradition of honoring one's ancestors, is a very indirect approach to forgiveness. Quite simply and concretely, we wouldn't be here if it weren't for our parents, our grandparents, our great-grandparents, and so on. Visualize your family lineage as far back as you can remember and as far back as the family stories go. Then imagine beyond that, ever farther back to your unknown ancestors. They have all contributed to your being right here, right now. Notice the linkage from generation to generation, including the generations following you. For example, I have her freckles; I've passed on his musicality; I identify with their spiritual searching; I have her metabolism. Whatever the linkages are, just notice the connections across generations.

passed, Christina felt closer to her mother and experienced a greater sense of wholeness and confidence in her ability to create a good and lasting relationship with her own daughter.

Christina's story shows how one retreat can smoothly lead into another, advancing along the path to forgiveness. After weeks of visualizing the connection among the three generations, Christina was ready to work on opening her heart to her mother. This was a very big step in her process of letting go of her anger and forgiving her mother for past mistakes. By practicing breathing through her heart in her mother's presence, Christina opened her heart to love her mother. In this way, she integrated her visualization retreat with her actual relationship with her mother.

*R*etreats to Cultivate Forgiveness

Being with Your Anger

This retreat is based on the concept of the shadow from Jungian analysis. The shadow is the part of your personality that you don't want to face.

"Being with Your Anger" is designed to help you become more conscious of your shadow by accepting your feelings of anger and resentment, especially if you tend to deny these emotions, think you *shouldn't* feel angry, believe anger is bad or unacceptable, or presume you *should* be more forgiving. Authentic acceptance of your anger or resentment is one of the first steps in the process of forgiveness.

Step 1: *Entering into Retreat:* While sitting on the floor or on a chair, please begin with three minutes of simply observing your breath. During this quiet time, just notice how your inhale flows into your air passages. How much effort do you exert when you begin your inhalation? Can you use less effort, allowing the inhalation to begin spontaneously? As the air moves in through your nostrils, how does it feel: cool, humid, scented? Remember, there are no right or wrong experiences, only observations.

Step 2: For the next ten minutes, please invite feelings of anger or resentment to arise. You can do this by thinking of a time when you were wronged or harmed. You may have to literally give yourself permission to feel angry for the purpose of retreat. Take three deeper and larger inhalations to intensify your experience.

Allow your feelings to exist, pure and simple. Do nothing to change them, minimize them, or layer them with guilt. Refrain from judging or denying your feelings. Also, don't add details for justification; don't remember every single possible reason to be hurt from beginning to end. Resist the urge to enlarge the anger or resentment

As you focus on your feelings, doing nothing to minimize or exaggerate them, allow your imagination to come into play. How do you experience your feelings in your body? Can you visualize an image to symbolize your emotions? If so, what form or shape is it? What color? Is there a sound that expresses your feelings? These questions will help you to perceive your anger in a more objective way, creating some distance between you and your feelings, yet giving them full permission to exist.

Reminder: As you observe your anger, please continue to be aware of your breathing, the experience of your inhalation, how the air feels as it enters your nostrils. At this point, you may be feeling bored, as if you are "just hanging out with your anger." Or your feelings may begin to subside or flatten. This is a sign that you are now ready to shift your focus.

Step 3: Take about four minutes to think once again of the original incident that helped you to get in touch with your anger and resentment earlier in this retreat. Do you have the same emotional reaction as before? While keeping this incident in mind, visualize your anger or resentment in its symbolic form — as a shape, color, sound, or body sensation.

Is it possible to imagine that you could now have a different reaction to this same incident?

Step 4: *Returning to the World:* Take about three minutes to make your transition from retreat time to your daily life. Begin by paying attention to your breathing again. Notice what parts of your body move as you inhale and as you exhale. Feel the floor or chair underneath you, the temperature of the air around you. Listen for any sounds in your environment. Feel a wonderful spaciousness inside of you that can accept both anger and non-anger. That inner openness is what will allow you to move toward forgiveness.

---

*Awareness can be called upon to be a companion
for our anger. Our awareness of our anger does not
suppress it or drive it out. It just looks after it.
This is a very important principle.
Mindfulness is not a judge.*

—Thich Nhat Hanh

Write an "I Resent" Letter

Let me be very clear from the beginning that you do not mail an "I resent" letter. Writing one is for your own healing, not for communication. This retreat is based on Dr. Fritz Perls's practice of Gestalt therapy. When he worked with someone who was stuck in their feelings of anger or resentment, he would often have them follow these same instructions verbally, rather than in writing, in the actual therapy session. Composing an "I Resent" letter is a good retreat for you if you can't get an incident or a person out of your mind. You keep replaying what someone did, and you keep getting angry or upset all over again. This is the perfect person to focus on for this retreat.

Writing an "I Resent" letter will take more than one day. You need to "sleep on" the experience and give yourself enough time to get every single thought down on paper. This retreat may take three to five twenty-minute sessions for you to feel totally satisfied with what you've written.

You will need a pencil or pen and plenty of paper handy for writing. Some people may prefer working at a desk, while others will like to curl up with some pillows. Sit however it is easiest for you to write, and you can always alter your position for comfort.

Step 1: *Entering into Retreat:* Take three minutes to quiet down, shifting into a time and space set aside solely for you. Attend to your breathing, especially your inhalation. For another two minutes, imagine you are breathing in powerful energy and that you can send it into your writing hand. You may feel that hand becoming warmer or have the unusual sensation that it is becoming larger.

Step 2: Let your mind generate every single incident in which you resented your focus person. Think through every situation, memory, disappointment, disillusionment. Allow the bitterness to build. When you are overflowing with outrage, begin to write. Give yourself the remainder of the retreat time to write, saving just three minutes at the end for transition back to the world.

Begin with the words "Dear [focus person]:"

Now, continue with the sentence "I resent . . ." Every sentence begins with "I resent . . ." and then you complete it with a specific message:

> I resent the time you forgot our anniversary.
> I resent that you spend too much money.

Just keep writing, and don't worry about whether or not it makes any sense. Tell yourself something good about what you've written so far, like "This is really true," or "At last I'm getting this out."

Step 3: *Returning to the World:* Use the last few minutes of your retreat to breathe quietly, this time noticing the movement of your exhalation. With every exhale, imagine you can let go of any tension associated with the anger you have been carrying around. Now that you are putting it down on paper, you no longer have to keep going over it in your head.

Repeat these instructions as long as you continue to recall instances that produce any angry feelings. Eventually you will be satisfied that you have recorded every single hurtful event.

Burning the Letter: A Personal Choice

Now you have a very private decision to make. You may want to hold on to this letter for a while. Some people find comfort having one document that chronicles all their rage, as if retaining it on paper keeps it out of their heads. If you hold on to your letter, please be careful to place it in a very private spot.

If you decide not to save your letter, you may be ready to burn it in a special ritual. If this is your choice, dedicate an entire retreat to this ritual burning, which is based on the ancient practice of ritual magic. Burning the letter is the outer symbol that magically brings about the inner transformation of your resentment. As your letter burns, your feelings will change, allowing you to let go and move on with your life.

Step 1: First prepare to burn your letter safely. Of course, a fireplace is ideal. You can also use a cooking pot for the burning. Remember, the bottom of the pot will get hot, so place a trivet underneath and keep pot holders and water handy. You could also go outside to burn the letter on the pavement as long as the wind is not strong.

Step 2: Begin the ritual burning retreat with a few minutes of quiet breathing. Find the words to make one clear statement as you set fire to your letter. For example, "With this match I am burning my old resentments," or "I am now ready for this list of resentments to be transformed by fire into ashes."

Solemnly watch the paper burn. Notice how it smokes and catches fire, how the color of the paper changes, how the letter dissolves into ashes. Watch the smoke rise and disappear. Stir the ashes, making sure the burning is complete.

Step 3: After letting the ashes cool, you can throw them to the winds or bury them in an indoor or outdoor garden.

Step 4: End this retreat with some quiet breathing, allowing yourself to feel the completion of the whole process. Notice the extra space inside your head now that it is no longer consumed with resentment. Allow this feeling of inner spaciousness to grow. Let a feeling of lightness arise within you. This is the openness you need for forgiveness to happen.

You Were Wrong

This retreat uses the same format as the "I Resent" letter, but it is practiced for an entirely different reason. Some people forgive too easily and too quickly. Perhaps they have trouble feeling or expressing anger, or they may assume they don't have a right to feel these negative emotions. They mistake submission and acquiescence for forgiveness. These people have difficulty asserting their rights, setting boundaries, or limiting the unacceptable behavior of others. The following may seem obvious to some, but I assure you it isn't to everyone: if someone keeps offending you repeatedly, forgiving them without setting healthy limits is like giving them permission to continue their offensive behavior. This retreat is designed to remind people of their rights.

Forgiving the unrepentant is like drawing pictures on the water.

—Japanese proverb

As with the "I Resent" letter process, you will need more than one day to complete this retreat. You will also need to choose your focus person before you begin. It's okay if you don't feel angry at this person now. Be certain that it's someone who has overstepped the limits with you more than once. Maybe she borrows things and never returns them; asks you to do more for her than she does for you; expects you to always respond to her needs but is unavailable when you need her. One important difference between the two retreats is that I don't suggest you burn your "You were wrong" list. Instead, keep it in some very private yet accessible place, so you can pull it out when you need help reclaiming your right to your feelings or boundaries. This list will remind you not to forgive as a way to avoid healthy self-assertion.

The "You Were Wrong" retreat ends with a special exercise from the Four Elemental Breaths of the Sufi Order of the West. By visualizing a fire in your chest and fanning the flames with your breath, you strengthen yourself to set limits. Then the instructions show you how to practice using this self-assertive energy in your daily life.

The one-minute retreat "Accessing the Fire" builds on the "You Were Wrong" retreat. Use it when you are in a real-life situation that calls for stronger boundaries and limit setting, when you need the strength to assert yourself.

In these two retreats, we are using cognitive therapy techniques to construct a bridge between retreat time and daily life. In the "You Were Wrong" retreat, we use imagination to practice applying the courage to be self-assertive when needed. In daily life we remember to use the one-minute retreat "Accessing the Fire" when we need the inner strength to set limits. Thus we build a bridge in both directions—from the retreat to life, and from life to the retreat.

Step 1: *Entering into Retreat:* You'll need the writing materials described in "Write an 'I Resent' Letter." Also follow the "Entering into Retreat" instructions also from that retreat.

Step 2: Write down all the ways your focus person has interfered with your life, harmed you in any way, been unfair, taken advantage of you, expected too much, been selfish. Begin with the words "You were wrong when you . . ." Feel free to include minute details. No complaint is too petty. The challenge for this retreat is to hold back nothing.

Step 3: *Returning to the World:* We will end this retreat with a special breathing exercise designed to generate the courage you need to assert yourself rather than retreating into forgiveness as an act of submission. Stand up and raise your arms, with your elbows bent and the palms of your hands facing forward. This is the standard "hands up" position from childhood pretend games or cowboy movies. Then, inhale through your mouth, holding your breath in the center of your chest. Imagine that your

> ### ONE-MINUTE RETREAT—
> ### ACCESSING THE FIRE
>
> When you find yourself in a real-life situation requiring courage
> and healthy self-assertion, you can take a few breaths to stoke the
> fire in your chest center. Subtly inhale through your mouth, hold-
> ing the breath inside for an extra second to intensify the inner fire, bringing
> back the experience cultivated by the "You Were Wrong" retreat. This will
> access the inner strength needed to stand up for yourself.

held inhalation is like a fire flaming inside your rib cage. As you exhale
through your nose, visualize the heat from the flames radiating out into
the space in front of you. After a few minutes of this practice, think of a
situation in which you are likely to be too forgiving, too passive, too
acquiescent. Breathe for a minute or so more while you imagine yourself
in that predicament. Then let your arms and hands return to your sides
and just relax. You're ready to face the world.

Communing with a Loved One

As in William's example with his dying father, our unfinished business
with a loved one who has passed on is one of the heaviest burdens to bear.
It's difficult to forgive ourselves for a mistake of omission or commission
when the person is no longer here to accept our apology. Likewise it is difficult to forgive someone when it's no longer possible to work through all
of your feelings, from pain and anger to loss and yearning.

This retreat is based on the concept that death is not an end but rather
a transition to another world just beyond the veil of our perceptions, a
belief shared by many world religions and cultures. As with other twenty-
minute retreats, this one begins a process that will need a series of "Communing with a Loved One" retreats. Usually we need more than one visit
to complete all our unfinished business.

Step 1: *Entering into Retreat:* Begin by paying attention to your breathing. Let your breath be light, even, and quiet. You will need a good five minutes to slow down, become quiet, and reach a calm stillness. You want to create the still silence necessary to perceive the presence of a loved one who has passed away.

Step 2: This next stage is the core of the retreat, taking about twelve minutes. Evoke the memory of your loved one. Remember how he or she looked, how his or her voice sounded, what he or she smelled like. Replay experiences you had with this person, both positive and negative. Allow whatever communication wants to happen, either in silent communion or with words. Such communication may be one-sided (from either side) or a lively two-way dialogue. This is your chance to complete your unfinished business, and you can return to this communing retreat as often as you need.

Step 3: *Returning to the World:* The final three minutes are to say goodbye. Again notice your breathing and the quality of the atmosphere surrounding you. If you sense a great stillness, you may have communicated everything you needed to. If the atmosphere seems a bit agitated, then it's likely you need to return to this retreat another day.

ONE-MINUTE RETREAT—FORGIVE US OUR GUILT

Guilt seems to be inevitable in our western culture. I explain to mothers, especially, that a certain amount of guilt goes with the job. It cannot be alleviated by therapy, only lightened by humor and, perhaps, this small retreat.

Imagine that you can take one specific feeling of guilt and throw it up in the air, just as you might toss a bird up in the air, encouraging it to take wing. Toss the guilt up. Let the wind carry it away. Repeat, if necessary.

Breathing through Your Heart

This is a wonderful retreat that can be used as a regular twenty-minute practice or, as Christina uses it as a one-minute retreat to help her open her heart to her mother. Either way, it works to open your heart, creating a greater capacity to love and be loved.

I learned of this technique through the Sufi Order of the West, although many religions are concerned with the subtle qualities of the heart. Thomas Merton writes of the prayer of the heart in the Christian monastic life, while Buddhists refer to the purification and illumination of the heart.

"Breathing through Your Heart" is designed to open the heart, which is a spiritual process. Psychologically speaking, it's very important for you to realize that this is not the same as forgiving everyone. Some people you can forgive, yet not forget the harm they've done. Others you can forgive, then choose not to deal with them. However, by breathing through your heart you can soften any hard-heartedness—you don't have to put someone out of your heart, whether or not you forgive them or ever see them again. This retreat is concerned with the subtle quality of your spiritual heart.

Step 1: *Entering into Retreat:* For the first three minutes, sit quietly and simply enjoy the flow of your breath. The movement of your breathing is the very essence of your being alive.

Step 2: Begin to imagine you can breathe directly through your heart center, inhaling and exhaling straight from the middle of your chest. This practice can continue for the next twelve minutes as your awareness gradually becomes increasingly sensitive, refined, and subtle. It's almost as if the flow of the breath gives a gentle massage to the heart, allowing layers of protection to lift off and float away. Any time your mind wanders, just gently return your attention to breathing through your heart.

Step 3: *Return to the World:* For the remaining five minutes, you will need to gradually shift your attention from the rarefied air of your heart to the reality of the world at large. This is quite a transition. Shift your awareness back to the physical movement of your breath. This will begin to move you solidly into your physical body. Gently open your eyes and

---

FIVE-MINUTE RETREAT—WE ALL NEED FORGIVENESS

The reason this is a mini-retreat is because I think it's such a difficult challenge to our egos that we can't sustain it for a full twenty
minutes. Think specifically of something you've done for which
you'd like to be forgiven. Imagine being forgiven by the other person. Imagine
being forgiven by yourself.

---

begin to let in your surroundings. As you're ready, stretch and move slowly
to standing up so you can stretch some more. Notice how your inner heart
space feels. Is it lighter? more open? clearer? more spacious?

Practicing Compassion toward Yourself

We are sometimes our own worst enemy, judging ourselves with a fierce-
ness we would never express to others. Understanding this self-imposed
suffering, the Buddhists practice compassion toward themselves and "all
beings." This retreat is literally about finding the compassion in your heart
to forgive . . . yourself. Compassion and forgiveness are closely related
within the heart, with one leading almost seamlessly into the other.

Step 1: *Entering into Retreat:* Use a full five minutes to sit quietly, just
being present in the moment. Allow your breath to flow smoothly, slow-
ing down gradually and peacefully. Be very gentle with yourself. If any
thoughts arise, gently guide your attention back to the rise and fall of your
breathing.

Step 2: For the next five minutes, center yourself in your heart space,
keeping your awareness in that inner space of your chest. Notice how that
space changes with the movement of your breath.

Imagine that you can breathe in compassion with every inhalation.
Your heart space expands, creating an interior spaciousness. With every
exhalation, breathe out anything that is not compassion, like old self-talk,
harsh judgments, guilt, or self-blame.

Imagine you can fill up your inner heart space with the warm, gentle flow of compassion. Take five minutes to experience the spaciousness and compassion in your heart. This is you being kind and gentle with yourself.

Step 3: *Returning to the World:* You will need the remaining five minutes to gently prepare yourself for reentry. Begin to shift your attention from your breathing to the physical outline of your body. Feel what parts of your body touch other parts. Are your hands on your lap? your legs crossed? Slowly begin to change your physical position and to stretch in whatever ways feel good to you. During the next twenty-four hours, take one-minute retreats in which you re-create this feeling of being centered deeply in your compassionate heart.

Hold On/Let Go Retreat

This is a series of three retreats using art therapy for the purpose of facing the cost of holding on to anger and resentment. Arrange your paper and oil pastels or crayons in a comfortable way for drawing (see page 22).

DAY 1

Step 1: *Entering into Retreat:* Get in touch with all your anger, rage, disappointment, hurt, grief, and frustration embroiled in not forgiving a specific person in your life. Hold on to these feelings. Solidify them and identify with them. For some this will take two seconds, but give yourself three minutes to summon up the depths of these feelings.

Step 2: Do a nonrepresentational drawing of this emotional mix. Really get into the energy and colors that best express your feelings. Use as much time as you need, up to fifteen minutes. If you complete your drawing early, you can use a separate piece of paper to jot down words or phrases that express these same feelings.

Step 3: *Returning to the World:* Save the final two or three minutes to admire your drawing. Note its intensity, movement, color, depth. Hang it up in a private place where you can see it.

DAY 2

Step 1: *Entering into Retreat:* Give yourself three minutes to imagine how you would feel if you could totally forgive the same person used in day 1 of this retreat. Imagine you could let go of all negative emotions and feel free. Get in touch with whatever feelings accompany and arise with such forgiveness.

Step 2: As on day 1, use up to fifteen minutes to do a nonrepresentational drawing of how you imagine you would feel after forgiving this person. Again, if you finish early, on a separate sheet of paper jot down words or phrases to express your feelings.

Step 3: *Returning to the World:* For the final two or three minutes, admire your drawing. Appreciate it as an outward illustration of an inward possibility—forgiveness. Hang this drawing next to the first one.

DAY 3

Step 1: *Entering into Retreat:* Place both drawings side by side in front of you. If you have accompanying words, add those papers next to their respective drawings. For the next ten minutes, simply look at the two drawings (and the words). Notice as many details as you can about each of them and admire them both. Pay attention to what feeling states are evoked in you by each of the drawings. If you need a break from this concentration, simply allow your eyes to close. Return to looking at the drawings when ready.

Step 2: Get up and move to different places in the room so you can look at the drawings from all different angles. Continue doing this for five minutes.

Step 3: *Returning to the World:* For the remaining five minutes, sit anywhere you like in relation to the two drawings and just be in their presence. You can look at them or close your eyes as you wish.

The contrast between your two drawings may make it very clear to you what impact your anger and resentment have on you. There is always a cost to holding on to these feelings, and sometimes it helps to literally see it on paper. With the completion of this three-session retreat, please don't make any precipitous decisions or attempt to force yourself to forgive. Simply allow the process of forgiveness to unfold in its own way from within you.

And through all eternity
I forgive you, you forgive me.

—William Blake

5

Gratitude

*If the only prayer you would say in your whole life is
"thank you," that would suffice.*

—Meister Eckhart, thirteenth-century
Christian mystic

It's easy to be grateful when our lives are going well, when we're getting what we need and doing what we want. However, feeling grateful becomes a spiritual practice when we can truly express gratitude even when our lives are not going well. This is a far more difficult time to give thanks or express appreciation. It's much easier to fall into negative emotions like resentment, blame, bitterness, or disappointment. To feel gratitude at these times has to come from an inner decision to be grateful, no matter what.

This inner decision is not at all related to a Pollyanna philosophy; it's not a blind sort of optimism. It's actually a deep, spiritual decision of how you want to relate to life. I want my attitude toward life to be independent of the inevitable ups and downs. I want my philosophical stance to be consistent, not reactive to other people, circumstances, or luck.

A thankful person is thankful
Under all circumstances.
A complaining soul complains even if
He lives in paradise.

—Bahá'u'lláh, founder of Bahá'i faith

Brother David Stendle-Rast, a Benedictine monk, has made a personal study of gratefulness. In his book *Gratefulness: The Heart of Prayer*, he presents a quite radical belief: everything is a gift. All of life is a gift. This attitude goes beyond an optimistic outlook or even the ability to see something positive in any situation. This depth of gratitude arises from an overflowing heart. We are grateful for the very fact of being alive. Children are far better at this than we grown-ups are. They live closer to feelings of awe and wonder at those precious moments of being alive that we seem to hurry past, missing completely. We may learn much about gratitude by watching how excited and joyful children can become and trying to incorporate those feelings into our daily lives.

Heartfelt Thanks

Children move easily from feelings of gratefulness to love, to celebration with great enthusiasm. At the moment we see a child's heart overflowing with these feelings, we can receive a spiritual lesson in gratefulness.

If you were lucky enough to have a wonderful teacher in your early school grades, first through third, I'm sure you can remember something from her classroom—her name, the desks, the new boxes of crayons, the decorations, her smile. Can you also remember how you and all the other kids adored her, and how you were so grateful to have a year with her?

Ms. Bidler was just such a beloved first grade teacher. She had taught for twenty-five years and was retiring at the end of the school year, so her class had to say good-bye to her not only for the summer but forever. As part of their good-bye ritual, the children made thank-you cards, not on the computer but small works of art, printed by hand.

The drawings on these cards were a child's version of the "Heartfelt Gratitude" retreat in which you do an emotional drawing of what being grateful feels like in your heart. The kids did this spontaneously; they didn't need the structure of retreats as we grown-ups do. As my client, Ms. Bidler brought the children's cards into my office to share them with me during a psychotherapy session. It was exciting to see the love expressed so directly and to see how deeply Ms. Bidler was touched by them. The children's cards were all quite different, yet they shared an intensity and openness of expression. They were pure in their expression of loving gratitude.

This is the quality of the emotional drawings called for in the "Heartfelt Gratitude" retreat. This pure expression of gratefulness, even when it's a bittersweet situation like saying good-bye, is incredibly healing. Heartfelt gratitude means you feel it in your heart, you literally feel the flow of positive energy radiating out from your chest. Oh, if only we adults could open up to these feelings as freely and easily as the children in that classroom! By practicing this "Heartfelt Gratitude" retreat we can reconnect with that youthful impulse once again.

Gratitude and Marriage

Couples need to commit to look consciously for the positive aspects of their relationship, to find things to appreciate, and to be grateful for each other if they are to create a fulfilling long-term marriage. When husbands and wives are not able to maintain this attitude of gratefulness, they often find a million reasons to criticize each other. In any marriage, there are always disappointments, hurt feelings, and conflicts. But in most marriages there are also strong benefits, like love and support at the end of each day. The decision to be grateful for the good things helps spouses to overlook the smaller affronts that are inevitable in day-to-day living and stay focused on what's positive in their relationship.

When I'm practicing marital therapy, part of my evaluation of a couple who come in for help has to do with each partner's ability to be grateful for the positive aspects of the other. Nora and Phil were a two-career couple with no children who came to see me when their marriage was in trouble. Nora said she couldn't see anything in Phil for which she could be grateful. As we began to talk, she was focused on what her husband didn't give her, how he neglected her, and how often he didn't do what she asked. She was partly right; Phil did have room for improvement. But, even as Phil's behavior improved in marital therapy, Nora remained as dissatisfied as ever. She was so used to seeing the negative, she wasn't able to open up to see the positive and be grateful for the effort Phil was making to rebuild their marriage. Many of us fall into the trap of seeing the world from a negative perspective and often are not aware of just how much our outlook colors our experience. When this happens we have to step away from our usual point of view to gain another vantage point.

To this end, I suggested Nora and Phil do the "Appreciate Your Spouse" retreat as a homework assignment between therapy sessions. The retreat encouraged Nora to discover positive things about Phil for which she could be grateful. As a result, she began to see him differently and even to understand that having gratitude for her relationship and all it had to offer was an inner decision she could make, regardless of his behavior. Nora realized that being grateful allowed her to enjoy her marriage and her life and therefore was a far better attitude for her to adopt than being dissatisfied. This change in Nora's attitude was a breakthrough in their marital therapy, motivating both of them to open up to each other in a newly intimate way.

You might want to take a moment to consider your general attitude toward life. The practice of being grateful can enliven your relationship to life and open your heart. Reflect on the following clues to see if you need to cultivate gratitude.

SIGNS THAT YOU NEED A GRATITUDE RETREAT

1. You complain a lot and often contribute a negative comment no matter what the topic.
2. You have trouble getting started in the morning, as if you've lost your enthusiasm for life.
3. You overlook the presence of beauty in the natural world.
4. You have resentment about events in the past.
5. You have trouble asking for help.
6. You frequently feel like a victim.
7. It's difficult for you to be dependent on others.
8. You haven't enjoyed the sunset or sunrise in the last few years.
9. You don't take care of your body.
10. Time seems to pass by too quickly for you to really enjoy life or live it to its fullest.

11. You have trouble enjoying the present moment.
12. You can't remember the last time you spontaneously hugged someone.

*H*elen's Story

For many of us, the easiest time to feel gratitude is when we're in a natural setting. The grandeur of the outdoors often forces us to open up and expand beyond ourselves. The horizon over the ocean, a canopy of trees that extends as far as we can see, the view from a mountain, a few moments spent by a running stream, or the crashing surf calls our hearts to overflow with awe, wonder, and yes, gratitude.

One of my friends has confided in me that his spiritual life is rooted in his boyhood summers exploring the forests and seashore along the New England coast. He was happiest alone with nature and, from those early years, developed a love for all the things of the forest—plants, rocks, animals, and birds. To this day, at age sixty-five, his connection with nature continues to feed his soul, keeping his heart open and filled with gratitude. He tries to get out for hikes and walks weekly, but simply spotting an unusual bird from his car window can brighten his day, making him feel grateful to be alive. We can all take note of what lifts us up each day and make a point of pursuing even a moment of that pleasure.

We can all count on the natural beauty of the wilderness to awaken deep feelings of gratitude. You can probably recall wonderful moments in nature from your own life, when you were overwhelmed by beauty. For me, these moments are almost like postcards in my mind, and when I take them out for review, they have almost the same effect on me as when I was actually there.

Helen, an investment banker, began to use the "See Beauty" retreat to balance her twelve-hour days in the office, most of which she spent at her computer. She felt she was losing touch with the natural world, that her reality was reduced to commuter traffic, E-mail, and office buildings with windows that never opened. On her way to the office, Helen began to pay special attention to small scenes of beauty—a person's face, a window box of flowers, the sky at early morning.

> ### ONE-MINUTE RETREAT—THANK YOU
>
> Saying "Thank you" is something we do every day, usually auto-matically, to strangers and loved ones alike. This retreat is a very simple approach to gratitude. Simply say "Thank you," consciously and from the heart, whenever the opportunity arises. You'll be sur-prised how total strangers will respond differently to these words when they are spoken consciously, with real meaning.

This retreat worked for Helen, reconnecting her to the beauty of nature and opening her up to experience gratitude for being a part of the world, for being alive. She brought flowering plants into her office, an admittedly excessive number of them, but she felt better at work being sur-rounded by beauty. Helen spontaneously began practicing the one-minute "Thank You" retreat, finding that the more she expressed her gratitude, the easier it was for her to have positive feelings flowing through her heart.

Imagine that at every moment we each embraced the world as the gift it is: An apple is a gift; the color pink is a gift; the blue sky is a gift; the scent of honeysuckle is a gift.

—Rabbi Marcia Prager

Retreats to Cultivate Gratitude

Heartfelt Gratitude

The feeling of gratitude opens the heart more than any other emotion except, perhaps, love. As we practice feeling gratitude, we expand our heart's capacity to experience and express love and joy. This opening of the heart is part of the subtle spiritual process in Sufism, the mystic path of Islam, and inspires the purpose of this retreat.

Step 1: *Entering into Retreat:* Have your paper and oil pastels available (see page 22), and sit however suits you best for drawing. For the first five minutes of this retreat, close your eyes and consciously decide to feel gratitude. Think of all the things for which you can be thankful. Pay careful attention to how you experience these feelings in your heart.

Step 2: Make an emotional drawing (see page 27) of this feeling in your heart. Remember, this is not a drawing of people or a scene. It's a free-form expression of feelings. You have a full ten minutes here. Some of you may spend all the time on one drawing, while others will do more than one drawing.

Step 3: For three minutes, close your eyes and again experience the feelings of gratitude in your heart.

Step 4: *Returning to the World:* In the final two minutes, look again at your drawing(s). Plan a time, just a minute during your busy day, when you will remember this drawing and the feelings in your heart.

Appreciate Your Spouse, a Friend, Family Member, or Anyone at All

You don't have to be married to practice this retreat. You can choose to be grateful for any person in your life. The more intimately you know the person, however, the more detailed you can be in the way you appreciate them. This retreat can also be used for people you don't know at all. I practiced it once while focusing on an elderly man whom I never met, who stood on the same corner every morning waving to the cars going by. No, waving to the *people* in the cars. He was such a friendly character, he was easy to appreciate. Indeed, sometimes it's easier to feel appreciation for strangers than one's own spouse. If you are having a tough time feeling gratitude for your significant other, that's a sure sign you need this retreat. Most couples can benefit from a structured reminder to help them maintain a positive attitude in their marriage.

This retreat integrates psychological and spiritual techniques. The cognitive-therapy aspect of the instructions helps us focus on the ways we

FIVE-MINUTE RETREAT—THE TIBETAN PERSPECTIVE

From the Buddhist perspective of reincarnation, we can be reborn in any form. As far as we know, the highest form for rebirth is as a human being, which brings with it the greatest opportunity for spiritual development. Take five minutes to consider what it would be like to be reborn in the form of a squirrel, a cat, a giraffe. Consider the spiritual opportunities you have as a human being to expand your awareness, exercise your freedom, and learn to love. Feel gratitude in your heart for being born human, with all that this opportunity implies.

think about our spouse in order to influence how we feel toward them. The mindfulness training gives us the technique for dealing with our negative thoughts toward our spouse as they arise, which expands our ability to concentrate and be grateful for the positive aspects of our relationship.

Step 1: *Entering into Retreat:* Spend the first three minutes committing yourself to doing this retreat. Promise yourself that no matter what negative thoughts arise, and no matter how valid they may be, for the next twenty minutes you are going to think positive. Trust me, if there are important complaints that arise, you will have no trouble remembering them at a later time.

Step 2: For the next fifteen minutes, think of your spouse. Imagine him sitting with you now. See his face, sense his energy, remember his smell. Allow yourself to feel gratitude toward your spouse in a general way, as well as specifically, such as how he laughs at your jokes or calls you during the day. Fifteen minutes is a long time to do this. You can repeat reasons to be grateful and things to appreciate as needed to fill the time. The discipline in this retreat involves dealing with the inevitable negative, disgruntled thoughts and feelings that doubtless will arise. Don't push them down; it's normal for the other side to come out. Simply acknowledge them, saying "That's one" silently to yourself, then return to appreciation and gratitude. These instructions are similar to those used in mindfulness meditation.

Step 3: *Returning to the World:* For the final two minutes, simply appreciate yourself for doing this retreat, for exercising the discipline to choose gratitude in one of your most important relationships.

See Beauty

Beauty surrounds us all the time; however, we are not always capable of seeing it, much less feeling grateful for it. It's amazing how much our perception of the world around us changes depending upon our inner attitude. This is a wonderful retreat to use when you are actually in a beautiful natural setting. Perhaps we need it most, though, in our regular daily schedule, hurrying from home to work and back again. We arc so used to our routine, we often miss the beauty surrounding us every day.

Step 1: *Entering into Retreat:* Use the first five minutes of this retreat to slow down. Close your eyes. Focus on your breathing. Count slowly for each inhale and exhale—1001, 1002, 1003 . . . See if you can extend your breath for a number or two without feeling stressed. Try to keep your inhale and exhale the same length.

Step 2: Gently let your eyelids open, allowing your focus to be soft. For the next eight minutes, look around you and intentionally see what is

---

ONE-MINUTE RETREAT—TWENTY-FOUR WONDERFUL HOURS

Thich Nhat Hanh is a Buddhist monk and a prolific poet with a wonderful way of expressing gratitude for being alive for a whole new day. He faces each day as twenty-four wonderful hours and suggests that each of us do the same. This retreat is inspired by his morning outlook. The attitude we choose upon awakening, even without that first cup of coffee, can set the tone for the whole day. As you awaken, before you leave your bed, take a moment and be grateful. Notice how this simple change of focus enhances your day.

beautiful. Gradually your eyes will see more and more detail. A cobweb in the corner of a small room can be beautiful.

Step 3: Close your eyes again and, for the next three minutes, repeat the counting of your inhale and exhale the same as you did in step 1. Notice if your breathing has grown quicker without your being aware of it. If so, extend the count a number or two.

Step 4: Open your eyes again and, for three minutes, look around you to see what is beautiful, *as if you are seeing it for the first time*.

Step 5: *Returning to the World:* For the last minute, simply take an extra deep breath and let it go all the way out. Continue to see beauty in your surroundings as you go about your day. Allow yourself to feel gratitude for both the presence of beauty in your world and your ability to see beauty.

Death, the Great Teacher

In many spiritual traditions, there is no better teacher than death. Novices in Tibetan Buddhism are sent to meditate in graveyards to face their own mortality and to learn that life is precious. Nothing makes us more grateful for the life we have than the realization of its inevitable end.

Preparation for Retreat: Draw the Death card from your tarot deck and place it in full view. Also have your book interpreting the tarot cards close at hand (see page 24).

Step 1: *Entering into Retreat:* Find a comfortable position for this retreat. If you like, lie down with pillows and blankets to create a cocoon of comfort. For the first three minutes, just settle in, feeling the movement of your breath through your body.

Step 2: For the next ten minutes, let your mind travel through all of your thoughts, images, associations, and memories related to death. Include symbols and images from movies, artwork, and literature. Then concentrate on the Death card from your tarot deck, noticing all the exquisite detail.

Step 3: For the next five minutes, consider the inevitability of your own death and what you need to accomplish, experience, and complete

FIVE-MINUTE RETREAT—OPEN FUTURE

There are times in our lives when it's difficult to be grateful for either our past or our present. These are the times when we need to be careful to remain open to the possibilities in our future. So sit in front of a vista, either at a window, outdoors, or in front of a painting. Then close your eyes and sense the vista in front of you. Imagine your vision extends through your closed eyelids into the space in front of you, into your future. Spend these five minutes being grateful for the future possibilities that await you.

before you go. Be grateful for the time you have to do this. Then read the meaning for the Death card in your tarot book. You will see that this card is symbolic of transformation and change. Consider this interpretation of death and its meaning in your life.

Step 4: *Returning to the World:* In the last two minutes, feel gratitude for the whole length of your life, from birth to death, and for all your experiences.

Donation

A donation is only part of the gift we give to our favorite charity. The larger gift is our gratitude that the charity exists so we can support it. You can do this retreat anytime you write a check to support a worthy cause.

Step 1: *Entering into Retreat:* Use the first three minutes to sit with pen and checkbook at hand. You have made a clear decision to give away some of your money. Be aware of any ambivalence you might have and reaffirm your decision.

Step 2: Take a minute to write the actual check.

Step 3: For the next twelve minutes, concentrate your awareness in your heart center. Allow feelings of gratitude to flow through your heart

ONE-MINUTE RETREAT—WEATHER

Weather is probably the most common topic of conversational complaints. It provides a great opportunity for agreement and bonding; however, the conversation doesn't really have to be negatively oriented, which it so many times is. Consider the possibility that every conversation on this subject might be an expression of our gratitude for some aspect of the weather. "I saw some beautiful lilacs this morning, just beginning to bloom. Thank heaven for the rain." "I'm enjoying the new frost and the incredible colors of the trees this fall." "Isn't the snowstorm great?" is something I overheard from a child in the snow belt of upstate New York. In any conversation about the weather today, focus on adding a positive remark that will enhance your gratitude for whatever nature has to offer.

for the abundance you have that allows you to donate to others. Be grateful for the existence of the charity you have chosen to support, and the opportunity they give to you contribute.

Step 4: *Returning to the World:* For the final four minutes, simply focus on the quality of feeling in your heart center. The experience of gratitude purifies our heart energy, so notice the subtlety of how that feels. As you enter your day, allow your heart to remain as open as it feels when you give. One outward, physical way of maintaining this feeling is allowing your facial muscles to be soft.

Pleasure

It's a tradition among Hindu spiritual teachers in India to give something sweet, like hard candy or raisins, to their students. Sometimes, also, in the West, a teacher from that religion will toss candy into the attending crowd at the end of a lecture or meditation. This is great fun, and people of all ages love it and feel blessed. The candy is given as a reminder that life is sweet.

We have many experiences that remind us that life is sweet—basking in the warm sun, relaxing in a hammock, enjoying the glow after lovemaking or the elation after exercise. In this retreat we use these moments to remind us to be grateful for our physical pleasure.

Preparation for Retreat: You can do this retreat at the actual time of experiencing these pleasures, or you can imagine them for the purposes of this retreat. If you like, you may do this retreat while holding a hard candy in your mouth to help you focus on life's sweetness.

Step 1: *Entering into Retreat:* Use the first three minutes to become more aware of your physical being. Feel the movement of your breathing, the outline of your body from head to toe, the contact with whatever you're sitting on.

Step 2: Either place a sweet candy in your mouth or imagine a time, like those mentioned above, when you physically experienced the pleasure of being alive. For the next seven minutes, feel gratitude for those experiences, for that pleasure.

Step 3: For the next seven minutes, focus your gratefulness toward your own physical body. Do not get sidetracked into being grateful about your appearance. Stay concentrated on the ability to experience pleasure.

FIVE-MINUTE RETREAT—EVERYTHING IS A GIFT

Adopting this attitude, that everything is a gift, will change your perception and experience of daily life. It's irrelevant whether this attitude makes sense to you or not, whether it seems rational or irrational. This brief retreat is not about faith or even belief but, rather, simply about the decision to adopt a particular perspective on your world. Once you take the philosophical stance that everything is a gift, then no matter what happens, you will look for the positive lesson, outcome, or potential inherent in any situation you face. It's your looking for the gift that makes each experience a gift. Pause at any time during your day and devote five minutes to seeing everything in your life, right now, as a gift.

Be grateful for your physical existence, your rhythmic breathing, your ability to exercise, your sense of taste, your eyesight. There are many aspects to your physical existence that give you pleasure and for which you can be thankful. Review them and remember their pleasure.

Step 4: *Returning to the World:* Use the final three minutes to enjoy the pleasure of stretching. Allow yourself to stretch in whatever ways feel good to your body. It always helps to stretch full length on the floor, reaching with your hands overhead on the floor and extending your heels downward. Be grateful your body will now carry you onward in your day.

To be grateful is to recognize the Love of God in everything He has given us—and He has given us everything.

—Thomas Merton, Trappist monk

Long and Winding Road

We will acknowledge the philosophical influence of the Beatles with this retreat, which encourages us to reflect on the paths our lives have taken, with all the curves, setbacks, and expressways. We've all been lost along the way but have found our path with help of one kind or another from teachers, loved ones, and strangers. When someone helps us in this way, they are acting as a spiritual teacher, guiding and enriching our unfolding. For example, even a total stranger can appear in our lives at just the right time with the message we need to hear. This is why the Sufis suggest you always talk with the people you meet when you're traveling. The encounters you have on the road may appear to be serendipitous, yet there may be a hidden spiritual purpose behind your meetings. Spiritual teachers can appear in our lives at any time and in many different forms.

This retreat offers an opportunity to express our gratitude to those who have acted as our spiritual teachers, guiding, encouraging, and supporting us when we needed them the most. For the truth is that none of us would be where we are today without this help.

I recommend you do this retreat before the "Self-Gratitude" retreat. They are similar, but it's generally far easier for us to appreciate others' qualities.

Step 1: *Entering into Retreat:* Find a comfortable position in which you can write in your journal. Use the first three minutes to settle into a self-reflective mood.

Step 2: Begin this five-minute step by writing down headings for the major stages in your life: early childhood, school, adolescence, college, young adulthood, marriage and family, career, retirement. Write in the name of the person who influenced you most positively during each of those times, who made a difference to your future and the type of person you are now. You may write in more than one person for a specific time in your life or you may include none at all.

Step 3: Choose one of these people and concentrate on him or her for a full ten minutes. Think of the gifts they gave you, how they helped you, and how you changed as a result. Reflect on the qualities you admired in them, what you learned from them, and most importantly, what you have incorporated into your being as a result of knowing them. Write these thoughts and feelings in your journal, documenting this person's imprint on your life.

Step 4: *Returning to the World.* In the final two minutes, imagine you can send this person, whether living or dead, your best wishes, positive energy, and gratitude. You can hold them in your heart, think of them surrounded by white light, or imagine them having fun doing whatever they loved. Wish them well.

Self-Gratitude

This retreat is best done following the "Long and Winding Road" retreat, as mentioned earlier. This is generally one of the more psychologically challenging retreats, since so many of us have difficulty recognizing and appreciating our own positive qualities. By expressing our gratitude to

ONE-MINUTE RETREAT—GIVE THANKS

The most common way of expressing gratitude in daily life is the saying of grace before a meal. Whenever you take a bite of any snack or sit down to a meal, think of where the food comes from— air, ocean, earth. Think of the spirit of the animal that is now part of your meal. If your food was harvested, consider the people who grew or caught the food and those who brought it to you. Internally, say a brief grace that expresses how grateful you are for the nourishment on your plate.

others first, we may be more willing to express and accept these feelings for ourselves. This retreat follows the same format as the "Long and Winding Road," using the same categories in your journal.

Step 1: *Entering into Retreat:* Use the first three minutes to settle into a comfortable position with your journal. Be grateful that you can give this time and attention to yourself.

Step 2: For the next five minutes, reflect on these times in your life: early childhood, school, adolescence, college, young adulthood, marriage and family, career, and retirement. Write down the qualities inherent in you that helped you the most during each of these stages in your life.

Step 3: Dedicate ten minutes of concentration to yourself for one of these qualities. Feel this quality resonate through your inner being. Appreciate it as a part of who you are. Reflect on how this quality is expressed in your life and what a difference it has made to you as the years unfolded. How can you nurture this inner quality in your current life? Write these thoughts and feelings in your journal, even if it's difficult for you to give yourself positive feedback. Write down whatever beneficial observations come to mind.

Step 4: *Returning to the World:* Use the last two minutes to become aware of how you experience this quality right now, in your current life, today.

Right Here, Right Now

This retreat is a meditation on being in the moment and being grateful that we have this opportunity to be, here and now. Being present in the moment is one way to cultivate gratitude for being alive. If we are totally right here, right now, we don't have the same worries that accompany our memories of the past or thoughts of the future. We can be grateful for the present.

The technique of focusing on your breathing is the basic instruction for mindfulness meditations such as this one. I have added the intentional shift in mind-set to the past or future to contrast with and highlight the experience of being in the present.

Step 1: *Entering into Retreat:* Sit comfortably in an upright position, with back support if you need. Allow your eyes to close gently. Use the first three minutes to begin to pay attention to the flow of your breathing. Feel the temperature of the air as it enters and exits your nostrils.

Step 2: For the next five minutes, keep your attention focused on right here, right now. If your mind begins to drift, gently return your focus to your breathing.

Step 3: Now intentionally begin to play with leaving the here and now. For the next ten minutes, consciously think of something in the distant past so you can fully experience the shift from the present to another time. Stay for a moment in that memory, and then come back to the present. Notice what it feels like to arrive again in the moment. Travel back and forth between the here and now and the distant past, the recent past, the distant future, and the near future. Always return to the present.

Step 4: *Returning to the World:* For the last two minutes, imagine your day today. Remember you can always return to the present moment for a brief respite when the demands of the past and future are too much.

Grateful for Music

We can be as grateful for music as we are for nature. Both are capable of brightening our world and filling it with beauty. When NASA sent the

Voyager out into space as a messenger from our planet to whatever form of life may greet it in the universe, cassette tapes of many different kinds of music were included in the spaceship, from Elvis Presley to Johann Sebastian Bach. Music can express a divine aspect of our shared humanity and can raise our spirits to exalted heights.

For this retreat, use any music you love, because whatever you love, you will be most grateful for. Some of my favorites are: "Claire de Lune," by Debussy; Piano Concerto No. 1, by Tchaikovsky; and the Brandenburg Concertos, by Johann Sebastian Bach.

Preparation for Retreat: Set up your tape player so all you have to do is push a button to start the music.

Step 1: *Entering into Retreat:* Lie down on a carpeted floor, arranging pillows for your comfort. Give yourself a full five minutes to relax. With every exhale, allow yourself to let go, then let go even more. After you are as relaxed as possible, you will find that you can still let go a little bit more.

Step 2: Start the music. For the next ten minutes, experience how the music moves through your body. Feel the vibration of it within you. Imagine you can hear the music with your body, instead of just your ears. Be particularly aware of your experience of the music in your heart center, being sensitive to the effect the music is having on you.

Step 3: During the next three minutes, while still listening to your chosen music, allow feelings of gratitude to arise from within your heart center. This may feel like actively loving the music. Also, be grateful that you're capable of this level of appreciation for music.

Step 4: *Returning to the World:* Use the last two minutes to stretch and move slowly to return to everyday life. You can turn off the music to end the retreat or, if you like, use the music during your daily activities to stay connected with the feelings of gratitude in your heart center.

It is gratefulness which makes the soul great.

—Rabbi Abraham Joshua Heschel

6

Healing

Healing is transformation.

—Himayat Inayati,
of the Sufi Healing Order

We all need to be healed, to feel more whole. Deep down inside ourselves, we know there's more to life, more that we can be. We dream of transformation, like a caterpillar dreams of becoming a butterfly. However, no matter what we do to seek or encourage it, the process of healing proceeds according to its own timetable for each of us. Rarely can we see or guess what the next step of healing will be. There is always an element of mystery to it, far beyond logical comprehension.

It is this elusive component that makes all healing sacred healing. More is happening at the different levels of healing—physical, emotional, and spiritual—than we can know or imagine. Sometimes we can help with this process of healing, and other times we need to just allow it to follow its own course. One paradoxical aspect of healing is that someone can be healed during their illness and yet still die. Inner healing, spiritual healing, is not the same as remission of physical or emotional symptoms or cure. Healing is related to our capacity to experience and embrace life as it is. Often this means accepting the unacceptable, making peace with disintegration, and loving whatever we face. These are the signs of healing. They illustrate how healing transforms our relationship to life.

Healing, then, is part of our life's path, and as Stephen Levine, a Buddhist teacher who works with the dying, says, healing is what we were born for. What did we come into this world to heal, and what do we need, within ourselves, to be healed? What can we give and what can we receive? The amazing thing is that sometimes the healing we need can only come from the experience of giving to others. For example, when I am totally stuck with a psychotherapy client, I will suggest he or she try doing volunteer work, something that puts them in direct contact with those needing care, like being a hospice volunteer or a Big Brother. One man I counseled, an engineer, took up rocking cocaine-addicted babies in the neonatal intensive care unit. The babies gained weight, allowing them to go home earlier, and the engineer learned exactly what he needed to about giving and receiving love.

The potential for healing is always present, whether in the healing of our relationships, the healing of ourselves, or the healing of others. We must realize that healing is a spontaneous and essential part of our spiritual journey. The more we are able to heal ourselves and others, the more whole we become—we are transformed again and again.

Healing Our Relationships

Relationships sometimes need healing, just as the individuals involved do. We make a terrible assumption when we limit relationship healing simply to talking things out. Sometimes relationships improve with a seemingly minor emotional or spiritual shift in just one of the participants. In the following situation, a father changes his energy and then is able to handle himself differently with his son. The son, perceiving the change in his father, then responds better. With this kind of subtle reciprocity, relationships can gradually cycle in a more positive direction.

Ed was a master wood craftsman who still had his long ponytail from the sixties. He never imagined that he would have a communication problem with his teenage son. But Ed and James seemed to end up in conflict no matter what the topic of conversation was—borrowing the car, college decisions, football games, even the weather. Neither one of them meant to instigate a disagreement or create bad feelings. The conversations they had just somehow seemed to veer off in a bad direction as a natural course. Ed was sure they would both grow out of this tendency, but he didn't like feeling so much on edge with his only son. So he began to practice the "Smooth Your Energy" retreat before his talks with James. The retreat practice only took a minute and helped him to feel calm and centered. After a few conversations went better, James remarked on the difference in his dad's attitude. So Ed shared with James how he had been smoothing his energy field. James couldn't believe his father was into such a cool thing and couldn't wait to impress his girlfriend with the technique his dad had shared.

Relationships are complexly intertwined. When things are not going well, it doesn't often help to blame the other person. Rather, figure out what you can do differently to start a positive cycle and improve the relationship. It takes only one person to open the possibility for a healing dynamic.

ONE MINUTE RETREAT—SMOOTH YOUR ENERGY

Ancient esoteric teachings describe an energy field or aura surrounding the physical body. Some psychics like Rosalyn Bruyere and Barbara Brennan, who teach subtle energy healing in their respective books *Wheels of Light* and *Hands of Light*, can perceive this energy and describe it by color, size, intensity, or vibration. The aura changes depend on the person's state of mind and physical condition. Some psychic healers believe that physical healing can occur by working with this energy field alone.

Smoothing your energy field is a little like dusting. Imagine you can gently stroke the aura surrounding your body to soothe and purify your energy. Use your hands to dust the outline of your energy body, about six to twelve inches away from your physical body. Be sure to move around your entire body, from above the top of your head to the difficult-to-reach spot in the middle of your back and to the soles of your feet.

Healing can occur at many levels and in ways we don't understand. With the "Smooth Your Energy" retreat, Ed may have softened his non-verbal approach to his son, while appearing more available to listen and understand. James may have unconsciously noticed this more receptive attitude and become more open to his father. This could be the beginning of a more positive cycle, which may take father and son into a new, comfortable, and fulfilling stage of their relationship that could last for years to come.

Healing After a Loss

Mourning a loss is part of the healing process. However, healing occurs at a different level of being than mourning, because it involves a transformation of each of us as a whole person. It would be quite difficult to differentiate healing and mourning, and probably not all that useful when you are experiencing them, but it's important to recognize that healing is a larger process than simply mourning. In the following description, healing occurs at the same time as a person is in mourning.

Miriam was just in her early twenties when she lost her mother. She already had two children in diapers and could barely tend to them because of her grieving. Every time a holiday or birthday turned up on the calendar, she was again confronted with the fact that her mother was not there to share the joy. The empty space in her life actually made her heart hurt.

Psychologically, Miriam was doing everything she knew of to console herself. She cried as often as she needed and sought emotional support from family and friends. She organized a photo album of her mom's life and took comfort in wearing her mother's favorite ring. Still, the loss of her mother left her feeling empty and numb. Her children, sensing that something was amiss, seemed to cry and cling to her constantly. Miriam began to feel guilty that she wasn't able to be as responsive to them as she wanted to be.

Miriam began using the Shekhina retreat, because she thought connecting with this Hebrew goddess, the feminine aspect of God, would help to ease the pain of losing her mother. Even a goddess can't replace a mother, but Miriam thought that this retreat could be healing for her. The Shekhina is pictured as a beautiful goddess with expansive white wings, which Miriam imagined could enfold her in comfort and protection.

Miriam continued to miss her mother as much as ever, but by practicing this retreat on a daily basis, she also began to feel a deep, inner sense of being loved and nurtured. This was exactly what she needed, not just to survive the loss of her mother but to grow stronger and more whole. Miriam's experience with the Shekhina imagery seemed to fill her up so she could lovingly respond to her own children in the way she wanted. Healing at this level is transformational and goes beyond mourning.

We can all benefit from a healing retreat, since there is always something within us available to be healed. However, if any of the following indicators resonate with you, then perhaps you have a special need for a healing retreat.

SIGNS THAT YOU NEED A HEALING RETREAT

1. You suffer from chronic symptoms, such as headache, upset stomach, musculoskeletal aches and pains, with no clear medical diagnosis.
2. You don't feel rested and refreshed upon awakening.
3. Your sleep is disturbed.
4. You find you have more critical or negative things to say than constructive and positive comments.
5. The energy in and around your body feels imbalanced, jagged, edgy.
6. You feel too vulnerable, easily hurt, or weak.
7. You're overreacting to daily stress with impatience, frustration, annoyance, or irritation.
8. You're at a crisis or major transition in your life, and you need to reconsider your life direction, values, and calling.
9. It's your fiftieth birthday.
10. You have just suffered a major loss.

11. Your medical doctor has given you a serious health warning or medical diagnosis.
12. You have some uncomfortable relationships in your past or current life that you would like to heal.

Cynthia's Story

Healing needs to be an ongoing process, because we are continuously affected by life's ups and downs, whether by a major crisis or normal transition from one day's challenges to the next. Healing practices help us to move more gracefully through life changes and give us the strength to rise up to meet new challenges, as Cynthia's story demonstrates.

Cynthia was in her mid-thirties, and her career was building nicely. She carried significant managerial and bottom-line responsibilities in a major corporation and had a direct line to one of the senior vice presidents. She had worked hard to get to this level, postponing marriage and children. At this point, her company was acquired by a larger corporation and she was downsized, let go, fired.

Cynthia was shocked and flooded with a complicated array of feelings—anger, hurt, disappointment, fear, insecurity, vengefulness, shame. She spent the first few weeks after her last day at work sleeping a lot. Then she began to feel motivated to look for a new career opportunity. However, Cynthia's bitterness about her job loss made it impossible for her to face job interviews and explain why she had left her last position. She knew she wouldn't make a good impression because her negative feelings would be expressed nonverbally, and the interviewer would perceive her as disgruntled. After all, the first few seconds of an interview are the most important, and Cynthia knew she was not exuding positive energy.

In an attempt to change her outlook and energy for the better, Cynthia began to use the Native American practice described in the "Smudging" retreat to purify her energy. She lit the sage stick and circled the smoke from it all around her body as well as into the four corners of her bedroom and home office area. Then she would sit in the center of this

FIVE-MINUTE RETREAT—SMUDGING

 As a ritual, Native Americans harvest sage, dry the leaves, and tie them in bundles with string. They light this sage stick, which burns very slowly, creating a scented smoke for use in ceremony. You can buy already prepared sage sticks in health food stores. Smudging is a wonderful way to purify the energy in your aura, in your sacred retreat space, or your entire house. Purification refines the subtle quality of the energy in the atmosphere, clearing away any negativity.

Practice this retreat mindfully, honoring the sacred ritual. Light the sage stick and move it slowly to circle the smoke around your entire body. Be sure to include the top of your head, behind your back, and the soles of your feet. When you are finished, stand quietly for a moment and feel your feet connecting through the floor to the earth, and the crown of your head lifting toward the skies.

If you want to purify a space in your house, walk with the smoking smudge stick into each of the four corners of the room. Make sure the smoke enters hard to reach areas, such as behind doors or furniture. In this way you can purify your whole house, room by room.

cleansed space and practice the "Golden Light" retreat until she felt she was absolutely glowing.

These two retreats, used in combination, helped Cynthia to reduce the intensity of her negative energy. She also felt more open and ready to enter a new situation without being burdened by her old feelings. By practicing these healing retreats, Cynthia was able to view herself less as a victim and more as a warrior embarking on a new adventure.

As a transformational process, healing shifts our relationship to life. We perceive events differently, our reactions change, and our attitudes are uplifted. Cynthia wasn't just preparing herself for job interviews, she was shifting into a new attitude about her experience of being fired. The "Smudging" and "Golden Light" retreats saved her from getting lost in negative thoughts and feelings. Instead, she was able to heal and move on with her life.

The more light you allow to flow through you, the more wondrous your reality is.

—Rabbi Shoni Labowitz

Retreats to Cultivate Healing

Shekhina Retreat

This retreat is adapted from Rabbi Shoni Labowitz's book, *Miraculous Living*. She is a student of the Kabbalah, an ancient tradition of Jewish mysticism. In *Miraculous Living* she describes the Shekhina, the Hebrew goddess, as having wings to lift us into an altered state of consciousness so we will be more open and receptive to our healing. Images of wings have always transported us to other worlds, from the wings of angels in the Bible to those of the mythological winged horse, Pegasus. Prayer shawls, used traditionally in Judaism, are symbolic reminders of wings in that they draw awareness into the body at the same place where wings sprout: the heart center at the back. This retreat uses the imagery of wings to convey a loving, even maternal, embrace.

Step 1: *Entering into Retreat:* Sit comfortably with back support. Close your eyes. You can use a scarf or shawl around your upper back and shoulders to give your body a kinesthetic sense of wings. Give yourself three minutes to let your breath become easy and light.

Step 2: For the next fifteen minutes, imagine that pure white feathery wings are encircling you. This is a mystical embrace of love and light. You are fully surrounded. You can rest easy in these wings, allowing them to support, protect, and sustain you. Feel yourself being enveloped and cared for. Allow this loving embrace to soak through you, down into your bones. Let your face become as radiant as an angel's.

Step 3: *Returning to the World:* For the last two minutes, gently allow your eyes to open. See if you can catch a glimpse of the shimmering light quality of the other world coexisting in this present world.

Golden Light

Many subtle energy systems, which heal through the laying on of hands, use the visualization of filling up your physical body with light to enhance healing. A variety of colors can be used, from a blue-white to a pure white to pale green. As recommended in Structural Awareness, a system of body exercises and visualization, I usually envision golden sparks of light. In my mind, they are similar to those gold-colored handheld Fourth of July sparklers we used to play with as children.

ONE-MINUTE RETREAT—HEALING EYES

 Wilhelm Reich, the founder of body-oriented Reichian therapy, which is described in chapter 2, claimed that one of the most important ways we block the flow of subtle energy through our bodies is with our eyes. As with many other approaches to healing, Reich's goal was for our energy to be able to flow freely and unrestricted throughout our bodies. This retreat will help you to relax and heal any tension in your eyes.

At your desk, in front of the computer, or while reading, pause to give your eyes a rest. Simply rub the palms of your hands together in a vigorous fashion to generate energy and heat. Then quickly place your hands over each eye socket so that your eyes are at the centers of your palms. Let your eyes relax in this warm darkness for the full minute. You can experiment with keeping eyes open or closed.

Step 1: *Entering into Retreat:* Use the first three minutes to get seated comfortably, with back support if you need it. Close your eyes. Let your breathing become gentle and easy.

Step 2: For the next fifteen minutes, imagine you can breathe in golden particles of dancing light. Let the entire inside space of your body fill up with these particles of golden light. As you exhale, let go of any negativity.

Once your inside space is totally filled with golden light, let the light permeate through your body into the space around you, like the glow of a candle. Continue this process of filling up and glowing with golden light for the full fifteen minutes.

Step 3: *Returning to the World:* For the final two minutes, simply let your breathing return to normal. Be aware of your physical contact with the floor or your chair. Open your eyes and glance softly around the room. Move gently as you stand up.

Healing Waters

Water has been used for healing throughout history, from ancient Grecian temples to modern-day spas. When combined with aromatherapy, water provides both a tactile and an olfactory experience. This is incredibly powerful sensory input, because our skin is our largest sensory organ, and touch is one of the earliest senses to develop. Also, our sense of smell carries with it our oldest memories. For instance, notice how a whiff of a favorite smell from childhood, like freshly baked bread, floods you with images and details that are decades old. This retreat gives a soothing experience directly to your body through the scented waters. Lavender oil is recommended, as it is the most versatile of all the healing aromatherapy scents.

Step 1: *Entering into Retreat:* You will need a few minutes to prepare by drawing a bath of very warm water. Put a few drops of pure, essential lavender oil in the tub. Light candles. Put on music if you like. Some musical suggestions are: *Lullabies and Dances,* by Julianne Baird and Bill Crofut; *Jean-Pierre Rampal Plays Johann Sebastian Bach; Canyon Trilogy,* by R. Carlos Nakai; *Pachelbel Canon and Gigue in D,* by Pinchas Zukerman;

ONE-MINUTE RETREAT—GATHERING
BAMBOO

This is a polarity therapy technique designed to ease headache pain, soothe tiredness, and clear your vision. While in a sitting position, let your head hang forward slightly as if you were looking down at your lap. Place your thumbs in the corners of your eye sockets under the inner point of your eyebrows. You should feel a ledge there where your thumbs seem to fit perfectly. Allow your thumbs to support the weight of your head for a full minute.

The History of Trees, by Enya; works by Debussy ("Clair de Lune," *Deux Arabesques, Images* I & II, *Children's Corner*); J. S. Bach: *Six Favorite Cantatas*, by The Bach Ensemble and Joshua Rifkin; *Sacred Space Music*, by Constance Demby; or *Sea Peace*, by Georgia Kelly.

Step 2: For the duration of this retreat, simply soak in the tub, enjoying the lavender scent and the warm water on your body. Since we are all wounded in one way or another, imagine that whatever needs healing in you at this very moment can be soothed and cleansed by the healing waters. Give yourself up to the water.

Step 3: *Returning to the World:* Move slowly when you are ready to get out of the bath. As you towel yourself dry, rub your skin briskly for stimulation. You skin is your body's boundary with the world and literally defines your physical identity. Create a global image in your mind's eye of your entire body, and experience a sense of wholeness from head to toe.

Breathe into Chakras

The word *chakra*, Sanskrit for "wheel of light," refers to the energy centers along the length of the spine. According to Yogic and Tantric adepts, prānā, or energy, flows along the chakras from the base of the spine through to the crown chakra at the top of the head. For healing as well as spiritual development, we want our energy to flow freely upward through our chakras. In this retreat we use breathing and imagery to encourage this energy flow.

Step 1: *Entering into Retreat:* Sit straight in a chair or sit on the floor with a meditation pillow. Please use a back support if you need it. For the first three minutes, allow your breath to become calm and slow. Notice the temperature of the air as it enters and exits your nostrils. Let your breathing slow down naturally.

Step 2: For the next fourteen minutes, consciously direct your breathing to each of the seven chakras, spending two minutes at each energy center. The chakras are located in the following areas of the body:

First chakra—at the base of the spine
Second chakra—just below the navel
Third chakra—at the solar plexus
Fourth chakra—at the heart center
Fifth chakra—at the throat
Sixth chakra—at the forehead
Seventh chakra—at the crown of the head

Begin by imagining you can inhale energy from the universe and then send your exhalation into the root chakra at the base of your spine. As you exhale, direct the flow of energy into that area. Feel the warmth and energy circulation being generated there. Using both your imagination and your breathing in this way provides a very strong visual and kinesthetic message to your body and energy system.

Then do the same for all the chakras in the following order, moving up your body from the root chakra to the center two inches below the navel, the solar plexus at your midriff, the heart center, the throat center, the "third eye" in the middle of your forehead, and finally the crown chakra at the very top of your head. Notice the sensation of heat or energy swirling as you exhale into each of these chakras.

Please note: One convenient way to handle the timing involved is to count the number of breaths you take during two minutes. Then simply breathe into each energy center for that number of breaths.

Step 3: *Returning to the World:* For the last three minutes, imagine you can let your awareness float in the space directly above your head. When you're ready to return to the world, bring your awareness back down into your body. Feel what you're sitting on. As you stand, feel your feet solidly on the floor.

Where matter and energy are interchangeable, true healing begins.

—Deepak Chopra, Ayurvedic physician

Inner Words of Wisdom

When we live our lives according to our inner words of wisdom, we find that life itself is healing. Although there are times when we need a spiritual teacher to help us recognize our own wisdom or to reflect it back to us, we must never forget that we carry the source of our strength and wisdom within. If we pay attention to our inner source of wisdom, we will know how to live our lives in a way that is healing.

This retreat employs both imagery and journaling to help you access the inner guidance you need at precisely this moment in your life. The instructions are intentionally kept very vague and open to allow for whatever response that wants to emerge from within you.

Step 1: *Entering into Retreat:* Have a journal and pen on hand as you find a cozy way to relax. Use pillows and blankets to bolster you in the most comfortable position. Take the first three minutes to slow down your breathing and enter the present moment. Be right here, right now.

Step 2: For the next ten minutes, allow yourself to travel on an inward journey. Feel your feet walking along a path through a dense, green forest. Hear the sounds of small creatures scurrying through the underbrush and birds in the distance. Notice all the different shades of green in the woods. Smell the scent of plants and vines that surround you.

FIVE-MINUTE RETREAT—FOUR
ELEMENTAL BREATHS

This is the complete practice for purification from the Sufi Order of the West. Purification involves the removal of impurities, so that only the pure essence remains. It is both a spiritual and a healing process. This retreat coordinates your breathing with images of earth, water, fire, and air, the four basic elements composing your subtle energy. Its healing purpose is to cleanse these elements within your energy, releasing any toxins, so your subtle energy becomes more pure. Aspects of this practice have been described in other chapters for specific purposes, but this is the complete cycle. Do this retreat while standing up. It is a particularly wonderful experience when you are out in nature, at the ocean, or in the mountains. Spend approximately one minute on each of the following elements:

Earth: Allow your head to fall forward slightly. Bend your wrists so that your palms face the ground. Breathe in through your nose and out through your nose. Imagine you can inhale through the soles of your feet and the palms of your hands. Feel the weight of gravity.

Water: Tilt your head very slightly up, as if you were standing in a shower. Allow your arms to hang freely at your sides. Breathe in through your nose and out through your mouth. Imagine water raining down onto your face, all around you, and dripping off your fingertips.

Fire: Stand facing straight ahead. Place your arms in the standard "hands up" position from old cowboy movies. Breathe in through your mouth and out through your nose. As you inhale, imagine you are stoking the flames of a fire in your solar plexus. As you exhale, imagine you can radiate light in every direction from your heart center.

Air: Soften your stance. Let your arms hang at your sides with your palms facing forward. Breathe in through your mouth and out through your mouth. Imagine that the breeze can move right through your physical body.

Come to a glade in the forest where wildflowers grow in great profusion. It's warm and sunny in this clearing, and the breeze feels cool on your skin. Lie down in a soft mound of wildflowers. Enjoy the moment. Open yourself up to a great inner receptivity. Make the following statement: "I am receptive to inner guidance and words of wisdom." Feel spacious inside, allowing whatever wants to emerge to rise from within you. Listen for words of wisdom. Sense any inner message. Watch for inner images to emerge. Be open and patient.

Step 3: For the next five minutes, write in your journal. Just let your pen flow across the page. Don't even read or think about what you're writing.

Step 4: *Returning to the World:* Use the last two minutes to read quickly over what you've written, so the thoughts you've recorded can percolate inside you as you go about your day. Remember that this source of wisdom lies within you and is always available to you. Return to your journal and read your notes again at a later time. For instance, you might want to read these notes in bed just before falling asleep, so you can request a dream related to these inner words of wisdom.

Gender Dialogue

There seems little doubt that both genders need healing in order to understand each other with empathy and compassion. This dialogue approach uses a combination of active imagination and journaling to help you integrate your inner male and female. Please note that these instructions are appropriate for both men and women, because we all have both masculine and feminine aspects in our psyches. The imagination side of this retreat encourages you to become more conscious of these aspects of your personality. The dialogue part allows for communication and mediation, which together will lead to your greater internal gender harmony.

Step 1: *Entering into Retreat:* Gather your journal and a pen. For the first three minutes settle into a comfortable position either sitting or lying down. Sit if you're at risk of falling asleep. Unlike many of the other retreats, don't pay special attention to your breathing. Instead, luxuriate in this time for yourself, for your own inner healing.

Step 2: Spend three minutes imagining your inner male. He may pop into your consciousness fully formed, or you may have to daydream him up. Some people have role models that fit perfectly, while others construct their own inner male, borrowing qualities and characteristics from men they have known. Visualize your inner male so you see all the details, can hear his voice, can practically smell him.

Step 3: For the next three minutes, do the same for your inner female.

Step 4: For the next ten minutes, write a dialogue between your inner male and female in your journal. Have them both talk, hopefully moving toward respectful communication with each other. Allow each gender to have his and her own voice. Trust whatever your hand wants to write. Don't reread anything now; just get as much written down as possible.

Step 5: *Returning to the World:* Thank your inner male and female for existing and for participating in this retreat. Put your journal away in a safe place so you can read your dialogue later. I recommend waiting a week or so to read over this dialogue. This time will give you the advantage of distance and objectivity, so that when you read your journal, you will be better able to hear your inner male and female voices.

Sacred One,
Teach us love, compassion, and honor
That we may heal the earth
And heal each other.

—Ojibway prayer

Woundedness

We are all wounded. There is no other way to go through life. We are wounded by our parents and we are wounded as parents. We are wounded by love and we wound others in love.

The fact that we are wounded is not the problem. It is what we do with our wounds—whether our actions are driven by them, unconsciously wreaking havoc in our lives and our relationships, or whether we are inspired by our wounds to move toward greater intentionality and purpose in our lives. This retreat is very difficult because it requests nothing other than that you be present to your own wounds. No action, no quick fix, no goal. Just be with the pain, the scars, the unfinished business, and know that this is the first step in being healed and in becoming a healer.

Step 1: *Entering into Retreat:* Experience this retreat from whatever physical position you want. Some may sit in meditation, while others may curl up in bed with their favorite blanket. The choice is yours; trust your inclination.

For the first five minutes of the retreat, think about your woundedness. Your woundedness is the oldest, most familiar feeling of pain you can remember. Look for behavioral patterns that keep repeating throughout your life and the emotions that accompany these events. These patterns may seem frustratingly familiar, like becoming involved with selfish people, needing desperately to be loved, or having difficulty being self-assertive. Explore all the feelings and details. Think of all the ways your woundedness has influenced the course of your life and the ways in which your

---

FIVE-MINUTE RETREAT—HEART RHYTHM

 In *Living from the Heart*, Puran Bair, a teacher from the Sufi Order of the West, describes a technique to harmonize the rhythm of the heart with the breath. He teaches this meditation approach as part of his retreat seminars. Very simply, he suggests you use your heartbeat as a way to regulate your breathing. Locate your pulse in your wrist. Inhale for four beats, hold your breath for eight beats, and exhale for four beats. You can decrease or increase this number for your comfort, just so your breathing flows easily. However, be sure to maintain the ratio of holding your breath for twice as long as the inhale or exhale. By creating an inner harmony, the breathing practice in this retreat will help you to heal spiritually as well as physically.

woundedness is manifested in your life now. Feel your woundedness in your body, heart, and soul.

Step 2: For the next twelve minutes, just be present. Stay with whatever emerges when you explore your wounds. Follow the unfolding of layers as your woundedness reveals itself to you. Be willing to open your heart to your own experience. Give yourself permission to feel the whole range of emotions. Become the space in which your woundedness emerges. In other words, identify with your whole being, not just the wounded part. Allow yourself to expand so greatly that, no matter what the wound, your being is spacious enough to be a container for your experience.

Step 3: *Returning to the World:* There is still nothing for you to do but be present. Use the final three minutes to appreciate yourself for spending time with your own woundedness. Promise yourself that you will return to this retreat as often as needed to acknowledge your woundedness.

Laying on of Hands

Healing through a laying on of hands is an ancient tradition that continues today in religious circles as well as in modern medical centers. Some healers work on the body's energy field and never make physical contact; others lay their hands directly on the physical body; and still others purportedly perform psychic surgery by entering the body of the person needing to be healed. This retreat gives you the opportunity to experience all three levels of healing touch from the dual perspective of healing and being healed.

Step 1: *Entering into Retreat:* Lie down on a soft carpet or firm mattress. Arrange pillows for maximum comfort. Use the first two minutes just to smooth and quiet your breathing. Let out a long, audible sigh. Sigh again, louder.

Step 2: This second step is the essence of the retreat and will take a full fifteen minutes. Spend as much time in the following three phases of touching as seems right to you. Start by rubbing your palms together to generate heat and energy. Then place your palms about three inches above your physical body at your heart center. Feel the energy field of your body with your hands; feel the energy of your hands with your body.

Slowly let your hands approach your body until contact is made. Your palms may be overlapping on top of your heart center. Again, feel your body through your hands, noticing the rise and fall of your chest, and feel your hands through your body, noticing their warmth, weight, and quality of touch.

Now, imagine that your hands can sink into your body so that the touching actually occurs within your heart center. Again feel your body through your hands and your hands through your body.

Step 3: *Returning to the World:* In the final three minutes, gently let your hands lighten and very gradually lift off your body. Stretch slowly and prepare to sit up.

Healing is a cooperative venture between the conscious personality and the unconscious.

—John A. Sanford, Jungian analyst

7

Intuition

Between the conscious and the unconscious, the mind has put up a swing.

—*The Kabir Book*, Robert Bly's
translation of a fifteenth-
century Indian mystic

The definition of intuition that I like the best is: knowing without knowing how we know. We can recognize intuition when it happens, whether it involves an inspired leap, an educated guess, a gut-level hunch, or an elusive feeling. If challenged, however, we hem and haw, then admit, "I don't know how I know. I just know."

We all have intuition, although we each have a very different relationship with our ability to be intuitive, and that determines how much we pay attention to and trust our intuitive signals. Some of us ignore our intuitive signals, while others regard them as absolute truths. The reality is somewhere in between. It makes sense to learn how to recognize our intuitive inklings but also how to evaluate their validity and usefulness rationally.

I rely heavily on my intuitive faculties in my work as a psychotherapist. When a client says something that's very important, and that I shouldn't miss, I often see the sentence in my mind's eye as if it were being showcased on a movie marquee. This inner seeing happens spontaneously. I don't purposefully imagine the words; they just appear. And I've learned over the years to take this intuitive highlighting very seriously. I must add that this intuitive guidance doesn't happen so automatically in my private life. Personally, I miss important communications just like everybody else.

I tend to "see" my intuitive thoughts on a movie marquee because I am far more a visual learner than an auditory one. As a student, I always needed to read textual material; I couldn't learn from lectures alone. So, it makes sense to me that I get visual help with my listening skills. Each of us has certain preferences or sensory pathways for receiving information, and our intuition is likely to follow such preferences.

There was one exception for me, though, and this occurred when I received clear auditory information. I was passing through one of those small towns in Nevada where slot machines are everywhere. As I was paying a cashier for groceries, a slot machine called me over. I literally "heard" it say, "Play me." I responded without hesitation and won about $6.00. Unfortunately, this intuitive ability did not develop or expand.

By paying attention to how we receive messages from our intuition, we learn to be more sensitive and receptive to knowing without knowing how we know. We tune in to our own unique style of being intuitive and become more adept at noticing these messages. If we consciously want to develop our intuition further, we can intentionally invite it into our lives. We can notice and honor our intuition when it occurs. We can make a direct request for guidance from our intuition, and perhaps most importantly, we can maintain an open, effortless receptivity to our intuition.

Note that it takes a certain attitude to be effortlessly receptive, which is philosophically quite different from our cultural value of trying harder or striving toward a goal. Effortless receptivity assumes a degree of acceptance of whatever happens. Being open to your intuition is almost like calling a cat by name to get it to approach you. You sweetly call the name, then feign indifference as the cat gradually moves closer. If you appear too anxious, the cat will casually veer off away from you, just beyond reach. Our intuitive sense is similar. It can be honored, invited, and coaxed, but never forced.

This intuitive process is quite similar to the creative process. We can decide to write a poem or draw a picture, but then we need to be open to our creative impulse, following and expressing what wants to emerge. We intuitively recognize what sounds right in the poem, what looks right in the drawing. For me, intuition is central to my creative process; it's an inseparable aspect of my self-expression.

In her book *Awakening Intuition*, Frances Vaughan, a transpersonal psychologist, describes four different types of intuition: spiritual, physical, emotional, and intellectual. As you read through the retreats in this chapter, especially in the sidebars, you will find some labeled to fit into these categories, so you can experience every aspect of intuition. However, my focus here is on spiritual intuition, for this is the aspect most closely related to the experience of the divine. Our spiritual intuition can serve as a homing device, guiding us along our sacred journey. Sri Aurobindo, one of the late, great Hindu teachers of the twentieth century, wrote that "intuition is a memory of the Truth." No teacher or guru can give us the guidance or direction that our spiritual intuition offers. In fact, we should trust the guidance of our intuition to evaluate the wisdom in any advice given to us by others.

Intuitive Empathy

Some people understand immediately how others feel. Their ability to empathize goes beyond the information given, and they can sense what's bothering someone before a word is even spoken. However, not everyone is like that. Dianne was a kindhearted, forty-two-year-old woman who devoted herself to her volunteer work with autistic children. Unfortunately, she often missed important emotional communications from friends and, inadvertently, hurt their feelings. Dianne herself was frustrated and concerned with the fact that she so often "just didn't get it," didn't seem to have the emotional insight or perceptiveness to empathize with even her closest friends.

To develop her intuitive empathy, Dianne began to use the "Insight" retreat in this chapter. This practice increases sensitivity in the sixth chakra, or third eye, which is the energy center in the middle of the forehead, according to the Hindu tradition. Stimulating this chakra is supposed to increase insight into others, sometimes to the point of developing psychic ability.

Dianne liked using a candle flame as a point of concentration. This was a concrete task she could use as a focus to become very quiet inside and clear. In fact, Dianne felt that she was developing a center of stillness in her sixth chakra as a result of practicing this retreat. This new level of inner quiet and stillness allowed her to listen more carefully to what her friends said. Gradually, she was able to see into people in a way that allowed her to understand their feelings. Interestingly enough, Dianne's volunteer work with the autistic children also became more intuitive and, consequently, more effective. When her perception originated from this quiet center inside her, she had deeper insight into why people behaved the way they did. Although this level of intuitive empathy still did not come naturally to Dianne, she was learning that she could intentionally tune in, to be more insightful.

Only intuition gives true psychological understanding both of oneself and others.

— Roberto Assagioli, psychiatrist and founder of Psychosynthesis

Connecting with Nature

Intuition is not a rational, logical way of step-by-step thinking. On the contrary, intuition follows an irregular process of leaps and hunches, flashes of revelation, and pure guesses. Just as we court our creative muse, we can make ourselves available and receptive to intuition. One of the best ways to open up to our inner intuition is to connect with nature, especially if we have a special outdoor place we love. Whether we actually go there or just imagine being there, nature can help us to open up to intuitive ways of knowing.

For example, my neighbor Frank had spent every childhood summer at his family's cottage on the coast of Maine. There he learned to fish, read the signs of approaching weather conditions, and dig for clams. He knew the ledges where the seals liked to sunbathe and the evergreen trees where the eagles built their nests. This rugged coast was ingrained in his soul, giving Frank a quiet depth, an inner stillness learned from living close to nature. Although Frank was not a client, I felt as if I understood him completely. I had watched Frank grow up during those summers in Maine, where I also vacationed. Those of us who are lucky enough to be "summer people" on the Maine coast draw on our memories of clear August days to inspire us during our regular lives.

Now Frank worked as an engineer, spending his days in an office building, putting in long hours to build a successful business. His office was filled with old summer memories—photos of the sun rising over the ocean, an array of eagle feathers, a bowl of translucent sea glass, and a collection of smooth ocean stones in subtle shades from gray to green to purple.

Whenever Frank was frustrated with an engineering problem, he would use the "Nature" retreat to open up to his intuition. It often helped him find a whole new solution that he hadn't seen before. Frank had his own way of quieting himself to enter the retreat. He would pace around his office, looking over his summer photos, running his hands through the sea glass, and finally picking up one of the stones. Then he would sit in his chair, some distance from his desk, and just hold the stone in the palms of his hands. As he closed his eyes, the texture and weight of the stone would carry him back to the spacious summer sky and ocean.

Frank would reconnect with the intuitive part of himself, the part that had sat by the ocean's edge and walked through the deep forest. Frank would allow this intuitive part of his inner being to be present with his engineering problem. No pressure, no expectations. He would just sit with the stone in his lap and the papers on his desk.

Sometimes, after this retreat, Frank would experience an intuitive leap and see a creative solution to his work problem. Other times, he would have to put the problem away to work on a different project. Either way, Frank returned from the retreat feeling more whole and connected to his own source of intuition.

You can tap into your intuition and creativity as well. But to do so you must have your own touchstones for travel within. Everyone can benefit from a connection to their own intuition.

FIVE-MINUTE RETREAT—LEARNING TO SEE

A Native American elder gave these poetic instructions on learning how to see. They constitute a subtle training in shifting your perception, which is intrinsic to the development of intuition. They are quoted from *Everyday Soul*, by Bradford Keeney, a psychologist and student of shamanism.

"You must learn to look at the world twice. First you must bring your eyes together in front so you can see each droplet of rain on the grass, so you can see the smoke rising from an ant hill in the sunshine. Nothing should escape your notice. But you must learn to look again, with your eyes at the very edge of what is visible. Now you must see dimly, if you wish to see things that are dim—visions, mist, and cloud people, animals which hurry past you in the dark. You must learn to look at the world twice if you wish to see all that there is to see."

These are the best instructions I've ever read on learning to see through different eyes. They open up a magical world, ever present, waiting to be perceived. Try these instructions when you're out in nature and relaxed. Allow your eyes to learn a new way of seeing.

SIGNS THAT YOU NEED AN INTUITION RETREAT

1. You never remember a dream.
2. You feel disconnected from yourself.
3. You'd like to be more creative.
4. You feel a need for spiritual guidance or inspiration.
5. You've become cynical.
6. You feel a spiritual yearning.
7. Your meditation practice seems empty and forced.
8. You'd like to develop your inner life.
9. You want help with decision making.
10. You'd like to have more insight into interpersonal relationships.

11. You know there's more to life, but you don't know how to connect.
12. You're considering calling the Psychic Hotline.

Elaine's Story

Intuition plays a central role in the creative process involved in artistic expression or scientific discovery. In *The Intuitive Edge*, author and meditation teacher Philip Goldberg describes a vast array of inventions and research findings that reflect this intuitive process. The artist or scientist needs to cultivate intuition as an inner source of inspiration and creativity. If intuition is neglected or ignored, the creative process can become uninspired and empty, as illustrated by Elaine's story.

Elaine was one of the most dedicated teachers in the local middle school. She was a symbol of freedom and individuality, dressing in sometimes bizarrely colored vintage clothing. Kids knew who she was even if they never had her for a teacher. Even after teaching for twenty years, Elaine had never-ending patience with this most challenging of all age groups, and she was able to inspire the students to write poetry from their intense adolescent emotional lives. The kids loved her, parents were grateful to her, the administration valued her—but she was exhausted. For over a decade she had given all she had without replenishing her own creative wellspring. She had gradually fallen out of touch with her inner intuition and creativity. This past year even summer vacation did not revive her spirit. She had returned to her classroom in the fall with a fraction of the energy and enthusiasm she was used to having at the start of the school year. So Elaine applied for and received a sabbatical. She determined that this would be a time for her to work on her own creative writing, and possibly complete and publish that book of poems she'd been working on forever. Elaine knew if she didn't restore her own creative spirit, she wouldn't be able to inspire her students.

Elaine turned to the "Dream Poetry" retreat as a way to connect with her own intuitive resources. She hoped that the energy from her unconscious dream imagery would inspire her creativity, and so she began by keeping a dream journal. At the start Elaine could remember only a fragment or two of each dream, nothing coherent or even very exciting. But she kept writing in her journal, remembering more details and adding more story lines from each dream. Elaine's commitment to keeping her dream journal let her inner self know that she would pay serious attention to her dreams, that they were important to her. Soon she was recording complex, fully developed dreams in her journal.

Now Elaine was ready for the "Dream Poetry" retreat, and the poems that emerged were the best she had ever written. They tended to flow more smoothly, with richer imagery than those she had written previously. Elaine was pleased with her creative efforts and relieved to be in touch with her inner self the way she had been when life was slower and simpler. She was more intuitive about her own creative process as well, somehow knowing when to work even harder on a line to get the words just right, and when to quit and go for a walk.

Encouraged by her success, Elaine decided to try the "Mandala Drawing" retreat, even though she'd never before done any artwork. This was totally new territory for her creative efforts, and she felt like a kindergartner with a new box of crayons—thrilled and terrified.

Mandala drawings are laid out in a circular pattern, and this was very reassuring for Elaine, saving her from anxiety when facing a blank sheet of paper. She decided to structure her drawings even more by using them to illustrate her dream poetry. She found she could create mandalas with the same intuitive feel as each of her poems.

Working with these two retreats helped Elaine open up to deeper levels of her being. She once again felt a strong intuitive link between her unconscious and her creative expression. After her sabbatical, when Elaine went back into the classroom, she showed her students her published book of poems and, with equal pride, her unpublished mandala drawings. Once again, the kids were inspired.

---

*T*he poet puts into language that which we perceive
only through intuition.

—Adrianna Diaz, artist

Retreats to Cultivate Intuition

Insight

According to Hindu tradition, the third eye or sixth chakra, located in the center of the forehead, is often associated with intuition as well as insight and clarity. You can strengthen the energy from this center with this simple concentration exercise, which requires a lit candle. By using both a real candle flame and a visualization of an inner flame, this retreat helps you develop the flow of awareness between your inner and outer worlds. As you work with this retreat, you may begin to realize that this distinction between inner and outer, although convenient, is not real.

Step 1: *Entering into Retreat:* Light the candle and sit with it directly in front of you, ideally with the flame at eye level. Spend a full five minutes gently concentrating on the flame of the candle. Notice every shade of color in the flame, and how it changes as it moves and burns. Notice the halo of light surrounding the flame.

Step 2: Alternate closing and opening your eyes every other minute, for the next five minutes. Continue your concentration on the flame, noticing every detail. With your eyes closed, envision the flame burning inside you.

Step 3: For the next five minutes, keep your eyes closed and visualize the flame in the space behind your eyes, extending up inside your forehead. You may feel heat in this area.

Step 4: *Returning to the World:* Use the final five minutes to practice keeping the flame visualization burning inside you as you look around the room. When you need to strengthen your inner image, let your eyes return to the burning candle. Try walking around the room, even out of sight of the candle, to see if you can maintain your image of the flame independent of the actual candle. Return your attention to the burning flame as often as you need. At the completion of this retreat, please make sure you have blown out the outer candle, keeping the inner one lit.

Nature

The thirty-thousand-year-old religious tradition of Native Americans asserts that God is nature, nature is God. For us to be able to experience this reality, we need to suspend our limited ways of perceiving the world and use our intuition to see the sacred in the landscape. This is a new vision, one that leads to an intuitive way of knowing God in nature.

This retreat uses symbols of nature—sacred objects—to awaken our intuitive perception of God in a seashell, the divine in a stone. By taking the time to concentrate on these sacred objects in stillness and silence, we open ourselves up to the experience of nature as God.

Preparation for Retreat: Gradually create a collection of natural objects gathered from hikes, backyards, parks, or nature stores. Bring home stones, shells, driftwood, leaves, wildflowers, bones, feathers, pine-cones, or whatever catches your eye. Arrange your collection in a way that is aesthetically pleasing and meaningful to you.

Step 1: *Entering into Retreat:* Sit in front of your nature collection for about three minutes and become aware of your breathing. Realize that you, also, are another incredible manifestation of nature.

Steps 2–4: Select three objects, and concentrate on each one for five minutes. Contemplate each object in the following ways, discovering the style that allows you to connect most deeply: Close your eyes and feel it with your hands. Place the object over your heart chakra, in the center of your chest just over your breastbone or over the third eye chakra in the center of your forehead. These are two of the seven energy centers, according to the Hindu tradition. Hold it still in the palm of your hands. Smell it. Open your eyes and focus on the object, noticing every tiny detail.

Step 5: *Returning to the World:* For the last two minutes, sit quietly with these symbols of nature. Allow your intuition to sense the divine reality in these sacred objects. Remember you are, as well, a part of nature, a part of God.

Dream Poetry

As Old Testament stories illustrate, dreams are one of the most ancient methods of intuitively receiving knowledge from mysterious sources.

Shamans, the visionaries and healers in tribal cultures, enter into dream space and time to receive inspiration and guidance for themselves and their communities. This retreat is adapted from a workshop exercise by Henry Reed, a psychologist and author of *Edgar Cayce*. His approach encourages you to explore the meaning of your dreams through poetry.

Preparing for the Retreat: In order to do this retreat, you will need to be able to remember your dreams with some richness of detail. Begin by writing down in a journal whatever dream fragments and memories you have upon awakening. Some of you may remember a vivid dream as soon as you start paying attention, while others may need to write down their dreams in order to develop fuller recall. Within about a week this Jungian practice of journaling your dreams will enhance the memory of your time spent in dream space. Imagine that, instead of "just sleeping," you are traveling to another world, as real as this one, in which you will have meaningful experiences and learn lessons in life. Writing down your dreams then becomes more like a memoir of your travels.

Step 1: *Entering into Retreat:* Arrange yourself comfortably to write in your journal. Select a dream that you have already written out in detail, and read through it at your leisure. Then use the first five minutes to re-enter the time and space of the dream. Don't think about it or interpret it in any way. Just envision the dream unfolding around you. Dream it again.

Step 2: Take the next five minutes to read through your dream once more, underlining the words that seem to leap off the page, the phrases that resonate deep inside you, calling you into dream time and space. In your journal, make a list of the words or phrases that you've underlined.

Step 3: Take a full eight minutes to write a poem incorporating the words or phrases from this list, adding whatever other words you need. Don't worry about rhyme or meter, just let your pen flow in spontaneous, unedited lines. Or, if you prefer, write a prose poem, a few sentences based on words from your underlined list. Take more time if you need it.

Step 4: *Returning to the World:* When you feel satisfied with your writing, read it over one last time. Don't judge your poem or even interpret it. Allow yourself, in the final two minutes of this retreat, to imagine that you can travel between your night dreaming world and your day dreaming

ONE-MINUTE RETREAT—SYNCHRONICITY

Jung defined synchronicity as meaningful coincidence, as a magnetized moment when the outer world reflects the inner world. I don't know if some people are more tuned in to such coincidences, and so notice them more, or if synchronicity simply occurs more frequently in some people's lives than others. It's also possible that the more we respond to synchronous events, the more they appear in our lives.

Whatever the dynamics of synchronicity, we can always invite it into our lives by intentionally looking for unusual juxtapositions of events, by timing or pattern. Notice when you bump into people you know, when someone calls you unexpectedly, when someone lends you the perfect book. Recognize these coincidences and consider whether they relate in some way to the unfolding of your inner life. For example, I have one friend who pays attention to the song being played on the radio just at the moment she happens to turn it on. By assuming the message of that song will be meaningful to her, she listens more carefully and is less likely to miss a synchronous event.

world. Use your intuition to be open to the information that flows between these two worlds.

Mandala Drawing

The word *mandala* is Sanskrit for "circle," and Jung used this term to denote drawings based on a circular format. He did his own mandala drawings in his personal journal, and he also had patients do them as part of their treatment. The circular shape is symbolic of wholeness, so doing a mandala drawing encourages feelings of integration and healing. The instructions are kept purposefully flexible, because this type of creative expression follows your intuitive feelings. Just sense what feels right as you draw. Having the structure of a circle makes it easier to begin drawing. For those of us who face a blank page and art materials with fear and trembling, the mandala invites us into a reassuring, established structure.

Preparation for this Retreat: Gather paper and oil pastels (see page 22). Paper can be inexpensive newsprint or quality art paper. You can trace the outline of a dinner plate to create the mandala shape.

Step 1: *Entering into Retreat:* Sit quietly at a table with your art materials. For just three minutes, turn your attention inward to get in touch with yourself right here, right now. Don't look for words or images, just be aware of yourself at this moment.

Step 2: Use the next twelve minutes to do a mandala drawing. Since we each work with our creative intuition in very unique ways, follow any of a variety of suggestions to approach this drawing: allow your drawing to emerge spontaneously from your inner being as you are right now. You can stay within the confines of the circle, extend beyond it, or even ignore it completely. You can use the circle as a whole or divide it into quarters to further structure your drawing. You can use your entire retreat time to work on one mandala drawing, or you can work quickly and complete a series. You can use your mandala drawing to express your immediate feelings, to illustrate a "Dream Poem," or to reflect on a current conflict. Experiment with working in silence, or with music that you carefully select to reflect your inner state.

Trust your intuition in selecting any music and your approach to your drawing. You may find that you need extra time to complete it. Trust yourself and take the time you need to complete the drawing in one sitting. I do recommend that you not stop in midstream.

Step 3: *Returning to the World:* Use the last five minutes to sit quietly with your mandala drawing. Relate to it in a variety of ways: Allow your visual focus to soften and let the drawing come toward you. Look at it through half-closed lids. Imagine you are inside the mandala. Visualize the drawing in one of your seven chakras. These energy centers, derived from Hindu yogic training, are located at the base of your spine, below the belly button, at your solar plexus, at your heart center, in your throat, at the center of your forehead, and on the crown of your head. Imagine that the drawing can begin to move and shift, expand and enlarge, extend into three dimensions.

FIVE-MINUTE RETREAT—PHYSICAL INTUITION

Each culture has its own sense of personal space, and we all recognize immediately when someone invades our space by standing too close to us. However, the personal space extending behind our backs is experienced with far less awareness. This retreat sensitizes you to extend your intuitive awareness behind you, into the space you can't see with your eyes.

Whenever you're in a public place, strolling along the sidewalk, browsing in a department store, or shopping in the supermarket, give yourself five minutes to pay attention to how you experience your personal space. Intentionally notice the space behind your back. Take a rough estimate of the distance between your back and the closest person or thing. See if you notice as someone approaches you from behind. Pay attention to how far your physical space extends behind you. Compare that distance with how far your space extends in front of you and to each side. As you continue to practice this retreat, you'll notice that your intuitive awareness of your personal space will become more sensitive.

Write the date on your mandala drawing and save it in a private place. Your artwork is like a snapshot of your inner path, an intuitive expression of your unfolding at this moment. What you create is often interesting to look back upon at a later time, for clues as to where you have been and where you're going on your path.

Color Chakras

According to Hindu beliefs, each of the seven chakras (see below) has a corresponding color to which it vibrates in resonance, increasing the flow of energy between and through these centers. As the energy flows through the chakras, our intuition develops and begins to play a larger role in our life decisions. The way the colors are described for this particular retreat is taken from *Intuition*, by Patricia Einstein, a teacher and psychic. This retreat is designed to encourage an upward flow of energy through the seven chakras.

Step 1: *Entering into Retreat:* Sit in as upright a posture as is comfortably possible for you. Use pillows and back support if you need them. For the first three minutes, gently close your eyes and imagine that as you inhale, your breath travels up the inside space of your torso and all the way up through the top of your head.

Steps 2–8: Spend two minutes concentrating on each of the seven chakras. Imagine that you can send your breath into the chakra, and visualize each energy center intensely colored in the following ways:

First chakra, at the base of the spine:	red like a hot sports car
Second chakra, just below the navel:	orange like a tawny lion
Third chakra, at the solar plexus:	a golden yellow
Fourth chakra, at the heart center:	green like new spring foliage
Fifth chakra, at the throat:	blue like the sky
Sixth chakra, at the forehead:	royal purple
Seventh chakra, at the crown of the head:	white as angel wings

Clearly visualize the purest color possible in each chakra, as if you could hear the vibration of the color, taste it, and smell it.

Step 9: *Returning to the World:* Use the last three minutes to once again breathe up through the chakras with every inhale. Imagine a rainbow of color as each breath moves up through your seven chakras. Sense the white light radiating upward through your crown chakra.

As you prepare to move, open your eyes and notice all the colors in the room. Pay special attention to your depth perception. Often our vision improves after this retreat, and we see our surroundings more clearly. Move slowly as you once again become acclimated to the outside world.

ONE-MINUTE RETREAT—EMOTIONAL INTUITION

A high level of emotional empathy is often referred to as women's intuition; however, both genders have equal potential for developing this ability. In fact, many men use emotional intuition when they conduct job interviews, forming a positive or negative impression of a candidate in the first few seconds. Such first impressions are amazingly accurate predictors of later evaluations.

Do this quick assessment retreat just for fun, not as a way to seriously make a decision about another person, but as a way to become more aware of your emotional intuition that is already in use. As you encounter people you know and don't know, notice your first impressions and allow them to expand. Ask yourself: are they happy, stressed, tired, in trouble, anxious, misrepresenting themselves, lonely, secretive, straightforward, optimistic, depressed, fearful, confident, deceitful? Realize that this is your intuition working, and don't worry about level of objective accuracy. As with any muscular skill, the more you concentrate on building your intuition with practices like this, the more likely it will grow in its strength and accuracy.

Spiritual Intuition

This is the highest level of the four types of intuition mentioned earlier in this chapter: spiritual, physical, emotional, and intellectual. Spiritual intuition allows a direct perception of the divine, and it is often accompanied by awe or wonder and a great inner stillness. This is a mystical experience, and as such, it can't be created, programmed, or even imagined. If it happens, it happens spontaneously. You will do best to think of the development of spiritual intuition as a process of becoming more receptive to the eternal. You are gradually tuning in to the world of the spirit, refining your intuition to perceive the sacred within the ordinary.

Step 1: *Entering into Retreat:* Sit comfortably with your eyes closed. Use the first five minutes to focus your awareness right here, right now, by attending to the flow of your breath.

Step 2: For the next ten minutes, intuitively consider who you are beyond your personality, your physical appearance, your various roles and jobs, your mind and beliefs. Intuitively sense who you really are beyond who you think you are. At this level, you are an aspect of the divine. Tune your intuition to perceive this spiritual level of reality.

Step 3: *Returning to the World:* For the last five minutes, just allow yourself to be—no demands, no expectations. Simply be aware of a deep level of being, more than just the roles and responsibilities of your life. As you prepare to move and enter your day, take your time so you can continue to sense intuitively this deep level of being that is present within you.

Psychedelic

Psychologist Jean Houston teaches workshop participants to consciously train their sensory perception to cross over so they can, for example, see music, taste colors, and listen to movement. Expanding our ways of experiencing the world and expressing our creativity in ways such as these open us up to be more receptive to subtle messages from our intuition.

Step 1: *Entering into Retreat:* To enter this retreat, simply decide to pay primary attention to one of your senses—choose vision, hearing, touch, smell, or taste. Continue with your activities of the day, as this retreat requires sensory stimulation rather than isolation. For the first five minutes, simply notice as much spontaneous input to your selected sensory organ as you possibly can. It doesn't really matter which sense you select—it could be the one you favor most or your least developed.

Step 2: Continue with your day and, for the next ten minutes, intentionally try to blend your sensory experience. For instance, if you decided to pay attention to sounds, try to imagine you can see what you hear, feel the vibrations in your body, taste the sounds, or feel their texture.

Step 3: Use the last five minutes as a sort of sensory free-for-all— throw open all the doors of your senses and notice how many crossover experiences you can identify. Don't expect to get much done during this stage of the retreat, since most of your energy will be focused on experimenting with new ways of experiencing the world.

Step 4: *Returning to the World:* At the completion of this retreat, notice how you readjust to your familiar style of relating to the world. How do you diminish some sensory modalities in favor of others? How do you restrict sensory input so you can focus on your daily activities? And how does this affect your openness to your intuition?

Listening to the Silence

The Quakers have a long history of the practice of listening to the silence. At their weekly Sunday meetings, they sit in silence unless moved or called by God to speak. They wait for divine inspiration to guide their words, refraining from acting on personal impulse.

Listening to the silence means we use our intuition, not our ears. We become more sensitive to the experience of silence and intuitively receptive to what wants to emerge from that experience. This retreat employs the contrast of sound and silence to help you attune to the vastness of inner quiet.

Step 1: *Entering into Retreat:* Select a wonderful piece of music of any kind for this retreat. Experiment with world music   the more unusual to

---

FIVE-MINUTE RETREAT—INTELLECTUAL INTUITION

Since intuition can't be forced, we each have our own unique approach to coaxing our intuition to help in problem solving. Try this retreat next time you are facing a seemingly insolvable challenge.

Stop thinking about the problem. Instead, go for a walk, listen to music, eat a snack, take a nap, brush your dog, or go for a drive. We usually do these things to procrastinate. This time, do them to make time and space for an intuitive leap. Consciously shift from thinking hard to being receptive.

My best ideas often emerge when I'm in the shower. Perhaps this is one of those times when I am relaxed enough to be receptive to new thoughts and ideas. This retreat can help foster that open state of mind.

your ear, the better. Set yourself up so you can easily control the On/Off switch for the music. Give yourself five minutes to listen to the music, immersing yourself in the sound. Dive into it. Allow it to envelop you. Feel the vibration of the sound within you.

Step 2: For the next ten minutes, turn the music off and on at irregular intervals. Progress very gradually to longer and longer periods of silence. Pay special attention to the first moments of silence, just after you stop the music. Allow this dramatic contrast to sensitize your intuitive ability to listen to the silence.

Step 3: *Returning to the World:* Spend the remaining five minutes in silence. Feel the silence within you and without. Imagine yourself disappearing into the silence. At the completion of this retreat, inhale deeply and fully, and as you exhale, make a sound, a long extended sound. Feel the sound move from within you to without.

I call intuition cosmic fishing.
You feel a nibble, then you've got to hook the fish.

—Buckminster Fuller, architect and inventor

Transition Time

The transition between the dream world and the waking world is a very sensitive time. It's almost as if the dream body has to find its way back into the physical body as dawn approaches and the two need to "click" back into alignment. During the earliest moments of waking, we can almost be in two worlds at once, opening up the possibility for our intuition to flow between them.

Preparation for the Retreat: Place a clock where you can easily see it from your bed.

Step 1: *Entering into Retreat:* This is the most challenging of all retreats to enter, because you have to remember to do it at the very earliest moment of your awakening. As you fall asleep, you can experiment with concentrating on your intention to do this retreat, and it is hoped the intention will carry over to the next morning. Just trying to remember anything upon waking up can be difficult in itself. As you awaken and enter the transition time retreat, stay in bed, moving as little as possible for the first five minutes. Continue with slow, relaxed breathing, savoring this time almost as an extension of sleep.

Step 2: During the next ten minutes, remain in this slow, relaxed state while you mentally begin to travel over whatever issues are important to you in your life at this time. Don't think intentionally or sequentially. Just let your mind flit from one area to another, lightly touching on issues. You'll find you approach them in a very different way from your daytime logical thought processes.

As your mind wanders over the various aspects of your life, notice any intuitive thoughts or ideas that give you a new perspective or insight. Follow that line of thought another step or two. Tell yourself to remember this way of seeing things.

Step 3: *Returning to the World:* During the last five minutes, continue to stay relaxed, but use your rational daytime mind. Given a new perspective on an aspect of your life, reflect on the steps you would take today to begin to move forward with this fresh approach.

It is always with excitement that I wake up in the morning wondering what my intuition will toss up to me, like gifts from the sea. I work with it and rely on it. It's my partner.

—Jonas Salk, M.D., developer of polio vaccine

Collage of Many Selves

Even though we each think of ourself as one person, we are, in fact, an integrated blend of many different selves. We all know we behave one way in our professional lives, another way with close friends, and still another with our family. This gives us the creative flexibility to respond appropriately in a wide range of situations.

For teenagers, who have not yet established a strong sense of identity, this inner diversity can be disturbing: "Why am I one way with some friends and then another way with others?" The challenge is not to be the same person in all situations, but to be able to successfully integrate all the different aspects of ourselves. Maturity involves getting to know and accept these various selves, and intuition involves, in part, gaining access to how each of these selves sees the world.

Preparation for the Retreat: Gather together about twenty old magazines that have great photographs. Advertisements are as good a source of photos as articles. Select a variety of magazines that appeal to you personally. Also have scissors, poster board, and glue at hand.

DAY 1

Step 1: *Entering into Retreat:* Set yourself up in a comfortable situation to leaf through the magazines. Have scissors handy. Sit quietly for about three minutes, giving yourself a chance to reflect on all the varied aspects of yourself that you show in different situations.

Step 2: For the next fifteen minutes, simply cut or tear out any magazine photos that resonate with you in some way. You may simply like the photo, or it may reflect the way you feel in a specific situation. Trust your intuition. If you respond to a photo in some way, cut it out.

Step 3: *Returning to the World:* For the final two minutes, again reflect on the different aspects of yourself and how you are in the world.

Repeat this process until you have gone through all the magazines and are satisfied with your selection of pictures. You may have about ten to twenty pictures.

DAY 2

Step 1: *Entering into Retreat:* With poster board, glue, and scissors handy, spread out your preselected magazine pictures so you can see them all. For the next five minutes, simply sit quietly and allow your eyes to gently peruse the variety of pictures. Let the photos you selected mirror back to you all the different aspects of yourself. Don't think about this logically. Simply allow yourself to resonate and intuitively identify with the pictures.

Step 2: For the next ten minutes, experiment with arranging the pictures on the poster board to form them into a collage. They can overlap or be upside down. Any way you want to arrange them is fine. Use your intuition to see what arrangement feels right.

Step 3: *Returning to the World:* Once you are satisfied with the design of your collage, use the last five minutes to glue the pictures onto the poster board. Study your handiwork, and allow the wholeness of the new image you have created to reflect back to you the wholeness of your integrated self.

Inner Guidance

Many of us are at a point in our lives when we're ready for a change. Maybe we face a decision about a relationship, a new job or career, or a geographical move. Or maybe we face a transition concerning children, aging, or illness. These are the times we wish for wise advice. As much as we might be tempted to call a psychic hotline, our best guidance comes from within, if we can only quiet ourselves enough to listen to that still, small voice of wisdom we carry with us always. This retreat asks you to use your intuition to receive inner guidance. Your intuition can help you to sense inner feelings, internal images, or bodily sensations. With awareness you can move these internally experienced sensations into your full consciousness and, finally, into words.

Step 1: *Entering into Retreat:* I suggest you sit as you would for meditation, but with your journal handy. If you lie down, you may not be as alert to intuitive cues you receive. For the first five minutes, simply sit and breathe. As you notice any thoughts, feelings, body sensations, or other bits of mind content, just bring your awareness back to your breathing.

Step 2: For the next five minutes, ask for inner guidance to emerge: "I am ready to receive inner guidance." This is a most general request, trusting that whatever comes up will be what you most need. Focus on this statement without any expectations as to the answer or style of response. Maintain your intention, and be receptive.

Step 3: Remain receptive for another five minutes. Be sensitive to every inner sense or feeling, allowing any subtle clues to rise in your awareness, floating up like bubbles. As intuitions rise into consciousness, they move from dimly perceived sensations into symbols or feelings, and finally into words. Listen for these words.

Step 4: *Returning to the World:* During the final five minutes, jot down in your journal any words, phrases, or images that come to mind. These notes do not have to make sense. At the end of this exercise, be sure to thank your intuition for communicating with you.

Intuition, then, not reason is the source of ultimate truth and Wisdom.

—attributed to the Buddha

8

Joy

From joy I came, for joy I live,
in sacred joy I melt.

—Paramahansa Yogananda,
Hindu Yogi

oy is about celebration. So the real choice is, "What do I choose to celebrate?" If we celebrate only major events, like graduations, weddings, or the birth of a child, we won't have many opportunities for joy. Better to celebrate life itself, the fact that the sun rises every morning, that flowers bloom every spring, and that we are here to enjoy it all.

We have to see life through the eyes of the mystics to be able to celebrate being alive. If our focus is narrow, we will miss the sunrise because we're reading the front page of the newspaper. We have to see beyond our individual desires and not be limited by our egoistic disappointments. Our vision has to be broad to see all of life, to celebrate the ecstasy of existence.

Unfortunately, I'm personally not very good at joy, even on a mundane level. When I'm at a celebration, for instance, I find myself worrying about the excessive use of paper goods and the demise of the rain forests. I complete one book and immediately start another project without pausing to celebrate. You'll know which bird I am in this little story from *The Ramayana*, a sacred book from the Hindu tradition:

I see two birds in the same branch — one eats the sweet fruit, one looks on sadly.
The first bird wonders: in what prison does he live?
The second marvels: how can he rejoice?

There's an internal leap you have to make to feel joy so you can celebrate life exactly as it is, however it is. You have to embrace reality enthusiastically, with full acceptance. Alan Jones, dean of Grace Cathedral in San Francisco, says that this level of joy is one of the hallmarks of sainthood. It's clearly visible in the radiant faces of saints painted by old masters centuries ago.

Think of the joy in the wrinkled face of a modern-day saint, Mother Teresa, as she cared for the dying in the streets of Calcutta. This is spiritual joy, independent of external conditions. It is the celebration of the whole of life, the ecstasy in which pain and joy are inseparable. This is good news for me; I can worry about the rain forests and still experience joy. Joy arises from within and overflows into the world. It comes from a wonderful inner place of being exceedingly glad, even blissful. I am familiar with this source of joy and celebration; I just can't sustain it. I get the feeling of joy confused with happiness and fun. Am I happy enough and having enough fun to feel joy? Although highly overrated in our culture, happiness and fun are not necessarily related to joy.

Retreats for the Author

The retreats that help me to cultivate joy use the wonder of nature to overwhelm my personal hesitancies and limitations. "Cosmic Events," for instance, is a retreat straight out of my childhood. I have many memories of being woken in the middle of a warm summer night, to be carried outside to view some miraculous astronomical event. It could be anything from grand displays of heat lightning to a lunar eclipse. My mother enthusiastically followed the science news and was always ready to celebrate the night sky. These were joyous times, full of wonder and awe, as we marveled at the vastness of creation and then went back to bed.

One of my daughter's earliest memories is being carried out onto a pier in Key West, Florida, to look through binoculars. At age four, she witnessed Halley's Comet from the southernmost point of the continental United States. I hope the next time she sees it, she has a grandchild in tow and explains that middle of the night celebrations are a family tradition.

Rabbi Nachman of Breslov, a hasidic master of the eighteenth century, "taught that the only thing worth giving your children is joy." We create these moments of joy by celebrating the miracle of existence, not just our own, but the existence of the cosmos. Joy celebrating cosmic events carries us beyond our small personal lives to a spiritual perspective. Our concern with whether or not we had a good day today pales when we watch the drama of the universe played out in the night sky.

Music

Just as the wonder of the cosmos carries us to the heights of joy, so do certain pieces of music. My favorite is the climax of the Ninth Symphony, "Ode to Joy," by Ludwig van Beethoven, composed when he was completely deaf. He clearly heard ecstatic music in his head and wrote it down so that the rest of the world, centuries later, could be transformed by his shared experience of joy.

I recommended that Ruth, a client of mine, listen to the entire Ninth Symphony once and then listen to the "Ode to Joy" every day for one week as an antidote to her feelings of depression. Ruth was a housewife in her mid-forties who was just beginning to emerge from an extremely adversarial divorce. Her thoughts were a broken record of resentments, self-blame, what ifs, and pure rage. Her jaw felt permanently clenched. I was sure this ecstatic music could break through her negative thoughts, and at least remind her that joy was possible.

Ruth did her homework every day, listening to "Ode to Joy" one last time as she drove to her appointment to see me. When she walked into my office, she looked so much better, more animated and lively. She said that having listened to the music, she wasn't in the mood for having a psychotherapy session. We both laughed. I never expected "Beethoven therapy" to work that well. Of course, ecstatic music does not completely eliminate the need for psychotherapy, but it does have an enormous power to carry us into different emotional realms.

No matter how depressed we are or how dire our circumstances, music can give us a brief psychological vacation from our suffering. It can carry us into joyous feelings or at least remind us that joy is a possibility.

It may seem strange to think that we need to be reminded about the possibility of joy, but joy can silently slip out of our lives so gradually that we don't realize it's missing. Consider the following signs to reflect on the level of joy in your life.

SIGNS THAT YOU NEED A JOY RETREAT

1. You can't remember the last time you laughed until you cried.
2. You're too serious.
3. You haven't smiled at a baby in a long time.
4. You basically just try to get through each day.
5. You're not very generous.
6. You don't celebrate small events.
7. You think cards and wrapping paper are a waste of money.
8. You're not glad to be alive.
9. You don't enjoy your birthday.
10. You don't like your job.
11. You haven't had a vacation in a long time.
12. You don't notice when there's a full moon.

Barbara's Story

Joyful music is helpful in dealing with depression, but joy is not the opposite of depression. Joy is pure delight in being alive, ranging from deep contentment to ecstatic exaltation. When gratitude and love overflow, they bubble into joy.

However, as we mature and assume the responsibilities of adulthood, we often lose the feelings of pure joy we experienced as children. We sacrifice our joy in life to survival, maintaining our daily existence. Perhaps this is why babies and children seem closer to their joyous feelings, better at celebrating everyday experiences with exuberant enthusiasm for being alive.

Adults seem to express joy when they win something, either a sports event or money. But this is not true joy, because it's dependent upon winning. People are not joyous when they lose, and true joy is independent of such temporary external conditions as winning.

Barbara yearned for the joy she took for granted as a child, long before the stressful pressures of her education and her career began wearing her down. She was only in her late twenties, but she felt she'd been burdened with grown-up responsibilities forever. She had only dim memories of delight in play, carefree afternoons, and pleasure in everyday events.

Barbara thought the "Children's Joy" retreat was perfect for her, giving her a second chance to reconnect with childhood delight in being alive. She did have one crystal-clear memory of being on vacation with her family when she was about nine years old. She remembered the long hours of sitting in the backseat of the car, and finally arriving at their destination. As Barbara got out of the car, she heard the roaring sound of the falls — Niagara Falls. She remembers walking over to a viewing area with great excitement and being overwhelmed by the sheer power and glory of the falls. The sight was beyond anything she'd even imagined. Barbara felt carried away by her experience and could remember that feeling with great clarity two decades later.

ONE-MINUTE RETREAT—LOOK FOR BABIES

Babies are everywhere, especially if you frequent department stores and supermarkets. Look for them. Some will be asleep, others momentarily fussy. And some will be joyous and happy to share their joy with you. It's a blessing to make eye contact and smile at those babies. It's almost as if you share a secret in that split second of connection. This secret has to do with the miracle of birth and the joy of being alive. Look for those babies.

Using the "Children's Joy" retreat, Barbara can re-create her experience of seeing Niagara Falls for the first time. She could feel her childhood innocence and awe in response to so majestic a sight. As an adult remembering, she could consciously treasure these feelings of joy, surrendering to the glory of the moment. Re-creating this joyous experience transforms Barbara's interior world. It's almost as if she learns how to be more receptive or sensitive to feelings of joy. In her daily life, Barbara begins to feel lighter, less burdened with deadlines and stress. She starts using the "Look for Babies" one-minute retreat, which she previously had not taken seriously. Now when she sees babies in grocery stores or in parks, she can recognize the expression of joy that many of them have. They're just plain joyous about being alive. Barbara can now reflect back to their shining faces her own joy of being right here, right now.

Oh for the wonder
that bubbles into my soul.

—D. H. Lawrence

Retreats to Cultivate Joy

Cosmic Events

Goddess-worshiping religions, including witchcraft, have celebrated cosmic events for more than thirty-five thousand years, according to Starhawk, author of *The Spiral Dance*, in which she describes rituals for the waxing and waning of the moon, the new and full moon, the spring and fall equinoxes, winter and summer solstices, and other days of celebration. The most universal and recent cosmic event is the end of the millennium and the beginning of the twenty-first century, marked by joyous celebrations and rituals on every continent on the planet. On one level, these are just grand New Year's Eve parties, but on another level, they acknowledge the passing of a year and a century, the earth circling the sun, and a new beginning. How we celebrate cosmic events is our personal expression of how we relate to the universe.

Preparation for Retreat: For this retreat, you will need a candle, a match, and a calendar that includes the phases of the moon. The old-fashioned *Farmer's Almanac* is great because it also denotes solar and lunar eclipses, meteor showers, and visibility of the planets. Identify a cosmic event to celebrate. You will have to adapt these retreat instructions according to your situation, especially if you're outdoors.

Step 1: *Entering into Retreat:* Light a candle to represent the light in the universe. Use the first three minutes to simply observe your breathing while you concentrate on the candle flame. If you notice your mind drifting, gently return your attention to the candle flame and feel the movements of your breath in your rib cage.

Step 2: Transfer your attention from the candle flame to witnessing the cosmic event for the next ten minutes. Continue with your awareness of your breathing while you observe the sky. (Please follow all the warnings regarding *not* looking directly into the sun at solar eclipses.)

Step 3: For five minutes, alternate slowly between observing the cosmic event and closing your eyes to pay attention to the movement of your breathing in your body. Notice how this shift in focus between the universe and your inner world feels. Imagine you can allow your inner world to expand out into the universe.

Step 4: *Returning to the World:* For the final two minutes, feel the joy of witnessing the universe, being in the universe, and being a part of the universe.

Ecstatic Music

Joy that reaches spiritual heights includes feelings of ecstasy and bliss. We are carried away, beyond the limited confines of our everyday rational minds. Playing music, singing or chanting, and listening to music are frequent pathways to joy and bliss in every cultural tradition. The rhythms and instruments are different, but all the world's religions have sacred music.

The key to surrendering to ecstatic music is to listen with your whole body, not just your ears. Give yourself up to the music; let yourself be carried away.

Preparation for Retreat: Select music that, for you, is ecstatic. I recommend the Ninth Symphony, including "Ode to Joy," by Ludwig van Beethoven; *Appalachian Spring,* by Aaron Copland; or spirituals sung by Jessye Norman. You may want to experiment with a wider range of world music or traditional chanting. Set up the player so it's very easy to turn on.

Step 1: *Entering into Retreat:* This first step is very important, because the more relaxed you are, the more you can open up to the music. So take a full five minutes and lie down with pillows and blankets in a very comfortable position. You may appreciate pillows under your knees to give your back extra support. Lie on your back with your arms comfortably at your sides and your palms facing up. With every exhale, allow your body to relax a tiny bit more. Let the floor support the weight of your body. Feel the temperature of the air on your skin, especially on your palms.

Step 2: Start the music. For the next twelve minutes, give yourself up completely to the music. Feel it with your body. Let the sound enter, not just through your ears but through your palms, your heart center, or your third eye in the middle of your forehead. Imagine you can let yourself dissolve into the music. Lose yourself in it. Let the music carry you to whatever heights of joy you can reach. Surrender to the music so completely that you no longer exist separately from it.

Step 3: *Returning to the World:* You'll need the last three minutes to focus on your breathing. Feel the floor and pillows underneath you. Feel the movement of your rib cage as you inhale and exhale. Remember your experience of joy in the music so you can reconnect with it during the day.

Music is well said to be the speech of angels.
—Thomas Carlyle

Children's Joy

This retreat uses a visualization from a childhood memory of joy to remind us what joy feels like. As grown-ups, we can fall out of practice experiencing joy and forget not only what it feels like, but the fact that it's even a possibility. This technique is an application of cognitive therapy, illustrating how we can use visualization to consciously influence what we experience emotionally.

Step 1: *Entering into Retreat:* Choose a memory of joy from your childhood. It can be, as in Barbara's story, a memory from a family vacation, a birthday or holiday, a special surprise or celebration, or just a wonderful private moment. Then for the first five minutes, visualize this memory with as much sensory detail as possible. See the scene; hear what's happening; include any smells and physical sensations you can remember. You can do this remembering in your mind, in any comfortable physical position you like, or you can do it through journaling by writing down every little detail you can recall. Either way is just fine, whichever makes the memory more real and present to you.

Step 2: For the next ten minutes, feel the joy in this memory. Joy is often experienced as a full-body feeling, perhaps overflowing from the heart, but certainly spreading through the whole body and out into the energy field. Let yourself be swept away by the feelings.

FIVE-MINUTE RETREAT—SMILE

 This technique is suggested by Thich Nhat Hanh, a Vietnamese Buddhist monk. However, it follows the same principles as cognitive therapy. There are intentional things we can do or say to ourselves that will improve our emotional mood. A gentle half-smile is one of these things. Whatever you're doing in your normal activity, you can stop and sit quietly or you can continue being busy. Either way, consciously decide to smile just a little bit, an effortless, gentle smile. Notice how this small smile changes your emotional state.

Step 3: For just three minutes now, begin to reflect on what joy feels like. How do you experience it? What color do you imagine it would be? what shape? what sound?

Step 4: *Returning to the World:* During the final two minutes, as you prepare to return to your daily activities, imagine you can keep this experience of joy imprinted in your physical body and energy field. This is more than just remembering joy; it's integrating joy into your very being.

Laughter

This easy-to-do retreat is inspired by Norman Cousins's best-selling book *Anatomy of an Illness,* which describes his use of video comedies in his recovery from a life-threatening illness. His experience was that laughter was his best medicine. Laughter is sometimes part of the path to joy. It may not take you all the way to joy, but it's pretty difficult to get to joy without going through laughter.

Preparation for Retreat: Rent some videos that you find funny. Cousins said that the old comedy classics were the best for him—Charlie Chaplin, Buster Keaton, and the Marx Brothers. Have your remote control handy.

Step 1: *Entering into Retreat:* Give yourself full permission to watch the video without any guilt or thoughts about what you *should* be doing with this time. Use the first three minutes to relax into the chair, sofa, or bed. Sigh a few times with your exhalation.

Step 2: Enjoy the video of your choice for about fifteen minutes. Really let yourself relax, laugh, and delight in the silliness of the comedy. Notice how your body feels when you laugh.

Step 3: *Returning to the World:* Use the last two minutes to stretch, at first sitting down where you are and then standing up. Remember some of the funniest scenes from this video during your day.

Dance for Joy

Children spontaneously dance for joy, and this is a very clear example of how joy is a full-body experience. However, for me, the image that comes to my mind is Snoopy from the "Peanuts" cartoon strip. He expresses joy by levitating in the air and cycling his little legs in ecstatic circles while his expressive ears fly in the breeze. And he's usually joyous over a bowl of dog food.

Using your body to spontaneously explore the feeling of joy is a dance therapy technique. Specific encouragement is given in step 2 to explore novel ways of moving and to expand your movement repertoire. The emphasis remains on trusting your movement and experiencing joy as a whole-body feeling.

Preparation for Retreat: The most important element in this retreat is the music. Choose your favorite from any style of music as long as it's good dance music and it makes you want to move.

Step 1: *Entering into Retreat:* Use the first five minutes for stretching and gentle warm-up. Trust your body to know how it needs to stretch; just make sure you reach in all directions, stretching the backs of your legs and warming up your spine by bending over to try to touch the floor. You can use gentle music if you like or none at all for this step.

Step 2: Start your dance music. For the next twelve minutes, dance for joy. This doesn't have to be wild or exotic. Any way your body wants to move is fine. Experiment with moving your hips separately from your shoulders. Let the feelings of joy rise from deep within you to move your

---

ONE-MINUTE RETREAT—JUST SAY YES

 The feeling of joy originates from within, independent of external circumstances. However, the extent to which we can see everything as perfect will help cultivate the inner rising of joy. This retreat is inspired by *Dianetics*, written by L. Ron Hubbard, the founder of Scientology. At some point during your day, pause and look around you. Just say yes to whatever you see. Yes to the desk. Yes to the clock. Yes to the walls. You can do this one-minute retreat on your way to work. Yes to the tree. Yes to the traffic light. Yes to the car. Notice how this retreat influences your mood.

---

body. Remember to involve every part of your body, so you experience joy in your whole body.

Step 3: *Returning to the World:* For the final three minutes, cool down by walking around. It's a good idea to stretch your back and the backs of your legs again. Feel your whole body pulsing with joy.

The fullness of Joy is to behold God in everything.

—Julian of Norwich, fourteenth-century English mystic

Celebrate Yourself

You can plan to celebrate yourself at any time, for any reason, with your birthday being the most traditional day of celebrating. However, on any day of the year, this retreat is really a gift you can give yourself. And, of all the retreats, this is the last one most women will do. We are so used to taking care of others first, putting ourselves last, that we would just never get around to this one. And if we did try it, it would feel odd. If you identify with this pattern, then the "Celebrate Yourself" retreat is definitely for you!

Step 1: *Entering into Retreat:* Lie down in as comfortable a position as possible, using pillows, blankets, and whatever you need. Use the first three minutes to gently pay attention to the movement of your breath through your body. You don't have to change anything. Just notice what moves as you breathe.

Step 2: Imagine being present to greet yourself on the day of your birth. Ignore the realistic, physical circumstances of your birth and concentrate on seeing yourself as a newborn infant just entering the world. Spend ten minutes with this image of yourself. This is a magical visualization. You can talk to this baby, and the baby will understand. The baby may even communicate back to you. Remember, this baby is you at birth.

Step 3: For five minutes, reflect on the miracle of birth, how one moment you weren't here, and the next moment you were. Celebrate yourself for making that transition, for being born, for being alive.

Step 4: *Returning to the World:* Experience being alive in your whole body for the last two minutes. Joy is a celebration of yourself for being alive.

Yoruba Blessing

The practice of blessing the head with water is present in both Christian traditions and the Yoruba faith, an African religion that has survived in this country. This blessing is adapted from *Jambalaya,* written by Luisa Teish, a high priestess in the Yoruba tradition. You will notice that this ritual involves the same centers that the Hindus denote as the sixth and seventh chakras.

Step 1: *Entering into Retreat:* Sit with a small bowl of water handy. For the first three minutes, begin by paying attention to your breathing. Feel your body expand as you inhale. Imagine you can feel your energy field expand also with every inhalation.

Step 2: Dip your index fingertip into the water and then place it on the center of the top of your head. Focus your attention on this spot for three minutes, imagining a white light glowing there. According to the Yoruba tradition, this is the place where you were touched by the divine when you were born.

Step 3: Again dip your index finger into the water and touch the back of your head at the occiput. This is the bony ridge where your neck meets your skull. For three minutes, concentrate on this area which, since it's in the back, is usually out of your awareness. Imagine that the water blessing strengthens this area, providing protection.

Step 4: Dip your index finger again into the water and touch the center of your forehead. In the Yoruba tradition, like the Hindu, this energy center denotes clarity of vision. For three minutes, imagine a white light there.

Step 5: For another five-minute period, feel all three spots on your head simultaneously: the crown, the back, and the forehead. Imagine that a white-light energy from these three areas encircles your head.

Step 6: *Returning to the World:* Gently stand and begin to move around, entering into your daily activities. For at least three minutes, continue to feel greater awareness of your energy field surrounding your head.

Bon Appétit

We need to eat to live. It's just that simple. But we can easily lose this clear perspective by worrying about counting calories or wondering whether we're drinking the best possible coffee. It's rare to find someone who simply takes a joyful pleasure in their food.

Preparation for Retreat: Choose something healthy and yummy to eat so you don't have to deal with any guilt or self-recriminations. Personally, I prefer to eat what someone else has prepared. For instance, salads always taste better to me if I don't have to wash the lettuce. But this may not be true for you. Set a beautiful table for yourself with flowers and your best china.

Step 1: *Entering into Retreat:* Sit at the table and say grace for the food you are about to eat. Use these first three minutes to enjoy the anticipation of the meal and be grateful.

Step 2: No matter what your meal is, make it last for at least twelve minutes. When you eat, just eat, as the Zen saying goes. No TV, no reading. Pause to put down your fork and breathe every once in a while. Enjoy the texture of your food and how it tastes.

Step 3: When you're finished eating, notice how the meal feels in your stomach and the effect on your whole body. Just sit quietly for two minutes at the table. This is something we never do: enjoy having eaten well.

Step 4: *Returning to the World:* During the final three minutes, notice how your body feels as it moves, as you carry your dishes to the sink

---

FIVE-MINUTE RETREAT—SING IN THE SHOWER

There is nothing like singing. But most of us have few opportunities to really let ourselves belt it out. The car used to be a possibility, but now we're busy talking on the phone. So the shower remains our sacred space to sing our hearts out. Choose old familiar songs, turn on the water, and turn up the volume!

---

and tidy up. Remember, joy is a total body feeling, and enjoying food is experienced in your whole body, not just concentrated in a full stomach.

Joy in Giving

Some people are naturally more generous than others, and they're lucky to be so, for there is great joy in giving. If this is not our nature, then we would be wise to intentionally practice the art of giving. This involves remembering special occasions like birthdays, anniversaries, celebrations, and holidays. The gift itself is inconsequential to the remembering. A card is often enough of a gift. I promise that you will feel great joy when you spontaneously think of someone as you see just the right gift for him, and give it to him for no other reason than you thought he'd love it, too.

Step 1: *Entering into Retreat:* Sit with your journal. Use the first five minutes to make a list of everyone to whom you might, on occasion, give a gift. This includes those closest to you and extends to schoolteachers, hairdressers, associates, and acquaintances.

Step 2: For the next ten minutes, go through the list and make notes by each person's name with what you think might be a perfect gift for them. Gifts can be tokens of appreciation such as candles, poetry books, fancy cookies, or a bottle of wine. Think of each person individually and imagine what would surprise and delight them.

Step 3: Pause for three minutes to experience your inner generosity. Enjoy this feeling.

Step 4: *Returning to the World:* For the last two minutes, decide to carry this feeling of generosity with you as you go about your day. Let this feeling influence your behavior. Notice how you enjoy this day.

Giving brings happiness at every stage of its expression.
We experience joy in forming the intention to be generous;
we experience joy in the actual giving of something;
and we experience joy in remembering the fact we have given.

—attributed to the Buddha

Sun Worship

Ancient tribes, such as the Aztecs, worshiped the sun as the source of all life. We continue to worship the sun, despite dermatologists' warnings, because we feel more alive after sunbathing. The sun symbol stands for life-giving energy, power, and expansive, radiating energy. This retreat asks you to draw your own symbol of the sun as a way to connect with the joy of being alive.

Step 1: *Entering into Retreat:* Sit comfortably to draw with paper and oil pastels at hand (see page 22). For the first five minutes, visualize the energy of the sun in your heart center. Imagine that with every inhale, you are intensifying this energy, the source of all life. Feel the sun energy radiating from your heart in all directions.

Step 2: Make a drawing of this energy: what it looks like, what it feels like. Give yourself ten minutes, but please take longer if you need it to finish your drawing.

Step 3: Hold your drawing over your heart center for three minutes. Imagine the sun energy inside your body radiating out through the drawing. Imagine you can radiate joy.

Step 4: *Returning to the World:* For the last two minutes, imagine radiating this energy during the course of your day.

Celebrate Nature

The other morning I noticed a rabbit outside my window eating a dandelion. I was most grateful, as my lawn is covered with these yellow weeds, and then I began to laugh. The rabbit bit off the stem close to the ground, then chewed from the bottom up to the flower, just as a child sucks in a long piece of spaghetti. The rabbit paused for a split second with the yellow flower in its mouth, like a kiss on its lips, and then continued munching until the flower disappeared.

We have opportunities for joy all the time, because nature is always abundantly available. I had a friend who was bedridden with a terminal illness, and he only wanted to watch nature shows on TV. They brought him such joy! Even as he lay dying, he celebrated nature and life. Let's not miss an opportunity for joy.

Step 1: *Entering into Retreat:* It's wonderful to do this retreat outside, but you can also do it sitting by a window. Use the first three minutes to become very quiet and calm. Let your breath be light and silent.

Step 2: With this quiet attitude, begin to give your full attention to the natural setting surrounding you. For twelve minutes, consciously and methodically notice, in great detail, everything. See the ant working, hear the bird, feel the breeze, smell the grass, touch the flower. Lose yourself in nature.

Step 3: As you become more and more aware of this natural world, allow feelings of joy to rise up within you. For just three minutes, feel joy for the world, joy for life, joy for all of existence. And joy for how we're all a part of nature.

Step 4: *Returning to the World:* Stand and stretch for two minutes. Take a deep breath and let it go. Remember this feeling of joy and celebration of nature.

The beating of the heart of the universe is holy joy.

—Martin Buber, twentieth-century philosopher

9

Love

That Love is all there is,
Is all we know of Love.

—Emily Dickinson

ove will break our hearts. It's supposed to. That's the mystery of love. It breaks our hearts *wide open*. Then we have a choice. We can love again. Or we can close our hearts, clam up, freeze over, put up barriers, harden our hearts, and give up on love. But we know after our first heartbreak that there is no way to love without risking loss, sorrow, and disappointment. Those who do not choose to open their hearts to love again often become bitter, cynical, controlling, and selfish. Usually they don't even realize that they are not loving; instead, they blame others for not loving them enough.

I'm not just talking here about romantic love, passion, or even married love. Love is much bigger than that. We have many opportunities for love in our lives. Think of all the different ways we use the word *love*: I love spaghetti. I love to play basketball. I love children. I love my dog. Love can permeate everything we do.

For instance, I was browsing at a garden store the other day and found an extremely knowledgeable and enthusiastic salesman who gave me a guided tour through the roses, describing the qualities and history of each plant. After spending almost an hour noticing petal color, flower shape, and distinct smell, I was totally overwhelmed. "Which one shall I buy?" I asked.

He looked at me in surprise, after all his imparting of knowledge. "Why, buy the one you love," was his reply.

Love is many things, and no doubt my heart will break over my new rosebush. Will it survive, or be eaten by bugs and deer? I choose to love my new rosebush regardless and to love the deer, too. I'm working on loving the bugs.

Loving is probably the most important thing we do in our lives. Our ability to give and receive love determines our quality of life more than any other aspect. And our greatest regrets usually have to do with not expressing our love enough. Ultimately, the most important message at the end of life is "I love you."

Of course, we also have to let others love us. We have to accept their love and admit that we need their love. This means we have to be willing to feel vulnerable and dependent, and let others see us this way. Some of us are more comfortable and familiar with loving others than with being loved, and we find it embarrassing and frightening to be in the receiving role. We can learn to become more comfortable with the experience of being loved once we realize it doesn't come naturally.

We need to know for certain that we are lovable, that we deserve to be loved and that we are worthy of love—even with all our imperfections. This doesn't mean that we as adults should expect unconditional love. That's the nature of a parent's love for a child, and even then, not all parents are capable of it. Unconditional love is not a realistic expectation in adult relationships. We don't have to *be* perfect to be loved, but we do have to *behave* with care and consideration, if we expect to be loved.

We need to practice loving ourselves. I didn't say we have to love ourselves; I purposely said "*practice* loving ourselves." We can't wait until we feel spontaneous love for ourselves before we begin behaving in a loving way toward ourselves. We have to practice, whether we feel it or not.

Finally, if we're lucky or blessed, we will be consumed in love for the divine. Our hearts will open up so wide that our arms will embrace the world, and we will be united in love.

*L*ove Me As I Am

We all desire to be loved unconditionally. Maybe we didn't receive as much unconditional love as we needed growing up, or maybe we just yearn for the perfect lover who will appreciate us for who we are. Either way, the notion of being loved without demands or expectations sounds pretty good. It's terribly important for the health of our adult relationships that we recognize this wish as a regressive fantasy. First of all, it's not realistic, and second, it's a sign of immaturity to avoid the responsibility of behaving in loving, caring ways.

As adults, we have responsibilities in our love relationships. The psychiatrist M. Scott Peck, in his best-selling book *The Road Less Traveled*, describes love as an action verb: Love is as love does. And the main action of love is paying attention to the person we love, listening to them, thinking of them.

Many people are confused about unconditional love; they feel, "I should be loved just as I am, regardless of how I behave." This was the case with Bryant, a fifty-five-year-old physical therapist at a children's hospital who was caring and loving with his young patients but inconsiderate and selfish in his personal relationships. He had already been through two marriages and two sets of alienated children, yet Bryant persisted in his belief that he should be loved unconditionally. This belief precluded his having to face his own selfish behavior and lack of consideration. Bryant was the perfect candidate for the "Love Is Attention" retreat.

Wanting to improve his relationship with his teenage daughter, Bryant arranged to take her out to dinner. He decided he would listen to whatever she wanted to talk about for at least fifteen minutes during the meal and planned to set the timer on his watch. This turned out to be far more difficult than Bryant had imagined. During the fifteen minutes, he thought of at least fifty ways to interrupt his daughter. Instead, he followed the retreat directions, took a breath, and looked into her eyes. It helped that he could keep eating.

At the end of the meal, Bryant realized he had learned more about his daughter than he had ever known before. She had talked about her soccer team, her girlfriends, the teacher she hated, and her plans for college. And she had hugged him good-bye when he took her home.

It wasn't that Bryant didn't feel love. He literally didn't understand how to express his caring, that love is the action of paying attention, showing that we care.

It's Better to Love

As much as we may want to be loved unconditionally, it's far better for us to love than to be loved. Something magical happens when we generate love in our hearts, letting it overflow and radiate out into the world. This doesn't mean we should continue to love someone who doesn't treat us with care and respect. But it does mean we should seek opportunities in our life to love.

Shirley was in her late fifties and still as energetic as ever. Her husband had passed away, and her kids were involved with their own families, living far away. In her day-to-day life, Shirley was alone—she didn't even have a pet. But she was wise enough to know what was missing.

Shirley knew she wasn't loving enough. Even though she E-mailed her grandchildren regularly and volunteered at the hospital, she knew she didn't feel enough love flowing through her. So Shirley began using the "Flower Opening" retreat, and at the same time she become more involved at the hospital by training as a hospice volunteer.

As Shirley practiced the retreat, she began to feel an inner movement, a stirring in her heart. One of the first signs of this inner blossoming was that she began to develop close friendships with other hospice volunteers. She realized she was becoming more open to intimate conversations about life, death, and the meaning of it all. She was allowing herself to be deeply affected by her experiences of working with the dying and their families.

The "Flower Opening" retreat was helping Shirley to open her heart from within, and her hospice work was helping her to express her heart out into the world. Being with the dying is a spiritual training in how to live, and the major lesson has to do with love. As Morrie Schwartz says in

Tuesdays with Morrie, "The way you get meaning into your life is to devote yourself to loving others."

So at a time when her life might have begun to shrink and diminish, Shirley opened and expanded her heart, reaching out into the world with love. Life often works this way, with a transformation occurring on more than one level. For Shirley, the retreat deepened her hospice volunteering, and her work with the dying broke her heart open even more.

It may be painful to question whether we have enough love in our lives—either giving or receiving love. Too many of us are isolated, without daily opportunity to care for others or to be cared for ourselves. Be very honest with yourself as you peruse the following section, because it is possible to cultivate more love in your life.

SIGNS THAT YOU NEED A LOVE RETREAT

1. You're lonely.
2. Your heart feels closed.
3. Your response to situations is more cynical than you'd like.
4. You feel a yearning to experience the divine.
5. You don't notice beauty in your surroundings.
6. You want to learn how to love yourself.
7. You feel disconnected from your community.
8. You feel unlovable.
9. Someone you love has told you that you're selfish.
10. You're too isolated, not spending enough time with people.
11. You do nothing that is directly and immediately helpful to another person.
12. You question the meaning of your life.

Wendy's Story

Most of the signs that you need a love retreat don't show on the outside. You might feel them deeply, even painfully, but others would have no clue. You have to be very honest with yourself to admit, "I need more opportunities in my life to give and receive love."

No one would have guessed it, but this was the case for Wendy. She was an absolutely lovely young woman, bright, warm, and beautiful, with long wavy dark hair and shining dark eyes. Wendy was committed to her teaching career, and her young students loved her.

In Wendy's inner world, however, she felt completely unlovable, and she had well-developed beliefs reinforcing exactly why and how she was unlovable. During Wendy's childhood, her mother had been sick with arthritis and unfairly expected Wendy to take care of her physically and to cheer her up emotionally. Wendy grew up feeling that it was her fault her mother was sick, and that she was a selfish, inconsiderate person whom nobody would love. In adult relationships, Wendy felt guilty whenever she said no. She believed she had no right to her own needs, that if she didn't do whatever the man in her life wanted, then he wouldn't love her.

Wendy began using the "Why I'm Unlovable" retreat. She wrote in her journal every day, listing all the reasons she gave herself for why nobody would ever love her. Writing down her inner thoughts and beliefs helped Wendy to realize that they sounded very much like her mother's voice: "You think only of yourself. You just want to have fun. You won't make a good wife."

One statement at a time, Wendy went down the list, checking to see if it was really true. "No, I don't think only of myself; here are examples of how I think of others. I do want to have fun, and there's nothing wrong with that. I don't want only to have fun; I also like my work. And I will be a good wife, not a good traditional wife, but a good, sharing partner."

Wendy gradually saw that her feeling unlovable was rooted in old childhood beliefs, that when she reflected on them as an adult, she knew they were not true. Using the retreat to write out these old beliefs gave Wendy the opportunity to rethink these assumptions with a mature, objective perspective.

Feeling that she was ready to experience herself as lovable, Wendy moved on to the "Spiritual Love" retreat. Her personal image in this retreat was of a guardian angel, watching over her, protecting her, and loving her.

She felt the presence of this guardian angel most strongly during the retreat, but this feeling remained with her throughout her day.

*R*etreats to Cultivate Love

Love Is Attention

One of the favorite homework assignments that child psychologists give to parents of all children, no matter their age, is to spend fifteen minutes a day with their child. This seems like a very straightforward professional suggestion; however, most parents don't do it. They simply don't take the time. In my psychotherapy practice, I make the same homework assignment for couples. Usually, I suggest the husband spend fifteen minutes paying attention to his wife, but there are plenty of couples in which I give the assignment to the wife. Even if nothing else changes in the relationship, these fifteen minutes a day of undivided attention are a pure expression of love.

If you can't actually do this retreat with your child, significant other, or spouse, either in person or over the phone, then you can still do it in your imagination. If we really think about it, most of us know what our loved ones need us to listen to and understand. Even doing this retreat in our imagination will help us to be more sensitive when we see them.

Step 1: *Entering into Retreat:* Sitting comfortably, use the first three minutes to make a very strong inner decision: I'm going to devote a hundred percent of my attention to my loved one for a full fifteen minutes. Feel love in your heart for this person.

Step 2: The next fifteen minutes is practiced with your loved one; in person, on the telephone, or in your imagination. Give your full attention to your loved one by practicing mindfulness. Maintain comfortable eye contact. Listen to their words and hear the meaning of their communication from their perspective. Practice mindfulness to maintain your attention by being aware of your breathing. Just notice the physical sensation of your inhale and exhale. When you catch your attention drifting from your loved one, gently bring your awareness back to your breathing and

ONE-MINUTE RETREAT—BREATHE OUT "AAH"

In Hindu chanting, the "aah" sound is supposed to come from the heart chakra. With every exhale, breathe out the sound of "aah." Feel the sound arising from the center of your chest. Feel the vibration of the sound in your heart center. Let the sound call your heart into greater awakening.

your attention to your loved one. Be vigilant about drifting thoughts, such as what you'll do after this retreat is over, what you want to say, what you'd rather be doing now. When these thoughts come up, return to your breathing.

Please Note: You can be mindful and still engage in normal conversation. You don't have to be totally silent to listen. In fact, giving someone your full attention includes small comments like "uh huh" and "oh," as well as nonverbal responses like nodding your head in acknowledgment.

Also, this same retreat can be used with babies and small children. You are with the children in exactly the same way, practicing mindfulness. But instead of verbal conversation, you join the child in play. Be sure to follow the child's lead as you play together.

If you are doing this retreat with a loved one in your imagination, follow the same steps and just imagine what they would say. Maintain your awareness of your breathing as you pay attention to and listen to your loved one in your imagination.

Step 3: *Returning to the World:* Use the final two minutes to tell your loved one how much you appreciated this time together. Return your awareness to the love in your heart for this person.

Flower Opening

The Sufi Order of the West emphasizes the inner experience of the heart center. When I've asked people to focus on their heart center, they use a wide range of images to describe their experience. I remember that one young man saw only black when he looked inside, while another said he saw clouds. The variety of personal experiences is enormous when we look inside, so let the images come—from rainbows to fireworks.

This retreat uses a visualization of a flower opening to help the heart center open up and blossom.

Step 1: *Entering into Retreat:* You can do this retreat either sitting or lying down. I would recommend that you don't slouch or curl up, as you want your chest to be open. For the first five minutes, simply imagine you can breathe directly through your heart center, as if you were inhaling and exhaling through your chest. Imagine that with every exhale, you are clearing space in your heart center, opening up room for the flower to bloom.

Step 2: Visualize the bud of a flower in the inner space of your heart center. Choose any type of flower you like, and if you're not sure which to choose, try a rose. For the next twelve minutes, concentrate on this visualization, allowing the flower to open ever so slowly in the center of your heart. Notice the tiniest of changes, as the petals unfold gradually, the color of the flower changes, and the fragrance intensifies. Don't worry if your visualization blossoms before twelve minutes have elapsed. Simply spend the remaining time concentrating on the fullness of the flower in your heart center.

Step 3: *Returning to the World:* During the last three minutes, return your awareness to your breathing through your heart center. Feel your ribs

---

FIVE-MINUTE RETREAT—OPEN HEART

In Islam, there are many names for God, one of which is God the Opener (of the heart). This retreat uses movement coordinated with your breath to invoke this aspect of God. Breathe in through your nose, with your fingertips resting gently on the midline of your heart center. As you exhale out through your mouth, open your hands and extend your arms as wide as possible, symbolically opening up the doors of your heart. At the end of the exhale, return your fingertips to the midline of your heart center and begin again.

expand with every inhale. Sense the outline of your whole body. Notice what element of the flower stays with you. Often the scent of the flower's perfume lasts all day.

Why I'm Unlovable

In *Prisoners of Belief*, psychologists Matthew McKay and Patrick Fanning use a cognitive therapy approach to uncover the core beliefs limiting one's life. Believing that you're unlovable is a crippling example of a core belief. Often these beliefs work like a self-fulfilling prophecy: I believe I'm unlovable, so I choose someone who is incapable of loving, or I behave in unlovable ways. Either way, my belief is confirmed. I am not loved, and it must be because I'm unlovable. Now, reading this line of emotional logic, which is, of course, illogical, you are able to see the fallacy in the reasoning. But most of us don't examine our beliefs so concretely. We just assume they're true.

This is a three-day retreat, to give you plenty of time to work with each stage of the process. Take more time if you need it. "Why I'm Unlovable" gives you a chance to reconsider the facts and, possibly, change your core belief. After all, what would your life be like if you truly felt lovable and deserving of love?

DAY 1

Step 1: *Entering into Retreat:* Set yourself up comfortably to write in your journal. Use the first three minutes to focus your attention inwardly. Reflect on why you're unlovable, how long you've felt that way, and how this belief has influenced your relationships.

Step 2: For the next fifteen minutes, write down all the reasons why you're unlovable. List them, leaving at least half a page after each thought for more notes to enter later. Most of us have well-entrenched core beliefs, and it may take more than one day to list them all. In that case, add an extra day or two to this retreat.

You'll notice that your beliefs will fall into categories: *Appearance*— No one will love me because I'm too fat, have crooked teeth, too big a nose; *Personality*—I'm unlovable because I'm too shy, insecure, weird, hyper; *Achievements*—I'm unlovable because I don't make enough money, can't have a baby, didn't get the promotion, can't cook; *Possessions*—No one will love me because I don't have the right car, sexy clothes, good hair, the right friends; *Activities*—I'm unlovable because I don't play tennis, vacation in the right spot, dance well, like dinner parties. No doubt there are other categories. We're very creative in the development of our negative belief system.

Step 3: *Returning to the World:* Glance over what you've written and use the last two minutes to add other thoughts or jot down notes to continue this portion of the retreat another day. Appreciate yourself for investing this time and energy in the "Why I'm Unlovable" retreat, so you can be free of this negative belief.

DAY 2

Step 1: *Entering into Retreat:* Sitting comfortably with your journal, use the first three minutes to review what you've written from day 1.

Step 2: Consider each statement in your journal one at a time. Use fifteen minutes for this step, and add another day if you need it. In the space next to each statement, write down specific, realistic examples illustrating how this belief is true or false. For instance:

Belief	True	False
I'm unlovable because I'm too fat.	I don't like how I look in clothes.	George loved me and thought my body was sexy.
No one will love me, because I don't make enough money.	Wanda broke up with me.	Kim loved me and was satisfied with my professional level.

Step 3: *Returning to the World:* Use the remaining two minutes to glance over your writing and again appreciate yourself for doing this retreat.

DAY 3

Step 1: *Entering into Retreat:* This should be the final day of "Why I'm Unlovable," done after you've completed all the writing in your journal and feel you've completely uncovered your negative belief. Sit comfortably with your journal, and for the first five minutes, read over everything you've written. You can add more, if you like.

Step 2: Use the next five minutes to rewrite your core belief so it's more realistic and positive. Take great care with choosing just the right words and phrases that are accurate and reflect the journal writing you've done in this retreat. For instance, instead of "I'm unlovable because I'm too fat," write "I wish I were thinner; however, men still find me attractive and fall in love with me."

Step 3: For the remaining eight minutes, sit quietly with your new core belief. Be aware of how this new statement feels to you; psychologically, physically, and spiritually.

Step 4: *Returning to the World:* For the final two minutes, imagine how this new belief will make a difference in your life.

Your task is not to seek for love,
but merely to seek and find all the barriers
within yourself that you have built against it.

—*A Course in Miracles*

Spiritual Love

In Judaism, Christianity, and Islam, the image of blessing or grace is that it comes from above and descends upon us. This retreat uses that same image to enable you to experience spiritual love.

Part of my inspiration for this retreat came from Patricia, a young woman I saw in psychotherapy many years ago. Her mother had abandoned her and Patricia was, naturally, feeling very alone in the world. Psychotherapy could help her deal with this situation—how she understood her mother's behavior, how she felt about her situation, and what she did to cope—but psychotherapy couldn't change the facts. However, Patricia found a way to change her experience of being in the world. She began to concentrate on a picture of the Virgin Mary, especially when she felt lost and alone. Patricia was Catholic, so turning to Mary was quite natural to her. Within a few days, Patricia felt great love emanating toward her from the picture of Mary, and she let herself bask in this love. As a result of this experience of spiritual love, Patricia was better able to deal with her life situation.

The instructions for this retreat are written without reference to an image. However, you could easily use a picture of Mary, Jesus, Buddha, a goddess, an angel, or any image that you experience as full of spiritual love.

Step 1: *Entering into Retreat:* I suggest you sit up for this retreat, because one of the ways we experience spiritual love descending upon us is through the crown of the head. For the first five minutes, imagine that when you inhale, the energy of your breath travels up through the top of your head, and that when you exhale, the energy descends to your heart center and radiates outward. Use this imagery and subtle energy sensing with every breath.

Step 2: During the next twelve minutes, open yourself up to experience spiritual love. Imagine that this love radiates down onto you from above, almost as if you're being showered with love. Imagine that the crown of your head opens up, so you can receive the sensation of being loved directly into your body. Continue to radiate out through your heart center with every exhalation.

Step 3: *Returning to the World:* Use the last three minutes to bask in this feeling of spiritual love. Experience everything within you and around you as perfect. Remember this feeling during your day.

***W**e are put on earth for a little space*
that we may learn to bear the beams of love.
—William Blake

Metta

Metta is a traditional Buddhist term meaning "loving-kindness." This
practice of the heart was taught by the Buddha 2,500 years ago and is
a nonjudgmental embrace of others as ourselves, beyond separation, in
unity. Sharon Salzberg, a Buddhist meditation teacher, writes that through
metta meditation, we cultivate a loving feeling toward ourselves and all
beings equally. We learn to love others as ourselves and to love ourselves
as others. The following metta prayer is Lama Surya Das's version of
loving-kindness.

> May all beings be happy, content, and fulfilled.
> May all beings be healed and whole.
> May all have whatever they want and need.
> May all be protected from harm, and free from fear.
> May all beings enjoy inner peace and ease.
> May all be awakened, liberated, and free.
> May there be peace in this world, and throughout the entire
> universe.

Step 1: *Entering into Retreat:* Sit in a chair or on a meditation cushion
with as upright a posture as is comfortable. For the first three minutes,
simply watch your breathing, noticing the rhythm, the flow, the movement in your body.

Step 2: For the next fifteen minutes, repeat the metta prayer silently or aloud, taking a breath after each line. If your attention wanders, gently return to your breathing and the recitation.

Step 3: *Returning to the World:* For the last two minutes, stretch and begin to move. Notice the subtle feelings of love in your heart.

Love thy neighbor, even when he plays the trombone.

—Jewish proverb

Interbeing

The term *interbeing* is used by Thich Nhat Hanh, a Buddhist monk and poet, to describe the incredible interdependency in the web of life. He writes, "there is a cloud floating in this sheet of paper. Without a cloud, there will be no rain; without rain, the trees cannot grow; and without trees, we cannot make paper." Thich Nhat Hanh sees the interdependency in every single element in the universe, including ourselves. Everything coexists in everything else.

To see the world from this perspective of interbeing is to remember that the most ordinary artifacts of modern life play a sacred role in the grand scheme of things. And love is what keeps it all together.

Step 1: *Entering into Retreat:* Sit quietly for the first three minutes, paying attention to your breathing. Simply notice the natural rhythm of your breath, the flow, and the pauses.

Step 2: Slowly and methodically, begin to think through your day in great detail. Use a full twelve minutes to notice every person or object you'll come in contact with today. As you encounter someone or something, think of how you are interdependent with them. Trace all the connections from you to them through the environment you share, trade you exchange, people you know. Include the soap you use in the shower, the dishes for breakfast, the newspaper you read, the person you pass on the street, and so on. The way we all fit together on this planet is like an amazing, constantly moving jigsaw puzzle. We are interbeing together.

Step 3: For the next three minutes, go back to noticing the flow of your breath with the realization that you cannot and do not exist in isolation. The very air you breathe connects you to every other being on this planet.

Step 4: *Returning to the World:* During the last two minutes, become aware of your breathing through your heart center. Experience the reality of interbeing through your heart. Remember, love is what keeps us all together.

Love Our Planet

Not many of us are going to have a chance to go into space so that we can view our planet like a blue marble against a dark velvet eternity. Perhaps we all need that experience to realize that this planet is our home, but until then, we need to find other ways to love our planet. Try this one.

Step 1: *Entering into Retreat:* Sit or lie down comfortably, and for the first three minutes, gently become aware of your breathing. Feel how your body expands as you inhale. Love your body.

Step 2: For the next ten minutes, progress through the following awareness sequence. As you inhale, imagine your energy field expanding. Sense the boundary of your energy field. Love your energy field.

Become aware of the room in which you're sitting. Sense the size and shape. Love the room.

Sense the house or building around you. Notice the size and shape. How tall is the house? Does it extend into the ground with a cellar? Be aware of the outline of the house. Love the house.

In your mind's eye, mark the property surrounding the building. How far does it extend? Love the property.

Extend your awareness to the town or city. Visualize the limits of the town or city. Love it.

Do the same for your county, your state, the country, the hemisphere, and finally the entire planet.

The astronaut Edgar Mitchell saw the planet from space as "a sparkling blue and white jewel, a light, delicate sky-blue sphere laced with slowly swirling veils of white, rising gradually like a small pearl in a thick sea of black mystery. It takes more than a moment to fully realize that this is Earth . . . home."

Step 3: For the next five minutes, breathe lightly and love our planet. Imagine you can experience the weightless perspective of space travel. Our planet is one of millions in the galaxy.

Step 4: *Returning to the World:* In the final two minutes, bring your perspective back to earth. Return to this hemisphere, this country, this state, this city, this house, this room, this energy field, this body. Love your body. Love your planet.

The Heart As a Bridge

One of the Native American images for the heart is that it is a bridge between Mother Earth and Father Sky. This image shows how deeply and personally we are connected to the planet below and to transcendence above, and that love is the key in both directions.

Also, to experience personal love, we need to have our roots firmly planted, we need to be grounded. We all know the disasters that can result from falling head over heels in love with no base of support. So we want to be able to love with our feet on the ground. Then the love in our hearts can rise up to be expressed outwardly through our words, our eyes, our touch.

Step 1: *Entering into Retreat:* Stand with your feet slightly apart, no wider than your hips. Use the first three minutes to imagine that when you inhale, you draw energy up from the center of the earth, up through your feet and legs.

Step 2: For the next ten minutes, explore a wide variety of very slow movements, like an improvised Tai Chi, which is the traditional Chinese moving meditation, almost like a slow-motion dance. Coordinate your arm movements with your breath, so that as you inhale, you sweep your arms from the direction of the earth, and as you exhale, you raise your arms in another sweeping gesture toward the sky. You can do this standing in one place or moving and bending.

Step 3: For the next three minutes, feel your heart as the bridge between Mother Earth and Father Sky. You can send love out from your heart center by purposely turning in all four directions as you do the sweeping movements. You can also send love to specific people or areas of the world by facing in their direction, sweeping from below and above and gesturing from your heart.

Step 4: *Returning to the World:* Use the remaining four minutes to relax, either standing or sitting down. Let your breathing become gentle. Focus on your heart as a bridge between Mother Earth and Father Sky.

Send Love

There is growing evidence that prayer makes a difference. People who are prayed for recover better from surgery, newborns gain weight, and even plants grow faster. This retreat uses visualization and subtle energy sensing in a nondenominational approach to prayer as a way to send love.

Step 1: *Entering into Retreat:* Choose someone to whom you want to send love. Then sit comfortably and focus on holding this person in your heart for three minutes. Use your awareness of your breath to keep you focused.

ONE-MINUTE RETREAT—FLASH PRAYER

This is a mini version of "Send Love," inspired by Reverend Frank Laubach's practice of praying for strangers. Simply imagine you can radiate love from your heart to the heart of any person you encounter. Let this retreat be both random and secret.

Step 2: For the next fifteen minutes, visualize sending love to this person in a variety of ways or choose the way that works best for you. Imagine this person surrounded by white light. Imagine you can send loving messages to this person and that they will receive them. This is L-mail (love mail) as opposed to E-mail (electronic). Radiate loving energy from your heart directly to their heart. Visualize this person as happy and feeling loved. See them in your mind's eye doing what they most love to do. Imagine their energy field radiating and pulsating with golden light.

Step 3: *Returning to the World:* For the last two minutes, focus your awareness on your own breathing. Be unattached to any outcome of your sending love.

Love Yourself

Most of us have inner selves of all different ages—from children to teenagers to adults. If we think about how old we feel inside, many of us would answer an age quite different from our chronological age. John Bradshaw, the TV therapist who made "inner child" work popular, created a developmental approach for giving ourselves loving messages. Examples for life stages are:

Infancy—birth to 12 months—"You can trust me to love you and
    care for you and keep you safe."
Toddlers—1 to 3 years—"You're becoming a unique person able to
    stand on your own feet, and you have the right to say no."

Preschool—4 to 6 years—"You're learning how to do more and more things each day."

Latency—7 to 10 years—"You're learning how to manage yourself and your life and how to get along with others."

Early Adolescence—11 to 15 years—"You're becoming stronger in who you are and knowing what you want."

Late Adolescence—16 to 20 years—"You're finding your way in the world with confidence and optimism."

Young Adulthood—20 to 30 years—"You're doing well on your own and you're making good decisions."

Step 1: *Entering into Retreat:* Lie down in any position you like, making yourself comfortable with pillows and blankets. For the first five minutes, enter into a deep state of relaxation by imagining that you can sink into the floor with every exhale. Let go of any tension as you exhale. Imagine that your body can melt like water.

Step 2: Imagine yourself as a child or young adult in one of the developmental states. Go with any age that spontaneously comes to you. Use the next five minutes to listen to this child, giving all your attention. See the "Love Is Attention" retreat (page 157) for practice listening. Listen carefully for what this child needs from you.

Step 3: "Send Love" (see retreat on page 168) to this child for the next five minutes. Give your child accepting, loving messages by using the suggested sentences for the child's developmental stage as a starting point. Add messages in response to what your child has just told you in step 2.

Step 4: *Returning to the World:* For the final five minutes, recognize this child as a part of you. Identify with different aspects of this child's personality. Know that when you go about your day, this child goes with you. Stretch and rise.

Is It Love?

This is the question we all need to consider when making perhaps the most important decision in our lives: should I marry this person? The full

FIVE-MINUTE RETREAT—CHOOSE LOVE

We have a wide range of emotional reactions to people, events, and things during a normal day. We get upset with rude drivers; we don't like the sandwich we ordered for lunch. Just noticing the number of negative reactions we go through on a daily basis is a sobering practice. This retreat suggests that you choose love. This doesn't mean you have to like the rude driver or the stale sandwich. You can dislike something and still choose to experience love, instead of an automatic negative reaction. Your experience of love can be independent of what is happening in the moment. Breathe into your heart. Allow an expansive feeling of love to radiate in all directions.

question behind the title of this retreat is: Does this person treat me in a loving, kind, considerate way on a daily basis? The quality of your life will be determined in part by the everyday experience of relating to your marital partner.

Realistically, we know that feelings will get hurt in the best of relationships. Partners will offend each other, even deeply wound each other. The key behavior to look for is what the person does after they have hurt you. This retreat uses journaling to help you focus objectively on the behavior of a potential spouse.

Step 1: *Entering into Retreat:* Sit comfortably with your journal and spend the first five minutes writing down pros and cons about your prospective partner. This will help you clarify what you're already thinking.

Step 2: For the next ten minutes, remember a specific time when you got into a conflict with your prospective partner. Chart your interaction as shown in the following example.

Conflict: He came late for a dinner party, after other guests had arrived. He was playing tennis.

What I did: I expressed disappointment that he didn't arrive on time to help me greet guests and serve them drinks. I requested he come on time for the next party.

He responded: Said he lost track of time and was winning tennis game.

New behavior: None.

Repeat of old behavior: He is often late because he's involved in doing something of interest to him.

Step 3: *Returning to the World:* For the final five minutes, read over your journaling. Allow the objective information to sink in. Assume the pattern you have recorded will continue. Is this behavior loving, kind, and considerate? Do you want to live with it on a daily basis?

Prayer of the Heart

This retreat is inspired by the Jesus prayer described in *The Way of a Pilgrim*, written by an unknown nineteenth-century Russian peasant. The Jesus prayer is a way to "pray without ceasing" as mentioned in the Bible. A short, simple prayer is repeated internally as if in the heart, until it becomes continuous and without effort. The traditional Jesus prayer is "Lord Jesus Christ have mercy on me," but you can use any phrase that has meaning for you.

Step 1: *Entering into Retreat:* For the first two minutes, sit quietly with as good posture as is comfortable. Focus your attention on your breathing through your heart center.

Step 2: Begin to repeat your phrase with every inhale and every exhale. As instructed in *The Way of a Pilgrim*, "With your imagination look into your heart; direct your thoughts from your head to your heart." Continue this repetition for fifteen minutes. If your mind wanders, simply return to repeating your phrase with your breathing.

Step 3: *Returning to the World:* For the last three minutes of the retreat, begin to move around and start your day, while you keep the phrase repeating in your heart. To pray without ceasing means to have this phrase repeating in your heart all the time without effort. The phrase becomes as familiar an inner sound as your heartbeat.

> *I do not wish to dye my clothes saffron,*
> *the color of a holy order;*
> *I want to dye my heart with divine love.*
>
> —*The Kabir Book*, Robert Bly's translation of
> a fifteenth-century Indian mystic

10

Patience

The deep things do not come suddenly. Let us be patient with ourselves.

—Swami Paramananda

I think we must consciously learn to develop patience, for it's not a virtue that comes naturally, like artistic talent or mechanical ability. And in our culture, patience is not even valued. It's not written about very much, even in the spiritual literature. So we have to focus on valuing patience, recognizing this quality as a spiritual virtue, and then nurturing its development in our inner being.

There are levels of patience that develop over time, from learning to wait as children, to understanding that some things take time as adults, to a deep sense of inner patience in spiritual matters. We learn patience slowly on all these levels.

As children we learn to wait for birthdays and holidays, containing our excitement and counting the days. We look forward to greater independence, waiting for our driver's license, graduation, our future. Then as adults, we understand that we can't control whether or not we can get pregnant, or whether our promotion will come through when we need it. We plant a sapling knowing that it will take ten years before it gives shade. Our patience grows, shifting our perspective on time, from days or weeks to decades.

With patience, we gradually learn not to wait for "later" but to be in the "now." Zen master Suzuki Roshi said, "The problem with the word 'patience' is that it implies we're waiting for something to get better. . . . A more accurate word for this quality is 'constancy,' a capacity to be with what is true moment after moment."

This understanding of patience places us directly in the here and now, which is the only opportunity for deepening our acceptance of what is. The way we view our lives and make value judgments is influenced by this deeper level of patience. Priest Henri Nouwen tells the story of an old professor who said, "I have always been complaining that my work was constantly interrupted, until I slowly discovered that my interruptions were my work." Having patience shifts our perspective, allowing us to open to what is actually happening in the present moment.

Buddhist meditation teacher Jack Kornfield describes patience as one of the qualities of spiritual maturity. He writes, "True patience is not gaining or grasping, it does not seek any accomplishment." Patience accepts what is without resistance, letting go of personal goals and attempts to control.

My Way

We all know some people for whom control is an obsession or addiction. Roberta was an extremely competent executive secretary in her mid-forties. The only problem was that she thought she knew what was best for just about everybody. She knew what kind of car one friend should buy, where another should go on vacation. She had career advice for some, marital advice for others, and investment instructions for everyone. If there was a decision to be made, whether or not it was her business, Roberta was there with the answer.

Roberta didn't have the patience to listen to what others wanted. She figured it saved time and energy to go directly to the bottom line, her way. Roberta's friends asked her to do the "I Love to Control" retreat. This was a cute way to give her feedback, and they really hoped the retreat would help her recognize how out of control she was with trying to control everything.

ONE-MINUTE RETREAT—LET GO

When you feel yourself becoming impatient with a situation or a person, notice how you're trying to control to achieve a certain outcome. Take a deep breath and gently exhale through your mouth as if you were blowing out a candle. The exhale should be slightly longer than the inhale. As you exhale, let go of your expectations. Exhale and again let go of any expectations.

Roberta was enthusiastic about the retreat. It was clear and direct, and she didn't feel that she was being pressured to change in any way. She simply scribbled on a piece of paper all the ways she loved to control people, decisions, and events. She didn't think she needed a formal journal. A day or two later, Roberta thought of another way she exerted control and added that to the list. Then she caught herself trying to control when a coworker would have surgery. She added that to the list. After about a week of this, she bought a journal to keep track of all the ways she loved to control.

Roberta's "I Love to Control" journal became legendary. Her impatience with whatever was happening and her attempts to make things go her way were clearly documented. Reading over her journal, Roberta realized how out of control she really was. She began using the one-minute retreat "Let Go" as a way to develop patience with whatever is in the moment, rather than trying to control the future. What Roberta learned was that when she became impatient with a decision-making process, she could breathe and let go.

Surrender

The process of giving up our personal attempts to control and surrendering to God is an essential part of the mystical path. The word *Islam*, for instance, means primarily "peace" and secondarily "surrender," according to Andrew Harvey, a scholar of mysticism.

Parents also need to go through this process of giving up control, although we don't usually think of parenting as a mystical path. To respond to the needs of young children, we need to surrender our own egotistical desires. Frankly, I was so overwhelmed when my daughter was born that I practically surrendered brushing my teeth. Of course there has to be some balance of meeting needs within a family, but a mother usually surrenders an enormous amount of time and energy to care for the children.

As a first-time mother, I had no idea how many years of surrendering would be necessary to raise my daughter. I was familiar with the concept of seeing the child as a spiritual teacher, one who lives in the present moment, but somehow after sixteen-hour days (my daughter wasn't much of a napper), that didn't work for me. As we graduated from stroller outings to playgrounds, I thought that I, at last, would have a moment to myself, sitting on a bench in the shade, book in hand. But no, I was constantly on call to push the swing, watch her at the top of the monkey bars, and pick her up after a tumble. I spent many impatient hours in hot, mosquito-infested playgrounds, wishing I were *not* in this particular moment.

This was when I developed the "Parenting Patience" retreat. I surrendered. I gave up my desires to do other things, and I hung out in playgrounds. And this made all the difference. I became far more patient, as I was no longer resisting and resenting. I even began to enjoy my time, chatting with other moms, picnicking, and sometimes swinging on the swings myself. Do you feel that gnawing impatience at any point in your day, at work or at home? You may want to consider how you could approach your situation differently.

SIGNS THAT YOU NEED A PATIENCE RETREAT

1. You tend to tailgate cars while driving.
2. You're a Type A personality, always feeling an internal pressure to rush.
3. You often feel stressed and find it difficult to relax.
4. You overschedule your time, trying to pack too much into a limited period.

5. You're impatient with the people closest to you.
6. You underestimate how long something will take to do.
7. You're very impatient with yourself and self-critical when you don't live up to your own expectations.
8. You try to control too much.
9. You want things done immediately, if not sooner.
10. You have trouble going with the flow.
11. When you try to slow down, you get even more anxious.
12. It's difficult for you to bring silence and solitude into your inner life.

Linda's Story

Even as we develop patience for others, we usually have the most difficult time learning how to be patient with ourselves. We are our own harshest critics, expecting ourselves to change immediately, achieve goals at breakneck speed, and develop spiritually overnight.

Linda was a highly competent surgical nurse who, because of her work, was often in extremely tense situations involving life-and-death decisions. She had been reading self-help and spiritual books for a few years and knew how she wanted to live—she didn't want to be at the mercy of her emotional reactions. Instead, Linda wanted to be able to maintain a certain emotional composure no matter what was happening.

That this is not so easy to do will come as no surprise to those of us who have had ecstatic meditation experiences, only to lose our emotional composure over some insignificant event like a missed appointment or minor interpersonal conflict. Our expectations for ourselves are usually unrealistic; we lack compassion for our struggle, and we're impatient. This can be a devastating combination, expressed in the things we say to ourselves.

To take an honest look at the things she said to herself, Linda began using the "Impatient with Yourself" retreat. We all know we are much harsher on ourselves than on others. Linda recorded statements like, "I can't believe you made that same mistake again. When in the world are you going to learn? Surely you could have gotten this done faster."

Journaling her impatience with herself helped Linda to realize how she clearly needed to learn how to be kinder, gentler, and more understanding with herself. So she moved on to the "Very Slow Walking Practice," in which she took one step with every inhale and one step with every exhale. This makes for extremely slow walking, which Linda did privately around her own home. There were times she thought she would jump out of her skin, she was so impatient with this retreat, but she stayed with it and learned how to accept a very slow rhythm.

Our inner lives evolve slowly, unfolding over years and maybe even lifetimes. Part of our spiritual development is to learn to be patient with ourselves and with others who are moving slowly, literally and figuratively. For if we are impatient, we will miss the present moment, and that is when everything happens.

> **I** *have just three things to teach:*
> *simplicity, patience, compassion.*
> *These three are your greatest treasures.*
>
> —*Tao Te Ching*, Holy Book of Taoism

'Retreats to Cultivate Patience

I Love to Control

Some of us are out of control, trying to control things that are way beyond our sphere of influence. We have no patience for whatever is in the moment, as we're anxious about what will happen in the future. Realistically, there is more in life that we can't control than we can, and we would be wise to approach life with both patience and acceptance.

This retreat uses cognitive therapy, as described in chapter 2, to explore our unrealistic attempts to control the world around us. By journaling both our control fantasies and our actual actions and what the outcome was, we can realistically evaluate when we want to exert influence and when we want to be patient. In this way we can more objectively decide when to attempt to influence and when to accept things as they are.

Step 1: *Entering into Retreat:* Sit comfortably with your journal and, for the first three minutes, imagine the last time you tried to control an event or person. Reflect on how you felt both emotionally and physically. We tend to "get on a roll" with control and have difficulty letting go or switching gears to be patient and accepting. It helps to recognize the emotional and physical cues that accompany each of these approaches, so we can catch our control tendencies the next time they happen.

Step 2: For the next ten minutes, make a list in your journal of all the ways you try to control, influence, or "help" others. List all the ways you think of controlling under *Control Fantasies* and all the ways you really try to control under *Actual Attempts*. For instance, under *Control Fantasies*, I would list that I wanted to tell my daughter to wear a different shirt to school this morning, but I didn't say a word; and under *Actual Attempts*, I would write that I made reservations for a committee dinner meeting without consulting anyone about the choice of restaurant.

Step 3: Use the next five minutes to read over both your fantasies about controlling and your actual attempts. Journaling will encourage you to be more objective and less reactive as you reflect on your "I Love to Control" confessions. Write a note next to each entry about whether you'd rather choose patience and acceptance than control in that situation.

Step 4: *Returning to the World:* In the remaining two minutes, consider whether you want to change your "I Love to Control" pattern or not. Think about how it works for you and how it doesn't. Plan to catch one attempt to control today and make a decision to be patient instead, just so you can compare how it feels to choose a different reaction to a situation.

Parenting Patience

Those of us who are parents are most likely to lose our patience with our kids when we are resisting what is, when we'd rather be somewhere else, doing something else. These are not good reasons to be impatient with our children, who are probably only doing what kids normally do, asking for our attention. We have to be honest with ourselves about where our impatience comes from—it usually comes from inside ourselves. We can't force ourselves to be patient when we want to be somewhere else. We first have to be willing to be with our kids, and then work on patience. Here is a retreat to help you assess your mind-set as you approach time with your child.

Step 1: *Entering into Retreat:* Sit comfortably and, for the first five minutes, simply think of your children. Reminisce over treasured memories. Recall images of your children, imagine their voices, how they feel to you, how they smell, from infancy to their present age.

Step 2: For the next five minutes, think of how your life would be if you didn't have your children. Think of all the extra time and money you'd have, as well as how much you'd miss them, and the opportunity to love them and to be loved by them in return.

Step 3: Decide again to have your children. We can often benefit from deciding again and again to be parents, continually renewing our commitment to our children and our role in raising them. This decision takes only a minute, but give yourself a full eight minutes to willingly surrender to the reality of what having children means. Surrendering in this way can feel like an active letting go. The dictionary definition is "to voluntarily yield," and this is exactly what is called for in parenting. We voluntarily yield to the greater needs of our children. We don't sacrifice ourselves entirely, but we do surrender a significant portion of our desires in the best interests of our children. Reflect on what this means for you in your life.

Step 4: *Returning to the World:* For the last two minutes, envision the patience you will have with your children from this renewed commitment and surrender. Focus on the emotional rewards that come when you have been fully present with your children.

Impatient with Yourself

Most of the impatience we have with ourselves can be summarized as our frustration with not yet being perfect. You immediately see the irrationality in this perspective. We're not going to be perfect, ever, much less yesterday. For sure, we will make mistakes. It can be an important step to realize that impatience with ourselves is about unrealistic expectations and standards.

Addressing the true source of our impatience can help us become more kind and accepting in our expectations of ourselves.

.This retreat uses a combination of journaling and cognitive therapy to reveal our self-talk, or what we say inside our heads when we become impatient with ourselves. The very process of transferring our messages from our inner world into our journals in the outer world can change our impatient patterns. In this way, we bring our impatient messages to ourselves into the light of day, where we can take a good look at them. Then we can decide if we want to continue feeding ourselves these same words or choose alternative messages we'd rather give to ourselves.

DAY 1

Step 1: *Entering into Retreat:* Sit comfortably with your journal. For the first five minutes, reflect back to an incident when you became very impatient with yourself. Consider the following questions, but don't write down the answers, just think about them: What did impatience feel like emotionally and physically? What did you say to yourself? What would someone else have observed about you? Would they have even known you were upset with yourself? Do you have any memories from your childhood of a parent or other adult being very impatient with you? If this was a pattern in your family, what kinds of things were said to you out of impatience?

Step 2: Use the next ten minutes to write down all the inner messages you give yourself when you become impatient. Think back through a variety of incidents that left you impatient. On a separate page in your journal, write down any impatient messages that were said to you as a child.

Step 3: *Returning to the World:* If you wrote down childhood messages, what is the relationship between those and the impatient statements you now make to yourself? For the next five minutes, reflect on the impact of these messages.

DAY 2

Step 1: *Entering into Retreat:* Use the first five minutes to read over your journal writing. Add any other examples of impatient messages you give yourself, or those from childhood that you have remembered since day 1 of this retreat.

Step 2: In the next ten minutes, go through the messages one by one and rewrite them the way you would communicate to a child of your own. For instance, instead of saying to yourself, "How could you have forgotten the milk? Now you have to make another trip to pick it up," You might say, "I understand how you forgot the milk. You were in such a hurry. Maybe next time you could bring a list." The latter communication creates a whole different feeling. Perhaps you wrote down the classic childhood message of impatience, "Don't dawdle." You could change that to, "I have to be home by four o'clock and I need you to help me get there on time. Let's go." Stating a need and making a request has a much different effect than expressing impatience.

Step 3: *Returning to the World*: For the final five minutes, read over the new messages you wrote for yourself. Notice how you feel emotionally and physically as you read them. Use this retreat to help you catch times during the day when you become impatient with yourself, so you can more consciously choose what messages you want to give yourself.

Not *"Be perfect,"* not *"Don't ever make a mistake,"* but *"Be whole."*

—Rabbi Harold S. Kushner

Very Slow Walking Practice

The traditional Buddhist walking practice is usually done slowly. This retreat is done *very* slowly, with the emphasis on patience. When walking is used as a meditation, you don't go anywhere, either physically or mentally. There is no destination—you can walk in a circle or back and forth. You can walk around the house or in your backyard. However, you do need to consider where you walk. Privacy is important, because walking so slowly in public would attract undue attention.

The Buddhist meditation teacher Sylvia Boorstein, author of *Don't Just Do Something, Sit There*, suggests you focus your awareness on the physical experience of walking and then on the "feeling tone" or emotional state of the moment. The very slow walking practice allows us to experience time pressure, restlessness, and impatience in a meditative practice, giving us the opportunity to become more aware of how these feelings arise in us and how we can respond to them.

Preparation for Retreat: Decide on a private place to walk back and forth or in a circle. Wear flexible shoes or none at all.

Step 1: *Entering into Retreat:* For the first three minutes, simply stand, feeling your feet on the ground. How is your weight distributed? Do you stand more on one foot than on the other? Is there more weight on the balls of your feet than the heels? Do your toes grip the ground? Notice your breathing, the rhythm of your inhalation and exhalation.

Step 2: For the next fifteen minutes, take one step as you inhale and one step as you exhale. This is *very slow walking*. When your attention drifts, bring it back to your breath and the physical experience of walking. Notice how you become distracted, how feelings arise, how thoughts pop into your head. Be particularly conscious of feelings, thoughts, and body sensations related to time pressure, restlessness, and impatience. Please understand that it is not so easy to walk this slowly with full attention. We all lose our balance, our concentration, and our patience. Take your time.

FIVE-MINUTE RETREAT—TEND A PLANT

We have more patience for how our plants grow than we do for how we ourselves develop. We never say to a plant, "Hurry up and blossom," but, in effect, we give ourselves that same message all the time.

Get some plants, any kind, indoor or out, flowering or not. Water them, prune them, and encourage them. Notice small changes week by week. Be aware of how patient and accepting you are of your plants' growth.

This is an opportunity to be kind to yourself as you explore your feelings of impatience.

Step 3: *Returning to the World:* For the final two minutes, simply stand and notice the rhythm of your breathing. Feel how much you've slowed down. What a contrast with our usual way of rushing around. Be aware of your pace during your day.

Patience with Process

A young man left my psychotherapy office the other day, totally distraught and looking for reassurance. "This will be over soon, won't it?" he asked as he got up to leave.

"No," I answered honestly and maybe too harshly. "Divorce will go on emotionally for years for your children, and so for you, too. But the worst of it should be over in a year or so."

There are times in our lives when we're ill, someone close to us dies, we lose our job, or we simply feel overwhelmed by the demands of our lives and become depressed. When we face these periods all we can do is be patient and remember that this too shall pass. We hope we won't have too many life-shattering episodes. But we can help ourselves through any that do come our way by being patient and understanding with ourselves. We can practice an everyday version of this same process when we have a cold or the flu. Most of us lack the patience to give ourselves the full recovery time, so we rush back into our lives too soon and, most frequently, fall sick again. Next time you don't feel well, really take the time to recover and rejuvenate yourself completely.

The "Patience with Process" retreat is another way to help us go easy on ourselves every day and when times are tough. It uses movement in an inner visualization to help us move through our impatience during these challenging times.

Step 1: *Entering into Retreat:* Sit comfortably, with back support as needed. Use the first five minutes to become aware of your impatience regarding any situation in your life. Give yourself permission to feel the impatience. Become aware of how you experience impatience in your body, your thoughts, your feelings, and in the subtle energy field that surrounds you.

Step 2: Use the next five minutes for this step. Allow an image to emerge that symbolizes your experience of impatience. Trust whatever image appears spontaneously. It may be a stalled car, or an image of clenched teeth, or a bird with a broken wing. Set your imagination in motion, letting the symbol begin to move, interact with something, or change in some way. Allow the scene to play out as if it were a videotape. You need this imaginary videotape for the next step.

Step 3: Return to your experience of impatience from a real-life situation. Notice if it's changed in any way. For the next eight minutes, simply alternate between your real-life experience of impatience and the imaginary videotape of your symbol. Replay this video, letting the action continue to develop. Toward the end of the eight minutes, again look for any changes in your experience of impatience in your real-life situation. Visualizing action in your inner videotape can help you move through your impatience with a real-life situation. This may help you accept that sometimes things take longer than we think they should.

Step 4: *Returning to the World:* In the last two minutes, take a few deep breaths and exhale energetically, as if you were blowing up a balloon. Imagine you can release any impatience with your exhalation.

> **M**any of us are willing to embark upon any adventure,
> except to go into stillness and to wait.
>
> —Rabbi Abraham Joshua Heschel

Are We There Yet? When Do We Eat?

These are time-honored questions we all know well. We may even hear them from our own children, but that doesn't mean that we ourselves have outgrown them. The bottom-line question dealing with impatience

FIVE-MINUTE RETREAT—TRAFFIC

We've all been there, stuck in traffic. This is a great opportunity to work with our impatience. Notice how you experience impatience in your body. Make a game out of observing the slightest detail, such as "I feel tension in my left knee," or "I'm hardly breathing." This retreat is not about making you more patient, but purely about gaining more awareness of how impatience feels in your body. However, you may want to notice what happens to your level of impatience as you become more objectively aware of it. How does it change?

is, When are my needs going to be met? In some relationships, this is the central conflict: whose needs are going to be met first?

To a certain extent we are all children, impatient about getting what we want. This retreat gives us a chance to become more conscious of those parts of ourselves that are impatient, selfish, needy, demanding, and very young. Psychologically, the more we are aware of these aspects of ourself, the better we'll be at coping with these inevitable feelings.

Step 1: *Entering into Retreat:* Lie down so you're very comfy with pillows and whatever you need. Just asking the questions "Are we there yet? When do we eat?" stirs up in us childhood feelings of impatience. Give

ONE-MINUTE RETREAT—MAKE TEA

Put the water on, using either a stovetop or a microwave, and wait until it boils. Maybe this takes more than one minute, but we all know it can seem like an eternity. Make a decision to be patient while you wait for it to boil. Do nothing while you wait. Just practice waiting. Can you decide to be patient at other times in your life? Enjoy your tea.

yourself a full five minutes to become aware of these old feelings. Be open to remembering any specific scenes or examples when you said these words. Make one up if you can't recall any.

Step 2: Continue to be in touch with these old feelings of impatience, and begin to pay attention to your breathing. For the next ten minutes, simply notice the rise and fall of your breath, as you stay in touch with these old feelings of impatience. If your mind wanders, focus again on specific scenes or examples.

Step 3: *Returning to the World:* During the last five minutes, give yourself reassuring answers to the title questions, such as "We'll be there soon," or "You can eat when you're hungry." Notice whether these messages affect the rise and fall of your breathing or your feelings of impatience. Finally, stretch so you feel the whole length of your body as preparation for rising. Getting in touch with your full-grown body is a clear message to return to your present age.

Patience in Marriage

There are few relationships in which patience is more essential and necessary than in marriage. As a matter of fact, one of the native-born Maine philosophers and a personal friend of mine, Tina Tully, said it this way: "Get married. If it lasts, you've learned patience." Short and to the point.

Although designed for intimate partners, this retreat can be used for any relationship in which you're losing your patience or feeling out of control of your emotions. This retreat gives you a chance to calm down before you say or do something you'll regret.

Step 1: *Entering into Retreat:* For the first five minutes, lie down comfortably and do about seven exhalations by blowing the air out through your mouth as if extinguishing a candle. If thoughts or feelings arise to distract your concentration, bring your focus back to your breath, with the emphasis on the exhale.

Step 2: For the next ten minutes, let yourself replay the incident with your significant other up to the point where you lose your patience. Replay this same scene as if it were a videotape, and as you watch yourself, be aware of your breathing. Continue to emphasize the exhale, periodically

---

ONE-MINUTE RETREAT—WORK OF ART

 This technique is inspired by the work of G. I. Gurdjieff, a spiritual teacher who was famous in the mid-twentieth century. As mentioned in chapter 2, he taught a variety of techniques to help people "wake up" during daily life. Next time you start to lose your patience with someone, shift your perception so you begin to see that person as if they were a work of art. What would they look like as a Picasso painting, or perhaps a Van Gogh? You could envision them as a Rodin sculpture or an ancient Greek statue with slight damage. Altering the way you see someone will change your impatient response to them as well as how you deal with them. Try this technique and notice how it changes your response.

---

blowing air out through your mouth. Begin to imagine how you might have behaved differently, how you might have handled yourself better and responded to your partner with greater patience.

Step 3: *Returning to the World:* During the final five minutes, imagine the situation as you wish you had handled it. Be aware of your breathing. Make an inner decision to be patient, no matter what your partner says or does. Acknowledge that patience is an internal decision and inner state of being.

Marriage is half the tradition. (The other half is patience.)
—Hadith: *Sayings and Traditional Accounts of the Prophet*

Waiting for Sleep

This is a perfect opportunity to practice patience in a situation where we have little control. Although we can do things that encourage sleep, we can't force ourselves to fall asleep. This retreat is not intended to induce sleep. Instead, its focus is on the waiting time before sleep happens, and it's intended to help develop patience through accepting what we can't control.

Step 1: *Entering into Retreat:* Stay in bed and use the first five minutes to focus your awareness on your physical experience, right here, right now. Feel how the mattress supports you under different parts of your body. Experience the texture of the sheets on your skin, the weight of the blanket covering you. Notice how the pillows feel. Also pay attention to the temperature of the air as it enters your nostrils and as it exits your nostrils. Notice the movement of your breath in your body.

Step 2: Use the next five minutes to experience the reality of not having control over your mind or your body. This is a very intimate lack of control, since there's not much closer to us than our own mind and body. Notice what emotions and thoughts accompany this experience of not falling asleep. Don't try to change anything, just notice. For example, you might say to yourself, "Now I'm worrying about being tired tomorrow for that big meeting. Now I'm impatient with my body for not relaxing. Now I'm regretting having eaten that last piece of pizza." Don't get stuck on any one thought or feeling. Just continue to notice them as they arise.

Step 3: For the next eight minutes, continue to notice your emotions and thoughts about not being able to fall asleep, while you focus on your breathing. As you inhale, say the word *accept* silently deep within yourself, and as you exhale, say the word *patient*.

Step 4: *Returning to the World:* Please don't be concerned if you happen to fall asleep during this retreat. If you are still awake, use the last two minutes to decide how you want to use your time. Decide whether you want to stay in bed and rest or get up and do something.

Creativity

The poet Rainer Maria Rilke said "Patience is everything," in describing the creative process. No matter how disciplined or practiced we are in our art form, there is still a magical spark that we must patiently await. We can work without it, but our work will not be the same.

FIVE-MINUTE RETREAT—
IMPROVISATIONAL MUDRAS

Mudras are traditional Hindu hand gestures used during religious rituals or meditation. They are specifically choreographed ways of moving one's hands to form a variety of stylized positions. It's almost as if the two hands are dancing and moving in and out of complex ways of relating to each other. Each position carries a Sanskrit meaning, and the movements are done in a meditative state.

For improvisational mudras, select some New Age music that has a spacey quality, like Kitaro. Then sit quietly and just begin to move your hands in slow motion. Very slowly, allow your hands to be propelled by the advancing music. Let them move in very slow motion, almost floating in space, shifting effortlessly in their relationship to each other. Trust your hands and maintain the slow motion. You consciously start them moving and then allow them to continue almost as if on their own volition. Your patience will deepen as you maintain the slow, concentrated movement.

The technique used in this retreat is slightly different from an emotional drawing, since I'm not asking you to intentionally express feelings. The best approach to the "Creativity" retreat is to consider it play.

Step 1: *Entering into Retreat:* Sit so you can work with your oil pastels. Use the first two minutes to concentrate on the blank piece of paper.

Step 2: Take just a minute and do a random scribble on your sheet of paper. You will be using this scribble as the start of a drawing, but don't start yet.

Step 3: For the next five minutes, there are two levels of instruction. One level is to use your scribble as a focus for concentration. Be sure to turn the paper in all directions on the table and in the space in front of your face, so you can view your scribble from as many perspectives as possible. The other level of instruction is to notice what you want to do with the scribble to start your drawing. What ideas arise from within you?

What creative urges? What does your hand want to do? This is a chance for you to observe your creative process.

Step 4: Give yourself ten minutes to develop your drawing. You can do absolutely anything you want. As you work, just notice any feelings of impatience, which may emerge if you're not sure what to draw or if your drawing isn't going quite the way you had in mind.

Step 5: *Returning to the World:* For the last two minutes, admire your drawing. If any negative judgments or leftover feelings of impatience arise, gently return to admiration for your work.

Life of a Rose

This retreat extends over days, over the life of a rose. The instructions are the same for each day, so they are only given once. However, continue until you are completely satisfied that the rose is no longer changing.

"Life of a Rose" uses a visual concentration that will deepen your capacity for patience. By becoming still and quiet inside, you will gradually begin to see more and more subtle detail in the rose as it changes each day. The instructions use the same technique as mindfulness training (see page 25) in terms of dealing with the inevitable distractions. For instance, when distracting thoughts or feelings arise, as they will for everyone, simply notice them and gently return your attention to the visual concentration on the rose.

Preparation for Retreat: Buy a beautiful long-stemmed rose. Buy only one, and choose the color that you like best.

Step 1: *Entering into Retreat:* Sit comfortably with the rose in front of you. For the first three minutes, close your eyes and turn your attention to your breathing. Simply observe the physical experience of the rise and fall of your breath.

Step 2: Open your eyes and look at the rose, noticing the smallest details. This step is the core of the retreat and will take fifteen minutes. Notice the different shades of color in the petals, the size and shape of the blossom, the way the leaves extend from the stalk, and the angle of the thorns. After day 1, notice how the rose has changed from the day before. As you continue this retreat for the life of the rose, you will become more sensitive in your seeing. Be aware of your perception of the energy field of the rose, of the vitality or life force within the flower.

If you need to refocus, you can always close your eyes for a breath or two, and then reopen them to concentrate on the rose once again. When distractions arise, gently bring your attention back to the rose. Become aware again of the physical experience of your breathing.

Step 3: *Returning to the World:* In the final two minutes, thank the rose, especially on the last day. Feel how your capacity for patience deepens as you slow down enough to perceive the subtle life of a rose. This experience with the rose can help you when you find yourself irritable and impatient in your daily life. By focusing on subtle details, you can see the changes that are actually happening and be more patient with the process.

Patience with Transition

Rabbi Shoni Labowitz, a student and teacher of the mystical Kabbalah, tells the ancient story of the Israelites as they escaped from slavery and traveled through the desert to their new homeland. She says that "at times [they] waited three days before entering a new territory. That they stopped and waited is an indication of the need to empty." This was their transition from slavery to freedom. The Israelites needed to empty themselves of their slave identity, to let go of their past history so they could create a new future.

There are many times in our lives when we will go through a personal transition, maybe a job change, a marriage or divorce, or becoming a parent. We need to have the patience to take the time to let go of the old identity and prepare for the new stage of our life. If you are facing such a change, this retreat may be helpful as you make the transition.

Step 1: *Entering into Retreat:* For the first three minutes, sit quietly with posture as good as is comfortable for you. Use a back support if you like. Gently turn your attention to your breathing. Let each exhale you make float out of you.

Step 2: Gently allow your exhalation to begin to lengthen so that it takes half again as long as your inhalation. For the next ten minutes, keep your awareness on your exhale, never pushing it but just letting it float out of you and away. With every exhale, imagine you can let go of old ways of being, old relationships, old beliefs, and old ways of thinking and feeling. In other words, empty yourself of old, nonfunctional patterns. Make way for a new life. This is an important part of any transition, and we need to be patient with ourselves as we let go.

Step 3: Now shift your attention to your inhalation for the next five minutes. Allow your inhale to float in through your nostrils without effort. Imagine you can breathe in all the courage and patience you will need in the next stage of your life.

Step 4: *Returning to the World:* For the last two minutes, take this time to recognize the significance of this transition in your life. Appreciate the patience you have for your personal process of letting go of the old and preparing for the new.

---

*P*atience is the companion of wisdom.

—Saint Augustine

11

Peace

What most of us want for ourselves, for our loved ones, and for the world is peace. The Dalai Lama teaches that peace is based on love, compassion, and altruism, and that when we develop these inner qualities, we will be able to create an atmosphere of peace and harmony within ourselves. This internal atmosphere of peace is experienced as a deep feeling of going home to an inner spiritual home. The way I talk about this experience and have heard others describe it is, "I have a quiet, still place deep inside me that I call home. No matter what's happening in my life, I know I can go there and find peace." This inner atmosphere of peace can be expanded to encompass the whole world, the Dalai Lama explains. So world peace is really a reflection of the peace each one of us has individually. Each person must find their own inner center of peace in order for the world to be transformed.

The best definition of peace I've read is actually a Buddhist description of happiness. Happiness in Buddhist psychology is not the fleeting experience of pleasure that we usually think of. In her book *Lovingkindness*, Buddhist teacher Sharon Salzberg gives the Buddhist psychological definition of happiness: "a state of tranquillity in which our hearts are calm, open, and confident." I think this is a wonderful description of peace, conveying both an inner depth and serenity. This perspective means that we can be peaceful and happy within ourselves, no matter what our external situation may be.

For peace to be consistently available to us as an experience of having an inner center or home, it must be independent of whatever is happening in our lives. In fact, we most need the inner calm and quiet of our peaceful center when our lives are the most hectic and tumultuous. Personal peace that can be disturbed by external situations is not the depth of peace that we can call home. We want to be able to maintain our inner composure in all circumstances, by not being emotionally reactive. We want to have that calm place to visit whenever we need a moment to rejuvenate, reflect, or move into action with confidence.

Emotional Reactivity

The most obvious way we are emotionally reactive is when we "lose it" by saying or doing things we regret later. I don't need to give an example of this, since we all know too well what this looks like in our lives. But there are far more subtle ways of being emotionally reactive that we may not have considered in the same way, which also knock us off center, creating friction between our inner and outer worlds. For instance, if we observe our judgmentalness for even just one hour, we will be overwhelmed with examples. I know I'm a running judgmental commentary. As soon as I start paying attention, I realize I can hardly perceive something without judging, "I'm glad that's not me. I wouldn't want to live there. What a great car! How can he behave like that? I love her dress." I could go on, but I'm sure you have your own internal commentary to consider, and frankly, this infinite list of judgments becomes very boring, very quickly. "Who cares?" you might say. But just try and stop it.

If we tire of our reactive judgmentalness, we can observe our reactive desires to avoid or hold on to things or experiences. Every visit to the dentist is a lesson in avoidance for me, and I like my dentist. I have certainly experienced the romantic desire, "I wish this night could last forever."

FIVE-MINUTE RETREAT—CATCH YOURSELF

This retreat is intended to help integrate mindfulness training into your daily life and to nourish a quality of awareness that runs like an underground stream through your day. This is a quiet, watchful witnessing of each moment. When you catch yourself being reactive in some way—upset, irritated, insulted, jealous, insecure, and so on—simply notice the emotional surge and take a breath. Turn your full attention to the physical experience of breathing for a few breaths. Then return to the current situation and respond with as much consciousness as possible.

Who of us hasn't had that clinging thought? All these examples of emotional reactivity are body-mind experiences. I sit in the dentist's chair and my heart rate goes up. When we spend an evening with someone we love, our system floods with endorphins. When we are emotionally reactive, every aspect of us is involved.

Becoming aware of our emotional reactivity with a gentle compassion for ourselves is one of the paths toward peace. I have been working with the five-minute retreat "Catch Yourself," for most of my adult life. I see this as an integration of my retreat experiences into my daily life. I don't know if I've gotten significantly less reactive, but I have become more compassionate toward myself when I am reactive. The discipline of being aware of my reactions has been an important part of my lifelong spiritual path.

I've also started using the "Equanimity" retreat. I find this especially helpful when I face a recurring problem—be it an insolvable dilemma, a crisis, or a very difficult person. I think of a person I find irritating while I'm focusing on my breathing and realize how I have no control over how they behave. I find I am then more likely to be able to maintain a peaceful equanimity when I deal with this person during my daily life. You may find these retreats helpful in these ways and more as you consciously address the question of peace in your own life.

Cement Shoes

There are times, however, when we need a more active approach in dealing with very difficult people or situations. I do believe that peace is an internal state of being, yet I have to admit, there are some very difficult people in the world who seem to thrive on disturbing other people's peace. Jim was a great example of this, and he was driving Ralph crazy, as these troublesome people love to do. Ralph was a gentleman in his mid-fifties who had worked in real estate all his life. As a people person, he got along with everyone—that is, until Jim joined the real estate office. Jim constantly "forgot" to relay phone messages. He also would agree to cover for Ralph and then not show up. Finally, Ralph learned that Jim was totally untrustworthy, but by then Ralph was caught in his own emotional reactivity and quite frustrated and angry with Jim.

It's important to recognize and accept when an interpersonal problem is insolvable. This is when a retreat can help give us a new perspective. Understanding that he could not change Jim's behavior and would still have to continue working with him, Ralph began using the "Actively Letting Go" retreat for his own peace of mind. In this retreat he imagined dumping Jim's body in the deepest part of the ocean. Although this may seem extreme, it's important to remember that this is a fantasy, its purpose being to empower Ralph, not actually harm Jim. Ralph needed to repeat the retreat a few times to really feel emotionally free of Jim.

In the office, Jim continued to behave as before, but now Ralph was undisturbed. He knew not to depend on Jim, and he was able to maintain a peaceful inner center no matter what Jim did or didn't do.

We are responsible for creating our own interior peacefulness, and sometimes we need a reminder to take the time to cultivate this inner peace. When was the last time you gave yourself this gift of solitude and quiet?

SIGNS THAT YOU NEED A PEACE RETREAT

1. You are more emotionally reactive than usual.
2. You rarely give yourself solitude and quiet time.

3. Anxiety is a problem for you.
4. You feel that you're constantly fighting with yourself.
5. You have fantasies of retreating to a remote vacation cabin on your own.
6. You have trouble sitting still.
7. You yearn for peace and quiet.
8. You feel so stressed and pressured that it's difficult to relax.
9. You give other people the power to upset you.
10. You've had more crises recently than is usual in your life.
11. You feel overwhelmed with the human suffering in the world.
12. There has been too much suffering in your life.

Jennifer's Story

Jennifer was a newly hired accountant in the financial offices of a national department store. Almost as soon as she started working there, the office was given a huge project to finish within an unrealistic deadline. All of a sudden Jennifer was thrown into the office crisis, and, as a new employee, she had barely discovered the location of the ladies room.

Jennifer knew she would have to keep peaceful and calm within herself because she and everybody else was under such high stress. Every morning she would practice the "Peace/Calm Breath" retreat, and she would also practice this technique in bed as she was falling asleep. The morning retreat prepared her for her stressful day, allowing her to at least start from a quiet center inside. Then, using the technique in the evening helped her to let go of the day's stress and get a good night's sleep.

As the business deadline approached, Jennifer felt swept up in the office frenzy. She could recapture her calm peace at home, but at work, the pace was too frenetic. So Jennifer began using the "Smooth Your Energy" five-minute retreat during her workday. The visualization was calm and soothing, and Jennifer got so good at it that she could incorporate it while she was in the midst of working and benefit from the feeling of ease it afforded her.

I wish I could say that Jennifer shared these retreats with other people in the office, and that they began to take a retreat break together instead

---

FIVE-MINUTE RETREAT—SMOOTH
YOUR ENERGY

Imagine a wonderful smooth, calm lake. No boats, no people. Maybe a few birds. Nothing disturbing. The surface of the water is like glass, reflecting the surrounding trees. Then imagine a rock dropped in the middle of the lake, with concentric circles of ripples extending like small waves. They are dramatic at first, then slowly begin to disperse. As the surface of the lake is gradually restored to its original calm, mirrorlike quality, similarly allow the energy within and around your body to calm to a clear, quiet quality of mirrorlike reflection.

---

of a coffee break. But that's my fantasy. Most people haven't yet realized that taking a short retreat to restore peace will actually enable them to be more efficient during their workday.

Use these retreats to create an oasis of calm in your day. Share your techniques with those who talk to you about the stress they feel. Every additional moment of peace each one of us experiences moves the world to a more peaceful place. Don't underestimate the power and importance of your actions and what you share. One moment at a time is how we move toward a peaceful planet.

Retreats to Cultivate Peace

Equanimity

The Buddhist term *equanimity* means an inner balance or calm that accepts things as they are. In his book *Path with Heart*, Jack Kornfield writes, "*Equanimity* combines an understanding mind together with a compassionate heart." This balance between heart and mind lets us know that there are many things we cannot control in life and helps us to accept this fact.

It's admittedly quite a challenge to maintain equanimity when dealing with an insolvable problem or very difficult person in our lives. The more we can accept the fact that we can't control how such a person behaves, the less emotionally reactive we are likely to be. This retreat focuses on accepting this lack of control and offers traditional Buddhist phrases to cultivate equanimity.

Step 1: *Entering into Retreat:* Sit or lie down, whichever is more comfortable for you. For the first two minutes, pay attention to the flow of your breathing. Experience within yourself the possibility of combining your understanding mind with your compassionate heart. Notice how that feels inside you.

Step 2: For the next three minutes, imagine you can use the flow of your breath to help intensify that connection between your mind and heart. Here's the image that works for me: as I inhale, I imagine I can breathe up into my head. Then when I exhale, I imagine I can send the energy from that breath down into my heart. Continue this imagery and breathing for the rest of the retreat while you follow the other steps.

Step 3: Imagine your insolvable problem or a difficult person in your life. For the next five minutes, acknowledge how much of the situation is beyond your control. Accept the fact that you do not have control. Keep breathing with your understanding mind and compassionate heart.

Step 4: Continue following the first three steps as you add this step. For the next eight minutes, repeat to yourself the following phrases:

"May I be balanced and at peace."
"May I accept that there are things I cannot change."
"May I remain calm inside and in my behavior."

Step 5: *Returning to the World:* For the last two minutes, gently return your awareness to the flow of your breath and your inner experience of your understanding mind and compassionate heart. To rekindle your experience of the "Equanimity" retreat during your day, you could repeat the phrases quietly inside yourself.

Actively Letting Go

This visualization is so simple and straightforward that I'm surprised it works so well. Yet whenever I do it, I feel palpable relief. Make your visualization as real and alive as possible by adding other sensory details, such as "I hear the water sloshing against the side of the boat," or "I smell the salt air."

Use this retreat when someone is driving you crazy or you just have to let go of a problem or situation. If you're dealing with a chronic problem, you could even tape-record these instructions in your own words, so you can more easily do the retreat again and again.

Step 1: *Entering into Retreat:* Lie down and make yourself very comfortable with pillows and blankets. For the first five minutes, just let yourself relax. Imagine that with every exhale, you can let go of any tension in your mind or body. Allow your relaxation to deepen as you imagine that you are descending in a very slow moving elevator. With each floor you pass, your tension level drops another notch.

Step 2: Use the next twelve minutes to tell yourself the following story. See the scenery vividly in your mind's eye and feel yourself in the story, just as if you were dreaming it right now. This is a magical story. You will be able to do things in your visualization that you might not in real life.

Imagine you're on a beautiful beach. Listen to the ocean waves. Feel the warmth of the sun. You have all the equipment here that you need. Now imagine you can tie a rope around the problem, person, or situation. Really wrap it up in a good-sized package with lots of rope. Add lead weights, plenty of lead weights. Don't be stingy with any materials. Then, place this bundle in a convenient rowboat and row out past the waves, into the open ocean. Feel strong and powerful with each pull of the oars. When you can no longer see land, lift and dump this bundle in the deep part of the ocean. Watch it sink way, way down. Envision all those weights you put on it as it sinks lower and lower, never to surface again.

Now, row back to shore with a new attitude toward yourself. Step back onto the beach and feel the sand with your feet; let it sift between your toes. Lie down on the soft sand and enjoy the warm sun and the cool ocean breeze. Free of your problems, feel a new attitude of calm confidence and peaceful strength down deep in your bones.

Step 3: *Returning to the World:* During the last three minutes, travel from that wonderful beach to where you are right now. Feel your breathing and the floor underneath you. With every inhale, imagine that you are ascending in a very slow moving elevator. Take your time, and when you're ready, gently sit up and look around the room.

Peace/Calm Breath

The instructions for this retreat are very easy, so you can also use them for a one-minute or five-minute retreat during the day. Of course, these mini-retreats will be far more effective if you've practiced the twenty-minute version, building your focus and training your whole mind and body to respond to Peace/Calm. Use this retreat when you feel totally overwhelmed; use mini-retreats when you feel yourself heading for the panic button.

Step 1: *Entering into Retreat:* Sit or lie down, whichever feels more comfortable to you at this time. For just three minutes, allow your breathing to be gentle and easy. Just notice the rhythm of your inhale and exhale.

Step 2: During the next fifteen minutes, imagine that you can inhale Peace and exhale Calm. Let each word float like a feather on your breath. When you inhale, say "Peace" silently and deeply within yourself. When you exhale, say "Calm" in the same way.

Step 3: *Returning to the World:* For the last two minutes, notice the rhythm of your breathing. As you open your eyes, take a personal inventory and sense how different your body, mind, heart, and soul feel at the end of this retreat. Allow yourself to continue breathing in Peace and breathing out Calm as you go about your day.

To the quiet mind all things are possible.

—Meister Eckart

> ### *FIVE-MINUTE RETREAT—MAY THERE BE PEACE*
>
> The *Vedas*, or "sacred knowledge," of Hinduism were written thousands of years ago. The following Vedic quote on peace is poetic as well as comprehensive. I recommend copying this Hindu hymn onto a three-by-five card and carrying it with you. Read and reflect on this ancient prayer whenever you need to bring peace into your daily world.
>
> *May there be peace in the higher regions; may there be peace in the firmament; may there be peace on earth. May the waters flow peacefully; may the herbs and plants grow peacefully; may all the divine powers bring unto us peace. The Supreme Lord is peace. May we all be in peace, peace, peace; and may that peace come into each of us.*
>
> —The Vedas

Four Worlds

In his book *Renewing Your Soul*, Rabbi David Cooper teaches the Four Worlds of the Kabbalah meditation as a way to show that harmony exists at all levels. Part of this mystical perspective is that our lives are not random. Who we are fits perfectly with our destiny, and everything that happens is part of a larger plan. Realizing this harmony is a step toward peace with ourselves and our lives. This retreat is based on Rabbi Cooper's work.

Step 1: *Entering into Retreat:* Sit or lie down, whichever is more comfortable for you; however, alertness is necessary for the whole twenty minutes of this retreat. For the first three minutes, quietly observe the movement of your breath in your body.

Step 2: Become aware of your whole body from head to toe. During the next three minutes, consider your physical strengths and weaknesses. Please don't get caught in judgments about appearance. Focus on what you're physically well suited to do: What comes easily to you? Do you do better with activities requiring brute strength, or are you better suited for speed or gracefulness?

Step 3: Now consider your emotional strengths and weaknesses in this same objective manner. For three minutes, analyze your natural tendencies. Are you a people person? Do you handle stress well?

Step 4: Next analyze the strengths and weaknesses of your intellect for three minutes. How does your intelligence serve you? Do you have a photographic memory? Are you an analytical problem solver? We know we can't all be rocket scientists, but where do your talents lie?

Step 5: One of the basic principles in Kabbalah is that each of us is born for a reason. For the next three minutes, imagine your soul can speak to you, letting you know deep inside what your soul needs to learn in this lifetime.

Step 6: For the next three minutes, consider that who you are in these four worlds—physical, emotional, mental, and spiritual—is exactly who you're supposed to be. View your life with the perspective that you have everything you need in order to do whatever you need to do.

Step 7: *Returning to the World:* Return to quietly observing the movement of your breath in your body for the remaining two minutes. Feel at peace with who you are in your life right now.

Waves on the Ocean

The instructions for the "Mindfulness" meditation tell you to notice your thoughts, letting them float by like clouds across the sky, then gently return your attention to your breathing. Please don't assume this technique will stop your thoughts. I assure you, your thoughts, as well as physical sensations and emotions, will continue to demand your attention. The "Mindfulness" instructions will help you to notice when you're distracted and to become aware as soon as possible that you've drifted. However, it's equally important to be gentle with yourself, not judging or criticizing yourself for lapsing into unconsciousness or distractions.

The Tibetan Buddhist Lama Surya Das gives this advice for dealing with thoughts during meditation: "Thoughts are like waves on the ocean.

You don't have to iron out the ocean. Just notice the waves as they arise and disappear on the ocean's surface." This approach to meditation will help us to deepen our inner sense of peacefulness.

Step 1: *Entering into Retreat:* Sit with posture as good as is comfortable for you. Use a back support if needed. Close your eyes and turn your attention to the physical sensations of your breathing. For the first three minutes, observe with as much detail as possible how your body moves as you inhale and exhale.

Step 2: During the next fifteen minutes, notice when your attention wanders from the experience of your breathing. When any distraction arises—be it a thought, feeling, body sensation, or something external like a fly or a telephone ringing—imagine that the distraction is like a wave on the ocean. See it arise out of the ocean, peak, and then melt back into the ocean. Remember, "You don't have to iron out the ocean."

Step 3: *Returning to the World:* In Hinduism, personal identities are considered to be like waves on the ocean. We come from the infinite ocean, or God, and we melt back into the ocean, returning to God. Sit with this image for the final two minutes.

Walking Meditation

The instructions for walking meditation are almost the same as for the "Very Slow Walking Practice" (page 183). The only difference is the speed. This walking meditation is the more traditional of the two approaches to this traditional Buddhist practice. You take two to three steps with every inhalation and two to three with every exhalation. In this variation there's still plenty of time for you to expand your awareness of both your environment and your physical experience of walking. Handle all internal and external distractions in the same way as in the "Mindfulness" meditation (see page 227). Let them pass through your mind like waves. For a more detailed explanation of this approach, see the previous retreat, "Waves on the Ocean" (page 205).

One of today's most popularly known Buddhist monks, Thich Nhat Hanh, shares his inspiring attitude about walking meditation with the following words: "When we are able to take one step peacefully and happily, we are working for the cause of peace and happiness for the whole of humankind." How we step on the planet affects the whole wide world.

Step 1: *Entering into Retreat:* Stand with your feet at hip width apart in an area where you can walk slowly with privacy either indoors or outside. For the first three minutes, focus your attention on the soles of your feet. Notice your breath, and imagine you can inhale through the soles of your feet.

Step 2: Begin to walk slowly, taking two to three steps as you inhale and two to three steps as you exhale. Let your breathing be effortless; just let it float in and out. Continue walking for the full fifteen minutes. Whenever any distractions arise either within you or around you, bring your awareness back to your breathing and the physical experience of walking.

Notice what part of your foot touches the ground first as you step. Be aware of how the movement flows as you shift weight from one foot to the other. Then notice your back foot lifting and swinging forward to begin the next step. Feel the rhythm involved in your walking meditation. Step peacefully and happily for yourself and for all of humankind.

Step 3: *Returning to the World:* For the remaining two minutes, stand still and appreciate the quiet peacefulness in your mind and body.

World Peace

This retreat is inspired by the following statement of the Dalai Lama: "Although attempting to bring about world peace through the internal transformation of individuals is difficult, it is the only way." Certainly, the Dalai Lama is personally a living example of what he teaches. This retreat is one way we can embody our spiritual beliefs, bringing more peaceful energy into the world.

Step 1: *Entering into Retreat:* Sit comfortably, with back support if you need it. Turn your attention to your breathing. Use the first five minutes to gently let your breathing become easier, smoother, lighter, and more flowing. Don't consciously change the length or depth of your breathing. Just allow it to develop slowly into a more refined, peaceful breath. Feel the inner atmosphere of peace which this breath helps to create. Allow this quality of peacefulness to radiate outward into your personal energy field.

Step 2: For the next twelve minutes, continue being aware of your refined, peaceful breathing and continue to radiate outwardly this atmosphere of peace. Imagine this peaceful energy can expand to include your family and loved ones. Then extend it to include your friends and acquaintances. Continue your breathing, and imagine that this atmosphere of peace can expand to include your community and eventually every living being on the planet. Your awareness of your peaceful breathing is what helps to expand this atmosphere of peace so it is inclusive of the whole world.

Step 3: *Returning to the World:* Rest peacefully in this atmosphere for the last three minutes. Take this peace with you into your day.

There can never really be any peace and joy for me until there is peace and joy finally for you, too.

—Frederick Buechner, Protestant minister

Prānāyāma

In yoga philosophy, *Prānāyāma* is the science of breath. *Prānā* means breath, vitality, or energy, and *Ayāmā* means expansion, stretching, or restraint. This Prānāyāma retreat is adapted from a yogic breathing practice mentioned in the classic *Light on Yoga*, by B. K. S. Iyengar. Breathing

---

ONE-MINUTE RETREAT—LIGHT A CANDLE

Light a candle for world peace. This very simple retreat is an opportunity for an altruistic ritual, and altruism is one of the feeling states leading to peace, according to the Dalai Lama. This candle with its flame is not a personal request or even a request for a loved one. This is a request for all of us. It can be very nice to do this "Light a Candle" retreat in conjunction with the "World Peace" retreat (page 207).

exercises can create a great peacefulness deep in your body. However, if you feel uncomfortably lightheaded during this retreat, I recommend you stop, lie down, and breathe normally.

Step 1: *Entering into Retreat:* Sit with as good posture as you can. Close your eyes. During the first three minutes, intersperse three full, deep breaths among more normal size breaths. Exhale as much as possible. Breathe normally and gently between each deep breath.

Step 2: For the next twelve minutes, you will practice alternate nostril breathing. With the ring and little finger of your right hand, gently close your left nostril so you can exhale through the right nostril. Then inhale through the right nostril. Let go of your left nostril and using the thumb of your right hand, close off the right nostril. Exhale through your left nostril. Inhale through your left nostril. Let go of your right nostril and close off the left, so you can inhale through the right nostril. Continue this pattern.

Please note: You can take breaks during step 2 by breathing through both nostrils gently.

Step 3: *Returning to the World:* Sit quietly, breathing normally and gently through both nostrils for the final five minutes. Notice and enjoy the peaceful effects of the breathing practice.

If you would foster a calm spirit,
first regulate your breathing;
for when that is under control,
the heart will be at peace.

—Kariba Ekken, seventeenth-century
Hindu teacher

Anxiety

Anxiety is probably the most common psychological problem that interferes with personal peace. We all have anxiety, some of us more than others. Psychologically, the questions we should ask ourselves regularly are:

ONE-MINUTE RETREAT—NAMASTE

Namaste is a Hindu greeting meaning "the divine in me recognizes and bows to the divine in you." This is a very different way of seeing other people—they are not other, they are us. Peace is possible when we recognize each other in this way. Look around at other people when you're out in public. Really look at them with this thought in mind. Remember, the God in me recognizes and bows to the God in you.

Does our anxiety interfere with our daily functioning? Do we avoid certain situations because we are afraid of becoming anxious? Spiritually, anxiety makes it difficult to find peace in solitude. We tend to become fearful rather than peaceful.

This retreat uses emotional drawings, as described in chapter 2, to give you the opportunity to express your inner experience of anxiety outwardly in a creative way. You can symbolically pour your anxiety into your drawing, and then you have the chance to look at it with objectivity. This process helps you gain a sense of control over your anxiety. You can begin to learn how to deal with these feelings instead of avoiding them and in so doing giving them greater control over your actions.

Step 1: *Entering into Retreat:* Sit comfortably with your oil pastels and paper at hand. Take a full five minutes to remember a time when you felt anxious. Really re-create that experience so you can feel it in your body. Does your heart rate increase? Do your muscles tighten? Do your hands get sweaty? Allow your unique experience of anxiety to become very real to you.

Step 2: Do an emotional drawing that represents your experience of anxiety. You want to be able to look at your drawing when it's done and say, "Yes, that's what it feels like inside me when I get anxious." Use a full ten minutes to complete your emotional drawing.

Step 3: *Returning to the World:* For the remaining five minutes, prop your drawing up so it's directly in front of your eyes. Focus on your drawing as if you've never seen it before, and at the same time, become aware of your breathing. Notice details in your drawing and let your breathing gently become slower and deeper. This is the time for you to breathe peacefully in the presence of your anxiety.

Peace with Yourself

For us to make peace with ourselves, we not only need to accept ourselves, we need to find value in the parts of ourselves that we're tempted to reject. As our lives unfold, what we consider a personal problem often turns out to be a hidden treasure. For instance, Adam was a hyper child, very bright but unable to concentrate on one thing at a time. As a grown-up, he successfully handles a chaotic group of sales accounts. Adam still can't concentrate too well on one task for long periods of time, so he shifts his attention from one account to another as he's needed. This turns out to be the perfect strategy for his job. The other side of not being able to concentrate is being able to handle chaos well. Learning to find peace with ourselves means we see the silver lining in what we think is a problem.

Step 1: *Entering into Retreat:* Sit comfortably with your journal. For five minutes, reflect on your life from elementary school to the present, looking for recurrent problems or difficulties. Write down the central issues that seem to keep reappearing in your life. They could be problem behaviors, emotional reactions, or interpersonal patterns. Develop a list of about three to six significant concerns.

Step 2: For the next eight minutes, reflect on what the silver lining might be for each of these problem areas. What gifts arise from the pain, failure, and frustration of your recurring difficulties? Write down your thoughts for each issue.

Step 3: Now choose one of the areas and develop it further for the next five minutes. "If I didn't have this problem, then I wouldn't have . . ." "Without this difficulty, I never would have . . ." Following this line of thinking, generate as much information as you can about the benefits of this problem.

Step 4: *Returning to the World:* We are complex creatures, with enormous potential for learning and transformation. Use the final two minutes to appreciate how you've grown and developed as a result of this significant

---

ONE-MINUTE RETREAT—ONLY NOW

We can experience peace only in the present moment. Periodically during your day, remind yourself to become aware of the here and now. Breathe in the moment. Experience peace in the moment.

---

problem. Can you extend this appreciation so you can actually make peace with yourself around this aspect? Just for this moment?

Pause in Breath

There are two points in the rhythm of our breathing where we pause and do nothing. These are very rich moments of inner silence and stillness, opportunities for deep peacefulness. Breathing practices in both Buddhism and Hinduism focus on these pauses, often suggesting we extend them very gradually. This retreat takes a more gentle approach by merely suggesting you become more aware of your experience of these pauses.

Step 1: *Entering into Retreat:* Sit comfortably, with back support if needed. Close your eyes, and for the first three minutes, just notice your breathing as it is. Make no effort to change it.

Step 2: Become aware of the natural places in the pattern of your breathing where you pause. For the next five minutes, just notice the pause at the peak of your inhale and the pause at the bottom of your exhale. Let your breath flow evenly, so your inhale and exhale are about the same length.

Step 3: Now focus your awareness at the exact moment when your breath turns out of the pause—the moment when the next inhale begins and the moment when the next inhale starts to let go. For five minutes, focus on these precise turning points, allowing them to happen rather than controlling your breath.

Step 4: For the next five minutes, continue to focus on the pauses in your breathing. Really let yourself rest in the pauses. Let yourself experience a deep peacefulness in these moments of inner silence and stillness.

Step 5: *Returning to the World:* For the final two minutes, simply open your eyes. Your breathing and your awareness of your breathing will automatically adjust to returning to the world. Remember this deep feeling of peacefulness, so you can return to it again.

If we have no peace, it is because we have forgotten that we belong to each other.

—Mother Teresa

12

Relaxation

Learning to relax is at the heart of living well.
—Judith Lasater, Iyengar yoga instructor

We now know scientifically that relaxation training reduces a wide variety of physical and psychological symptoms. Physically, our heart rate slows, blood pressure lowers, pain decreases, and muscle tension eases. Psychologically, there is a decrease in anxiety, anger, hostility, and depression as well as improved quality of life for those suffering from life-threatening illnesses.

If that weren't a good enough reason to practice relaxation, it is also interesting to note that techniques for relaxation can be found in all of the world religions. Relaxation is part of every spiritual path, used daily to release worldly tensions. Regular relaxation retreats prevent the cumulative buildup of stress and tension, allowing us to be more receptive to the sacred. Relaxation reaches beyond the physical and psychological benefits and is essential for inner development and spiritual unfolding.

Relaxation softens us physically and psychologically, allowing us to loosen our grip on who we think we are—our beliefs, identities, ego, and conditioned responses. With relaxation we can gradually become less psychologically rigid, dense, and heavy. Then the way we relate to ourselves becomes lighter and more flexible, making more room for compassion and a sense of humor as we face daily challenges.

Relaxation retreats help us to loosen up at all levels of our being. In fact, the Latin root for *relax* is *relaxare*, meaning "to loosen." There is a paradox, however, in learning how to loosen up and relax. That is, it's not effective to work hard at relaxation. We can't force our muscles to relax or our minds to de-stress. We have to work *with* our whole body-mind to ease into a relaxed state. We must approach the process of relaxing in a gentle and accepting manner, without pressure.

The truth is, many of us not only don't know how to relax, we no longer know what relaxation feels like. We don't know how to get to that relaxed place, and we don't recognize it when we are there. Some people can even experience anxiety as they begin relaxation practices, because the relaxed body sensations seem so different from their usual tenseness.

When we're chronically stressed, as many of us are today, never relaxing, the tension accumulates, resulting in changes in our energy field, in our bodies, and even in the way we think. Because the tension accumulates gradually, we get used to ever higher levels of it and we experience it as normal. But at this point of chronic stress, we're actually at risk for illness. Relaxation retreats help us to break this chronic stress pattern, giving our bodies and minds a chance to recover a healthy balance.

The more you practice relaxation retreats on a daily basis, the easier it will be for you to relax in a stressful situation when you need to the most. The practical goal for relaxation training is that you learn to use it in daily life so you can let go of tension at any time, in any situation. In addition, the relaxation retreats will spontaneously evoke your softer, gentler side, enabling you to be more open, creative, and compassionate. Because of these personal changes, you will be able to respond to stress with greater flexibility and objectivity.

Preparation for Stress

Relaxation retreats can be used in the same way as childbirth preparation. Both approaches teach specific skills that can be applied at the anticipated stressful time, thereby reducing anxiety and increasing feelings of competency.

Tom was a gifted thirty-two-year-old computer programmer at an Internet start-up company. He was under a lot of pressure at work because he had to present a progress report to his boss and his boss's boss. Tom knew he was stressed out and that he needed to relax to prepare this report. So he began practicing the "Smooth Your Forehead" retreat. Tom had never before even thought about his forehead, so this was all new to him. However, this brief retreat is very specific and concrete, and Tom followed the instructions easily. He practiced nearly every day for about three weeks.

When it came time to deliver his report, Tom was nervous, and to make matters worse, his report was not all good news. But before going into the conference room, he told himself the magic words, "My forehead is smooth as silk." During the meeting Tom felt himself getting tense when he noticed a subtle clenching of his jaw. This was his earliest signal that he was feeling stressed. Tom was prepared. He nonchalantly stroked his silk tie and imagined his forehead was just as smooth. As Tom's fore-

FIVE-MINUTE RETREAT—SMOOTH YOUR FOREHEAD

In biofeedback training for muscle relaxation, the frontalis muscle of the forehead is often used as a focal point. This is because it has been found that as the muscles of the face relax, the rest of the body relaxes.

Depending upon your circumstance, you can do this retreat either sitting or lying down, in private or during your workday. Simply imagine that you can smooth the wrinkles out of your forehead. With every exhale, imagine your forehead becoming more relaxed. You can concentrate on different thoughts to enhance your relaxation. Imagine that your eyebrows let go. Your scalp eases. You can say to yourself, "My forehead is smooth as silk." You can use your fingertips to lightly stroke your forehead in a slow, soothing manner.

Notice that as you do this retreat, a general feeling of warmth and well-being arises in your entire body as you deeply relax.

head relaxed, his jaw also eased, and he felt a general sense of warmth and well-being. The meeting went very well.

By touching his tie during this stressful meeting, Tom gave himself a strong sensory cue to relax. This helped him to apply his newly learned relaxation skills in a stressful situation and integrate his five-minute retreat into his life. Tom now uses this technique whenever he feels he is becoming stressed, to help ease his body and mind. Just knowing that he has this effective technique at his disposal has helped Tom approach challenges much more calmly and effectively.

*E*scape

Relaxation retreats are very successful for reducing chronic pain. They give you a way to escape a current situation, even if only temporarily, as well as provide an important sense of hope that it may be possible to be pain-free. People report that their pain subsides for many hours following a relaxation retreat.

Theresa had suffered with chronic pain after a car accident almost a year earlier and was unable to work at her job as a bookkeeper. Theresa was a petite thirty-five-year-old who had never been seriously sick before the accident. Now she felt frustrated and hopeless about her pain. When she took enough medication to reduce the pain, she was too groggy to do anything. However, without the medication, she was in too much discomfort to do anything. When I told her about the "Vacation Visualization" retreat, Theresa was interested in trying it, because she wanted some time off from her pain.

For her visualization, Theresa chose a beach scene from a Caribbean island she had visited before the accident. She took great care to remember as many sensory details as possible. She remembered the breeze lifting her hair, the smell of the salt air, the sound of the surf, and all the colors of the water. As Theresa practiced this visualization day after day, it became more and more real to her. She felt it was her private beach, jellyfish and all.

This retreat gave Theresa a way to escape her current suffering, along with a renewed feeling of control. This retreat was something she could do for herself to reduce her pain. Theresa became more hopeful and determined about a full recovery. She started dreaming of a pain-free future that included her actual return to the Caribbean island and her private beach.

You can see from these two examples that relaxation retreats can be helpful in diverse situations. Take a look at the following signs to see if you might be helped by a little more relaxation in your life.

SIGNS THAT YOU NEED A RELAXATION RETREAT

1. It takes one week of vacation for you to relax enough to feel like you're on vacation.
2. Your speech is pressured, with words bursting out in a staccato rhythm.
3. Your life is even more stressful than usual.
4. You live with any one of a wide array of stress-related symptoms, such as digestive problems, sleep disorders, or high blood pressure.
5. You've lost perspective about what you truly value in your life.
6. You've become more tense, serious, and inflexible than you'd like to admit.
7. You can't remember the last time you did something unexpected, spontaneous, and fun.
8. You overschedule yourself and feel pressured by time.
9. It's difficult for you to soften and connect with your feelings.
10. You're having daydreams about running off to live on a South Sea island.
11. You're tired of the voices in your head, and you'd like more internal quiet.
12. Your life is out of balance.

Robert's Story

In my private practice, I have noticed that when people practice the relaxation retreats, they often begin to notice unexpected subtle changes in who they are. They may have turned to the relaxation retreats originally for relief from a stress-related symptom, but gradually they begin to notice a shift in their attitude and behavior, along with an awareness of a gradual spiritual opening. A spiritual opening is not a mysterious, mystical process; it's simply becoming more loving. This is a simple yet profound shift.

Robert's doctor was unusually blunt at his annual exam, and he delivered his somber warning purposefully in the presence of Robert's wife, Sarah. "You're a prime candidate for a heart attack."

Robert was an aggressive criminal attorney who had been working eighty hours a week for the past twenty years. His doctor's warning was not a surprise; it confirmed Sarah's worst fears. She took charge immediately. She cleaned up the family eating habits and insisted that Robert learn how to relax and meditate. She didn't want to lose her husband, the father of their three children. Robert reluctantly agreed and followed the instructions for the "Mindfulness" retreat. He didn't sense much happening during this retreat, but he was under pressure from Sarah, so he put in his obligatory twenty minutes each day.

After a few months of this new regimen, Robert's youngest daughter snuggled into his lap one evening, gave him a hug, and innocently proclaimed, "I like you better now, Daddy. You're nicer." Robert's two older children, who had been sitting on the floor nearby, heard this comment and glanced over with trepidation showing in their faces. Not only were they not used to their father's being home, they were not used to any expression of feelings. They expected their father to get up and walk out of the room, leaving their baby sister hurt and rejected. Instead, Robert stopped reading and really looked into his children's faces. He didn't say anything, but he gave his youngest child a real hug.

Robert got the message from all his children. He sensed the change in him was partly a result of the "Mindfulness" retreat, but he didn't quite understand how it worked. However, he didn't care. He just knew he was giving and receiving more hugs than ever before, both with his kids and his wife.

Robert added the five-minute retreat "Melting the Frozen Heart." It seemed like a natural next step and was easy to practice during the day. People at work began to treat Robert differently. They were not only friendlier but more willing to cooperate on projects and share information. At this point, Robert knew enough to realize that they were responding to

FIVE-MINUTE RETREAT—MELTING
THE FROZEN HEART

I have to confess, I used this same title for a five-day workshop one year and people signed up for the workshop in spite of the title. In our culture, this may sound more like a microwave cooking course than a spiritual retreat; however, the image of the heart softening and melting in order to open is found in the mystical practices of many religions, including Christianity and Islam.

Sitting quietly, close your eyes and focus your attention on your breath. Imagine that you can use your breath to massage your heart center. Allow the rhythm and movement of your breathing to melt away whatever is frozen and layered over your heart. You are melting the layers that have accumulated over a lifetime to protect your heart from being hurt. Instead of just protecting you, these layers have also frozen and restricted your capacity to love. Let these layers melt away.

changes in him. He guessed he was letting people in, allowing them to see more of who he really was. Robert had never realized how his tough, competitive exterior had frightened people. Although Robert needed that harsh demeanor in the courtroom, he didn't have to live it all the time.

There's a reason relaxation techniques are part of meditative practices in all the world religions. They soften the very structure of our personalities, allowing us to open up to new ways of being. When we relax, we are more open to our inner experience of the divine and more able to express love in our lives. Try these retreats, and observe the inner changes they bring over time.

*Something must give way, a native hardness
must break down and liquify.*

—William James

*R*etreats to Cultivate Relaxation

Floating

I learned this specific position for releasing the back from a Sensory Awareness class taught by Charlotte Selver, the founder of that method. This was more than thirty years ago, and I thought she was old then. I understand she is still actively teaching and must be in her nineties. She's a living testament to her approach. Her subtle, gentle classes have long been considered the Zen of body work and are often taught at meditation retreats.

Preparation for Retreat: Arrange a chair on a carpeted floor where you can lie down comfortably on your back with your lower legs resting on the chair seat. The edge of the seat should be behind your knees, so your entire lower legs and feet are resting on the chair seat.

Step 1: *Entering into Retreat:* For the first four minutes, let go of your legs with every exhalation, allowing the chair seat to support them. Notice specifically that as you practice this, there is a spontaneous releasing from your hip joints.

Step 2: Use your exhalations for the next four minutes to relax your back, allowing it to be supported by the floor. With every exhale, your back can relax even more.

Step 3: Continue for the next ten minutes to let go with every exhalation, and imagine that you are floating on a cloud that is supporting your entire body. Please notice any thoughts that pop into your head, and allow them to just float by as if they were passing clouds. Pay attention to the arising of the thoughts, their drifting by, and their disappearing into the distance.

Step 4: *Returning to the World:* Use the remaining two minutes to open your eyes, slowly stretch, and move gently toward sitting. Look around you, noticing the colors in the room. Reflect back on this easy relaxation exercise a few times during your day. Remember it in your body.

FIVE-MINUTE RETREAT—SPACIOUSNESS, NO HOLDING

This is another of the Elemental Breaths from the Sufi Order of the West. Standing, let your arms hang with your palms facing forward, slightly away from your body. Remember that according to the laws of physics, matter is composed mostly of space. Quietly inhale and exhale through your mouth. Imagine that a breeze can pass directly through you, through the spaces of your physical body.

You are spaciousness. Nothing accumulates. Any repetitive thoughts can be swept away by the breeze passing through you. Let go.

As each muscle is released from tension,
the mind's burden lightens.

—Mike George

Carried Away by Music

Just as music can tame the wild beasts, it can also help us tame our "monkey minds," a term well known to meditators. "Monkey mind" describes a mind that jumps from here to there, uncontrollably and unceasingly. Allowing ourselves to be carried away by music will calm our "monkey minds" and relax our bodies.

You may already have a favorite piece of music to use, but let me suggest some from the classical repertoire: Canon in D, by Pachelbel; "Moonlight" Sonata Op. 27, No. 2, First Movement, by Beethoven; *La Mer*, by Debussy; and *Pavane for a Dead Princess*, by Ravel. Current CDs might include *The Sky of Mind*, by Ray Lynch; *A Rainbow Path*, by Kay Gardner; *Music for Zen Meditation*, by Don Campbell; and *Canyon Trilogy*, by R. Carlos Nakai.

Preparation for Retreat: Find a cozy spot where you can listen to music and lie down in any position you find comfortable. Use blankets and pillows for extra support and comfort.

Step 1: *Entering into Retreat:* With the music on, use the first five minutes to scan through your body, from your toes to the crown of your head. Methodically move your awareness from your feet and legs, through your pelvis and torso, up into your shoulders, arms, and hands, and through your neck up to the very top of your skull cap. A full body scan never fails to give us the feedback we need to readjust our position in some subtle way to be more comfortable.

Step 2: For the next twelve minutes, allow the music to carry you. This will mean different things to different people. Some will *see* the music and be carried away by their vision, while others will *feel* the music in their body. Some people will *disappear* and *become the music*, while others will *experience waves of emotion* through the music. However you experience the music, allow it to carry you away, giving your body and your "monkey mind" a chance to calm down and relax.

Step 3: *Returning to the World:* Begin to stretch gently during the last three minutes so you can reenter daily life. Remember, some lucky people will live with music playing inside them throughout their day. I'm not one of those lucky people and only know about this type of music memory because

---

ONE-MINUTE RETREAT—YAWN, JUST YAWN

 Those are the complete instructions: yawn, just yawn. This retreat is for any time of day. For politeness' sake, you may want to excuse yourself to find a private place. This would also give you the opportunity to add a great stretch to your yawn. You can intentionally start to stretch as your yawn starts, and then just allow nature to take its course.

Yawning increases the amount of oxygen in your system, and Scientologists think it helps to shift your level of consciousness. Who doesn't like a good yawn?

my teenage daughter carries, I think, thousands of tunes in her head. If you have this ability, notice how long you can hear part of the melody in your head as you go about your business. Remembering the music can be a focal point for your mind, calming the tendency to jump from here to there.

Spontaneous Stretching

I find it mesmerizing to watch my cats stretch. They involve their whole bodies and seem so nonchalant and proud of themselves at the same time. And, of course, cats know how to relax. We have to remind ourselves to stretch and trust our instincts for how our bodies want to stretch. This is part of our learning how to relax. In the beginning, I am suggesting you do this retreat in silence so you can listen closely to your body's signals. Later, you can decide whether you want to include music.

Step 1: *Entering into Retreat:* Begin from any position. For the first ten minutes simply move and stretch in whatever ways feel good to you. This retreat approach is taken from dance therapy and is based on the notion that you can unconditionally accept and trust any way you move. Simply pay attention to your body's instincts and trust your flow from one stretch to another.

Step 2: For the next eight minutes, begin to consciously expand your movement repertoire: move in different spatial planes—up, down, behind you, in circles; try moving through space; work from the floor if you've been standing or vice versa; alter the rhythm or pace of your stretching—faster, slower, sharper, smoother. In other words, intentionally try something new.

Step 3: *Returning to the World:* For the final two minutes, just remain in stillness in any position you choose. Experience your physical reality, your warmth, your heart beating, your breathing.

> *This . . . sort of dancer understands that the body, by force of the soul, can be converted to a luminous fluid.*
>
> —Isadora Duncan

ONE-MINUTE RETREAT—RELIEVE TENSION

For many of us, whether we are sitting at a desk or in meditation, muscle tension accumulates in our neck and shoulders. The practice of rolling the shoulders to loosen up is well known, but important refinements are added for this retreat. These instructions come from the movement education system known as Structural Awareness. It's based on Dr. Ida Rolf's system of Structural Integration (also called rolfing) and is designed to improve your postural alignment.

Either sitting or standing, imagine you can breathe up your torso through the top of your head. Imagine that you are growing taller. Then, maintaining that height, roll your shoulders in backward circles. Feel your shoulder blades moving toward each other as you roll your shoulders back. The reason I don't suggest you also roll your shoulders forward is that most of us need to move our shoulders back for better postural alignment. Rolling shoulders forward only increases the tendency to fall into a round-shouldered slump.

After a few shoulder rolls, again imagine you can breathe up your spine through the top of your head. Maintaining a sensation of being taller, simply rotate your head to the right only as far as you can turn comfortably. Return to center and breathe up. While continuing to stand tall, rotate your head to the left. Again return to center and breathe up. These head rotations should look and feel very mechanical. Please do not try to increase your range of motion by stretching or pushing your head rotation. Breathe up one last time and return to your day, with a little less tension.

Vacation Visualization

I used this retreat with a client who was prone to anxiety and panic attacks. His vacation world was underwater, since he loved scuba diving. When he imagined himself scuba diving, his breathing was naturally slow and regular. This was the perfect antidote to his anxiety. I would have him enter into his "Vacation Visualization" retreat and then imagine he was in an anxiety-provoking situation. His breath remained calm. Then, when in real life he had to deal with stressful situations, he would imagine he was breathing through his scuba equipment—a slow, normal breath. This helped to relax and restore his sense of calm, no matter what situation he faced.

Step 1: *Entering into Retreat:* For the first two minutes, settle into sitting comfortably and noticing the flow of your breath.

Step 2: The core of the retreat will continue for fifteen minutes. Think back to an idyllic vacation spot or imagine an idealized one. Use all your senses to re-create the experience of being there: feel the tempera-

---

FIVE-MINUTE RETREAT—STRETCHING YOUR SPINE

Chiropractors know that the condition of your spine affects the neurological functioning throughout your entire body. Teachings on meditation from all the world religions recognize this same truth with their beginning instructions, "Sit up straight." Maintaining postural alignment and a flexible back contributes to the health of your spine and the energy flow within your body.

Begin this mini-retreat by standing in bare feet. Imagine that as you inhale up your spine and through the top of your head, you are growing taller. Then just let your head and neck gently hang forward. Take another breath now, into the back of your neck. Slowly allow the weight of your head to carry you forward, so you begin to bend over slightly. Shift your breath focus to your exhale. Feel each vertebra as you slowly curve your spine more and more. Keep your knees loose. Bend over only as far as you can comfortably go, staying down for only one breath. Then begin to unfold back up, beginning with the very base of your spine. Inhale into your spine as you gently unfold from the bottom up. Remember, your neck and head are the very last to come up. When you return to a standing position, imagine you can inhale your breath up your spine through the top of your head and feel even taller.

---

ture and humidity on your skin, smell the air, listen for sounds of nature, see the entire landscape until it recedes into the distance. Add greater detail. Remember or imagine the way the light shifts throughout the day, the first insect or animal sounds heard at night, the way the earth felt as you walked, the local housing, natural surroundings, or small stores, the way people talked. Even when you think you have all the details, go back and add more. Make your scene so real that it feels like an entire other world to which you can retreat. Move around in that world, breathe it in, soak it up. Let yourself disappear into that world.

Step 3: *Returning to the World:* Be very gentle with yourself during these last three minutes as you leave your "Vacation Visualization" retreat. Bring with you the feeling of total body, heart, and soul relaxation that you have just experienced. Return rejuvenated and revitalized.

Mindfulness

Through his research into the health benefits of the Relaxation Response, Herbert Benson, a Harvard physician, has helped to integrate meditation into the mainstream of our culture. The essential components of the Relaxation Response include having a gentle attitude and a focal point. The attitude is the first step toward Mindfulness—open, flowing, accepting, gently guiding you back to your focal point. Benson has claimed that the focal point can be the breath or any word used as a mantra, from "Om," "Shalom," "Hu," "Jesus Christ," to "Coca-Cola." However, mystics of many traditions believe that there is power in the sound of the word. For instance, the Tibetan Buddhists have mantras for every purpose: healing, wisdom, compassion, awareness, purification, wrath (to remove obstacles), and peace. They believe mantras like "Om" or "Ah" send energy vibrations to alter the inner and outer atmosphere of the meditator. I suggest we follow thousands of years of mystical training and use a mantra with spiritual meaning, like "Om." The mantra floats on the breath, repeated silently inside with every inhale and exhale.

Step 1: *Entering into Retreat:* Sit with as good a posture as is possible for you. For the first three minutes, scan your body, directing your awareness to flow through the entire inside space of your body.

Step 2: For the next fifteen minutes, simply maintain your attention on your breath. If you are using a mantra, repeat it silently within as you inhale and as you exhale. If you notice your mind wandering into thoughts, daydreams, physical discomfort, or some other distraction, gently guide your attention back to your breath. Mindfulness expects and accepts such wanderings and doesn't judge or worry about them. When it happens, simply return your attention to your breathing.

Step 3: *Returning to the World:* The last two minutes give you a chance to stretch and look around as if you were seeing things for the first time. As you begin to move and engage your world, maintain some small awareness of your breath, gently guiding your attention back to your breathing throughout the day as a way of checking in with yourself.

Muscle Release

In the 1930s Edmund Jacobson, a physician, discovered that teaching his patients to relax helped them with a wide range of illnesses—from high blood pressure to digestive problems. He asked his patients to alternately tense and let go of specific muscles so that they could learn how to recognize and induce relaxation.

Actually, this retreat is inspired by my father, who used to sit by my bedside when I had trouble falling asleep as a child. This happened often, since I was the youngest and had to go to bed first; I was sure I was missing something vitally important! My dad would talk me through this exercise. I doubt that he knew of Jacobson's work, but he did know the value of physical relaxation. These instructions are easier to follow than Jacobson's original work, because they focus on larger muscle groups rather than trying to isolate a specific muscle for relaxation.

Step 1: *Entering into Retreat:* Lie on your back on a soft mat on the floor or on a firm mattress. Place a pillow under your knees to give your back extra support, and place the flattest pillow acceptable to you under your head. Just settle in and get comfy for the first three minutes of this retreat.

Step 2: For the next ten minutes, you will systematically tense and release the major muscle groups of your body, starting with your feet and working your way up to your head. When you release the tension, let go in slow motion, so you are gradually relaxing the muscles. It's important that you isolate each body area as much as possible when you work with it. Tense and release each body part three times. After the third time of tensing and releasing, just continue to let go even more. You will find you can relax just a tiny bit more.

With all this in mind, let's begin. Tense both of your feet—scrunch them as much as you can without involving your leg muscles. Hold for three seconds, then let go gradually. Feel a rush of warm energy and blood circulation flow into your feet. Repeat this three times, and after the last time, relax even more. Continue this process with the following areas, in this order: calves, thighs, buttocks, stomach, chest, back, hand, arms, shoulders, neck, face. Tense your face by scrunching all your muscles toward your nose. Remember to tense and relax each area of your body, from your toes to your head, three times; feel the rush of warmth into your muscles during the relaxation stage.

Step 3: For a full five minutes, simply enjoy your state of relaxation. Let your breath be smooth and regular, without effort. Let yourself absorb this state of relaxation so it becomes imprinted in your consciousness. You will want to remember this feeling in your body, mind, and soul.

Step 4: *Returning to the World:* Use your final two minutes to begin to move very slowly. Take your time and gradually return to sitting. Pay attention to the feeling of relaxation in your body as you reenter the world.

Tension

Just as the "Muscle Release" retreat uses the physical tensing of muscles to relax, we can move toward deep release of tension by starting with our inner experience of tension. This retreat uses creative expression to capture a symbol of our emotional, physical, and spiritual experience of chronic tension. Then by breathing deeply and looking at our emotional drawing (see page 27), we can feel an inner relief and release.

Step 1: *Entering into Retreat:* Sit comfortably, with your oil pastels and paper ready (see page 22). Use the first five minutes to become more and more aware of how you experience tension on all levels of your being—emotionally, physically, and spiritually. Sometimes our tension is so chronic that we are used to it and no longer identify it as tension, thinking "That's just how I am." Look specifically for chronic patterns of tension.

Step 2: Give yourself a full eight minutes to do an emotional drawing of what your tension feels like inside. Use color and form to develop something that represents to you what you feel like inside.

Step 3: For five minutes, simply look at your drawing while you breathe slowly, gently lengthening your inhale and exhale.

Step 4: *Returning to the World:* For the last two minutes, notice if you feel any relief inside—perhaps less internal pressure or tension. You are now more aware of your chronic tension patterns and so more able to release them. Take a few really deep breaths and reenter your world.

Open Body

My favorite part of yoga class is the final posture—Savasana, or Pose of the Corpse. You imitate a corpse by lying completely motionless, allowing your breath to become fine and slow. In this retreat you will assume this posture and add a visualization along with a breathing technique for relaxation.

Step 1: *Entering into Retreat:* Lie on your back on a firm mat or soft carpet. Allow your arms to rest comfortably by your sides with palms turned up. For the first five minutes, just let your breath become gentle and fine. With every exhale, allow the floor to support your body and your weight a little more. Let your lower jaw hang loose and your tongue relax inside your mouth.

Step 2: For the next twelve minutes, imagine you can inhale through the soles of your feet all the way to the top of your head. Then imagine that you can exhale through the top of your head, sending the air out just as a whale spews air out of its blowhole. Experience your body as an empty reed, and allow your breath to move through your body with no obstructions.

Step 3: *Returning to the World:* For the final three minutes, simply allow your breath to return to normal. Stretch your legs through to your

ONE-MINUTE RETREAT—FOCUS ON FEET

Every ballet class, whether for beginners or professional training, begins with working the feet. Even Dr. Ida Rolf, in Structural Integration, focused on the breath in the first session and the feet in the second. Somehow loosening up the fascial sheath and the muscles of the feet helps to relax the spine and neck, affecting the whole body.

Place one hand on a solid chair or table for support. Do not try to balance without this additional support. In bare feet or soft socks, simply shift your weight to the ball and toes of one foot. Then while that heel is going back down to the floor, shift onto the ball and toes of your other foot. Your knees will bend and move forward as you go onto the ball and toes of your foot. The alternating movement has the same rhythm as when a cat is kneading with its paws.

toes, and your arms through to your fingertips. Sit up slowly bit by bit, and imagine you are waking up from a long rest fully refreshed.

*T*hrough relaxation, one opens the threshold
to inner sensing (that is, attentiveness to the inner self).

—Fran Levy, dance movement therapist

Calming Energy

We instinctively calm children, dear friends, and even our pets with a loving touch of our hands. It's important that we learn to do the same for ourselves. We don't have to wait for someone else to touch us; we can use the energy from our own palms to help comfort and soothe ourselves.

This retreat, based on Polarity therapy as described in chapter 2, is especially effective at bedtime if you have trouble falling asleep. This technique balances the subtle energy in your body according to ancient Chinese medicine. You can also use these very simple instructions briefly during the day, either sitting or standing, whenever you feel the need to calm yourself. The laying on of your hands will work to quiet both your body and your mind.

Step 1: *Entering into Retreat:* Lie on your back in bed, making sure that you are warm enough. Support yourself with pillows any way you like to be comfortable.

Step 2: Rub the palms of your hands together to generate warmth and energy. Place your right hand on your abdomen, just below your navel; place your left hand on your heart center. For a full twenty minutes, just allow your body to absorb the warm energy of your hands.

Step 3: *Returning to the World:* Allow yourself to simply drift off into a relaxed, good night's sleep.

We discover we can let go and trust, we can let the breath breathe itself and the natural movement of life carry us with ease.

—Jack Kornfield, Buddhist meditation teacher

13

Self-Acceptance

The curious paradox is that when I accept myself
just as I am, then I can change.

—Carl Rogers, psychologist

Self-acceptance refers to how much of ourselves we can accept and embrace. In essence, how broad is my embrace of myself? Can I accept my insecurities? Can I accept my mistakes? Can I accept my nose, thighs, or hips? Self-acceptance is not quite the same as self-esteem, although they are clearly related. I don't have to like all aspects of myself or hold them in esteem; I simply can accept them without judgment.

The broader our embrace of ourselves can be, the more we can treat ourselves with loving-kindness, understanding, and compassion. We need this deep level of acceptance so we can feel secure in who we are as we venture out into the world, take risks, learn from our experiences, and become resilient. This is how we become competent in the world. Then our self-esteem can grow as it should, based on our accomplishments and successes.

Let me give a few examples just so we don't confuse accomplishment and success with the cultural emphasis on money or fame. I remember a little girl in my daughter's kindergarten class who didn't like the orthopedic shoes she had to wear, but she accepted them and ran out to play during recess like all the other kids. She learned she could swing just as high as anyone else, and she felt great about herself. She may not have liked her shoes, but she accepted them and didn't let them affect the fun she had playing. Similarly, thirty-year-old Todd, who was transferred to a new department at work requiring many written letters and memos, acknowledged that his grammar was disastrous. His nonjudgmental acceptance of his weakness allowed him to ask for help more easily. He did this without getting nervous and, as a result, his memos and letters turned out fine and his self-confidence prevailed.

Our ability to accept ourselves is an important part of our inner psychological foundation. It affects small day-to-day ways of behaving as well as major life decisions. It's reflected in how we relate to others and how we expect them to treat us. Our acceptance of ourselves also determines our vision for ourselves now and in the future. It can influence our hopes and dreams for our whole lifetime.

Unfortunately, self-acceptance is a struggle for most of us in western culture. It's important to realize it doesn't have to be this way. During a meeting with western meditation teachers, described by psychologist Dan Goleman in his book *Healing Emotions*, the Dalai Lama was asked about people who feel they don't deserve to be happy, who "feel guilty, as if it would somehow be wrong for them to be happy." The conversation stopped. "After a long exchange in Tibetan, [the translator] comments that this concept is alien to His Holiness." The Dalai Lama finally admits, "I thought I had a very good acquaintance with the mind, but now I feel quite ignorant." The concept of not feeling good enough about oneself struck him as "very, very strange." The Dalai Lama's honest perplexity about a psychological phenomenon we take for granted gives us a broader perspective from which to view ourselves.

Our culture is becoming progressively consumed with unrealistic expectations and standards for what we're supposed to look like, what we have to accomplish, and what we need to possess. We cannot afford to let these extreme cultural values influence our inner capacity to accept ourselves. Self-acceptance implies a courageously honest self-confrontation: Who am I? What can I do? And where do I want to go in life? We reflect on ourselves with a vision based on our deepest values, independent of the external cultural media machine. Remember, we don't have to like every single thing about who we are or what we can do. We just have to accept ourselves in order to create the necessary condition for future self-development.

*B*ody Image Madness

One of the most common ways our self-acceptance of our bodies is compromised is by our near-constant exposure to the mass media, including TV, magazines, movies, and so forth. We all know that more women are unhappy with their bodies than ever before. But the most significant recent shift in this trend is that men are now joining in with their own dissatisfactions when it comes to their physical image.

Carol was one of the millions of women who had never felt good about her body. As she hit fifty, gained weight, and felt the effects of gravity, she became much more unhappy. Although Carol was a successful college professor with a long-term marriage, her feelings about her body were undermining her sense of herself. She understood intellectually that her body would never be perfect, but emotionally Carol couldn't accept the way she looked. She unconsciously avoided looking at herself in the mirror and began to buy loose-fitting clothing. Carol decided to use the "Mirror, Mirror" retreat because she thought she had to literally face herself, to confront the reality of her body and her feelings directly.

The "Mirror, Mirror" retreat requires a courageous commitment to face oneself. It is not for the weakhearted, since it involves nudity, a mirror, and dancing. Undaunted, Carol decided to practice the retreat every day for a week. She started on a weekend morning so she wouldn't have to rush off to work, and she set an alarm clock to ensure that she would spend the full allotted time. Carol slipped off her oversized nightie, turned on the lights, and stood naked in front of the mirror. The first day, all she could do was keep breathing; she never got to the dancing part of the retreat. But the next morning, she was back in front of the mirror. That day she did dance, albeit with tentative movements and great awkwardness.

By the end of the week, Carol was not much farther along, perhaps a little less tentative in her dancing but still harshly critical of her body. She realized she was just beginning a long but important process and decided to continue practicing the retreat until she felt more whole. Gradually she found that "just looking" at herself and breathing her way through her inner judgments and body hatred was becoming a little easier. Her dancing became more smooth, as if the movement itself were lubricating her joints. Carol began experimenting with the music, eventually trying salsa, African rhythms, and the Rolling Stones. She had come a long way. Carol had rediscovered herself—or perhaps, reclaimed herself. She felt better about her body physically from the inside out, rather than critically from the outside in. This shift empowered her as she stood in front of her students to lecture, encountered colleagues, or dressed up for a party with her husband.

The progression in the "Mirror, Mirror" retreat from "just looking" to closing your eyes and "just dancing" is a very important transition. At this point, one's experience of body image shifts from visual (out there) to kinesthetic (in here). Our body is less an object and more an experience of who we are. Making this transition was a breakthrough for Carol. She began to enjoy the dancing for the sheer pleasure of movement, reminiscent of a child's delight in "just playing."

I want to point out that the goal of the "Mirror, Mirror" retreat is *not* to develop a positive body image. That may in fact happen, but it's not essential. What we do have to learn is that we *are* our bodies. This retreat is focused on doing just that. Our bodies are not primarily objects to be judged and evaluated, but expressions of our uniqueness. Our ability to accept ourselves as we are comes from a much deeper place inside ourselves than even a positive body image. This way of accepting and nurturing ourselves through "Mirror, Mirror" can empower us, giving us a sense of ease with our whole selves, not just our physical bodies.

Y*ou might think that there are no others on the planet who hate themselves as much as you do. All of that is a good place to start . . . Start where you are.*

—Pema Chodron, Buddhist meditation teacher

---

*O*urselves in Others

Sometimes we can discover what we don't accept in ourselves by noticing what we dislike in others. Shelley thought she had been welcoming and friendly toward Anna, the new girl in the office. However, she distinctly felt that Anna didn't like her and, as a result, Shelley herself was beginning to dislike Anna. The two women had not had a disagreement, or even much contact. Nevertheless, Shelley was becoming very critical of Anna, and more and more uncomfortable with her presence.

One Friday evening, when Shelley was out to dinner with some office friends, she complained about Anna's poking her nose into everything that went on in the office. Later, Shelley's closest friend challenged her to identify exactly what was upsetting her about Anna. So Shelley began using the five-minute "Shadow" retreat in order to understand her own reactions to Anna. Whenever she felt negative toward Anna, Shelley would reflect back on herself: What's getting triggered in me? What meaning does this have for me? How is Anna similar to the parts of me I don't like?

As she started practicing this retreat, Shelley initially felt resistant, becoming even more irritated and annoyed with Anna. However, after a few "Shadow" retreats, Shelley had to admit begrudgingly that Anna reminded her of herself when she first started working in the office. Anna wanted to understand all the systems and how every procedure worked, so she asked lots of questions. Now Shelley realized why she had taken such an instant dislike to Anna. Shelley was embarrassed to admit that she herself could be intrusive, even nosy, always wanting to know everything that was going on. She saw herself in Anna and didn't like what she saw.

The "Shadow" retreat gave Shelley the chance to accept those parts of herself that she didn't like and could see only in Anna, not herself. Her realization also cleared the way for the two women to develop an easy friendship, because after all, they were so alike. In fact, together they cleaned out the office supply closet and revamped the whole system of ordering. Shelley could even laugh at herself for being so suspicious of Anna at the beginning, because now she really valued Anna's contribution to their island of organized sanity within the office chaos.

Self-acceptance is really about one's relationship with oneself, which is, perhaps, the most important relationship in life. Consider the following signs to reflect on how cultivating self-acceptance might improve the quality of your relationship with yourself.

SIGNS THAT YOU NEED A SELF-ACCEPTANCE RETREAT

1. Your inner critic is louder in your head than your speaking voice.
2. You stop yourself from trying something new out of fear of failure.
3. You're a perfectionist.
4. You're very dependent on others' opinions.
5. You feel as if you don't have a right to exist.
6. You don't seem to fit in anywhere socially; no one seeks to include you.
7. You think you should be thinner, smarter, richer, wiser, more spiritual, funnier, stronger, more vulnerable, more popular, more independent, less independent, ad nauseam.
8. At times, you feel as if you're invisible.
9. You're self-punishing in some way.
10. You're uncomfortable alone and you're uncomfortable with others.
11. You hate all the clothes in your closet.
12. You've lost your own authentic voice.

Gary's Story

Perhaps the biggest impediment to self-acceptance is the inner critic, our internal tape recorder that is constantly repeating self-defeating statements. This inner critic can be so loud and continuous that people assume it's their true voice and what it says reflects who they really are. It's not. The inner critic is merely one aspect of the psyche, definitely not the whole person. However, if it takes up too much psychological space, it can actually impact a person's life, discouraging them from exploring opportunities, learning new things, or accepting themselves as they are.

Gary was a twenty-something rising star in his corporate office when he first called me for an executive consultation. He was much younger than my typical executive client, and I asked how he was wise enough to recognize that he needed help.

"It's not wisdom," Gary replied, "it's desperation. I feel like such a fake. No one sees how little I know. I'm getting more and more responsibility, so when I blow it, there's going to be a major disaster."

In our consultation sessions, I soon discovered Gary had a very intense inner critic. His personal tape recorder was working overtime with messages like, "You'll never pull this off. You can't handle this. You've always been a failure. You're not good enough. You'll never make the team." Sometimes in his head he even heard his father's voice saying these things. These messages had been playing inside Gary's head for as far back as he could remember. He even knew the origin of the last one—Little League tryouts when he was about seven years old!

I asked Gary to do the "Self-Critic" retreat, writing down a complete list of every single statement he made to himself inside his head. Before doing this retreat, Gary had never realized how devastatingly negative his self-talk was, nor how continually these tapes were playing in his mind. At first he was afraid his list of statements would go on ad infinitum, but eventually he realized his self-critic was beginning to repeat, looping back over statements again and again. After doing this retreat on two consecutive days, Gary felt he had the complete list.

Just the practice of writing down his self-talk gave Gary a sense of objectivity and mastery over his self-criticism. "I didn't want those old thoughts interfering in my life now. I'll admit I never was a great Little League player, but those skills aren't relevant to me anymore. I'm in a very different ball game now."

The list of self-talk helped Gary become more conscious of his inner critic, and soon he was able to recognize the negative messages as they arose. With his growing awareness, Gary was becoming angry at the negative messages and how they were interfering with his career. He was ready to do battle with his critic. I understood his feelings and suggested we try a

ONE-MINUTE RETREAT—AHIMSA

The word *ahimsa* is Sanskrit for "nonviolence" or "nonharming," the philosophical core of Gandhi's satyagraha movement that eventually won freedom for India. The same philosophy can lead to personal freedom from your inner critic. Unlike cognitive therapy, which suggests you dispute your self-talk by logically arguing with it, the "Ahimsa" retreat encourages a soft, nonviolent resistance.

Whenever you notice your inner critic arising within you in words, feelings, or sensations, immediately take a full inhale through your nose and a long, light exhale out your mouth, as if you were trying to make a candle in front of you flicker with your breath. You can also label the critic by saying quietly to yourself, "critic, critic." This labeling is a technique from mindfulness training and will free you from taking the negative messages to heart. After this, return to your previous activity.

Please note that no one ever gets completely rid of their inner critic. That is not the goal. The goal is to loosen the grip the negative messages have on you and your life. Simply let them pass over you and move on. Don't get stuck fighting. You have made great progress when you can catch the messages immediately as they arise, notice them, and move on quickly.

different approach first. I gave Gary the "Ahimsa" one-minute retreat to use whenever he noticed a critical message arising from within. Based on Gandhi's teachings on nonviolence, this retreat appealed to Gary because it was not just a psychological technique but one rooted in philosophy and history.

Every time Gary heard his inner critic, he took a minute to breathe and consciously open his heart toward himself. He did not resist or try to stop the negative tapes. He merely accepted them and recognized that they represented a small part of who he was, and that his whole self was far more vast and magnificent. Gradually the voice of the inner critic shrank to minimal volume, allowing Gary to be more free and confident at work. In a follow-up interview a year later, Gary was very pleased to report an unexpected benefit. His personal relationship with his parents had steadily improved. Often his dad had given him critical advice as he was growing up, which frustrated Gary and caused tension in their relationship. Now Gary was able to listen nondefensively and still maintain his own independent ideas.

As soon as you resist mentally any undesirable
or unwanted circumstance, you thereby endow it
with more power—power which it will use against you.

—Emmet Fox, minister

Retreats to Cultivate Self-Acceptance

Mirror, Mirror

There is so much emphasis in our culture on how we look that the very concept of body image has become simplified to mean how we feel about our appearance. As a psychological term, *body image* refers to all the ways we experience and perceive our bodies. This is a broader definition that includes the ways we experience our bodies physically and in fantasy, not just in terms of visual judgments. In fact, it's very important that we take back our experience and perception of our bodies from the visual lens of our culture's fashion magazines, movies, and the media.

This retreat guides you from a confrontation with your body's visual reality to an experience of your body. Looking in the mirror is an exercise in desensitization, a standard technique in behavior modification. By the sheer willpower of continuing to face yourself, you will gradually become less reactive and judgmental of your body. Then, the second half of the retreat encourages you to discover the sheer pleasure of *being* a body, by dancing with your eyes closed. This removes the visual cues that can lead to self-criticism and inhibitions. Dancing with your eyes closed invites you to experience your body from the inside out and to expand your personal meaning of body image to include your perception of movement. In this way, you can rescue your body from cultural stereotypes and reclaim it for your own inner experience.

Step 1: *Entering into Retreat:* Begin this retreat by standing naked in front of a well-lit full-length mirror. Make a commitment to spend a full ten minutes there, no matter what. With a soft visual focus rather than a critical eye, allow the reflection of your body to enter your consciousness. Skim over your whole frame lightly. This is you. As soon as you feel any emotional constriction like fear, anger, judgment, hatred, or disgust, please take a deep breath. Release tension with your exhale, gently blowing the breath out through your mouth. Just look. Nothing more.

Play with your vision. Alternate between focusing on specific details or body parts and seeing the whole picture all at once. How do your inner reactions shift as your focus changes? Experiment with different angles, like looking at as much as you can see of your profile or your back. This is all of you.

Step 2: For the next eight minutes, give yourself full permission just to dance. Put some music on and move away from the mirror and into an open space. Close your eyes and allow your body image to arise purely from your inner experience of movement. Feel the pleasure of just dancing, with no judgments from others or yourself. Open your eyes as you need to for safety's sake, but do not use the mirror. Rely on your inner experience, not the mirror image.

If you work with this retreat over a period of time, experiment with a wide variety of music, such as: *Swing Kids* sound track; *The Immaculate Collection*, by Madonna, *Now and Then* sound track, *Franki Valli and the Four Seasons* anthology; *Bones or Totem*, by Gabrielle Roth; *The Buena Vista Social Club*; *Planet Drum*, by Mickey Hart, and anything by Babatunde Olantunji.

Step 3: *Returning to the World:* Simply breathe for the remaining two minutes in any position you like—standing, sitting, or lying flat out on the

ONE-MINUTE RETREAT—PERFECT IMPERFECTION

Rationally, we all realize we're not perfect and that we cannot ever be perfect. However, some of us create a lot of personal suffering by trying to be perfect. We can give ourselves more room to be perfectly imperfect by asserting our right to make mistakes. Take this time to recognize and value your mistakes. Celebrate your mistakes. Remember that mistakes are a natural part of learning, experimenting, and of course being spontaneous. You need all your mistakes in order to be the perfectly imperfect you.

floor. Keep your eyes closed, and enjoy the feeling of aliveness from deep within your body. This is also you. Concentrate on and remember this inner experience of your body image, so that it becomes stronger than the visual, culturally influenced one.

The Shadow

According to Carl Jung, the term *shadow* refers to those parts of ourselves that we reject or neglect, that we repress or split off from our identity. Accepting all of who we are entails recognizing and accepting our shadow elements as part of ourselves. Whenever we have a strong adverse reaction to someone, there's a good chance that we are projecting an aspect of our shadow onto them. This retreat will help you to see and accept your shadow.

Step 1: *Entering into Retreat:* Sit comfortably with your journal handy. Just quietly focus on your breathing for three minutes, making the inner commitment to be very honest and open with yourself.

Step 2: Think of someone in your life who consistently "gets on your nerves." Try to choose someone whom you don't know very well but toward whom you have an immediate antipathy. For the next seven minutes, remember, in detail, all the ways this person annoys or irritates you. Picture their nonverbal movements and facial expressions; hear their voice. Exaggerate the irritating things they do as if you were seeing them on a gigantic movie screen. Write down your description of them in your journal, saving lots of space for additional writing in the next step. Don't be shy—no annoying trait is too small to mention.

Step 3: For the next seven minutes, search within yourself for ways that you happen to be somewhat similar to this person. As you begin to self-reflect, remember your commitment to be honest and open with yourself. Can you acknowledge that these qualities exist in yourself as well? Make notes in your journal about the ways you fit the written descriptions. There should be extra space for these additional notes.

Step 4: *Returning to the World:* Now look again at this other person and just allow them to be however they are. Accept that they are who they are. Can you accept that some of their qualities are a part of who you are, blending in with the rest of you to form your unique personality? For the remaining three minutes, continue with accepting the other person and accepting yourself as you focus again on your breathing.

To hone and accept one's own shadow
is a profound spiritual discipline.
It is whole-making and thus holy
and the most important experience of a lifetime.

—Robert A. Johnson, Jungian analyst

The Self-Critic

We all have self-critical inner tapes. Problems occur when these tapes interfere with our lives, consume our energy, and demoralize our spirit. The more unconscious we are about these negative messages, the more power they have over us. By simply writing them all down, we literally move the messages from inside our heads into the outer world, where we can begin to view the statements objectively. This technique derives from cognitive therapy, in which the next step would be to dispute or argue with yourself to prove that the critical messages are irrational. My suggestion is that you use the "Ahimsa" one-minute retreat (page 240) instead.

The important thing about the "Self-Critic" retreat is to keep repeating it until you have written down absolutely every single thing your inner critic says to you. You have to make sure you get it all out of your head and documented. Writing this list down on paper will help you to deal with the messages in a way different from when you hear them inside your head. After all, you would never tolerate someone in the real world talking to you in this way.

When the statements begin to repeat themselves, you'll know you are near the end. Write down every version of a similar message. Don't worry about whether or not they make sense. You will see that your inner critic is not very creative. It has only a limited repertoire and then is reduced to repeating itself.

Step 1: *Entering into Retreat:* Arrange yourself so you can write comfortably. To some that may mean sitting at a table, while others will curl up with a notebook in hand. Take the first two minutes to relax, feeling the chair underneath you or the pillows surrounding you. Make sure you're cozy and comfortable.

Step 2: For a full fifteen minutes, write down every negative statement from your inner repertoire. What do you say to yourself in times of stress, upsetting moments, disappointments, or frustrations? How do you blame yourself? How do you put yourself down, diminishing who you are? The first three times you think you have a complete list, I assure you, you don't. Go back and add more. Remember things that were said to you as a child by your parents, siblings, other kids, or teachers. Have any of these statements become lodged in your self-talk?

Step 3: *Returning to the World:* Even if you're not finished, take a break. You can always repeat this retreat tomorrow. In the remaining three minutes, read over your negative messages. Notice how you feel about the things you say to yourself all the time. Practicing this retreat documents your critical tapes. They are now on paper. You do not need to carry them in your head or listen to them anymore.

ONE-MINUTE RETREAT—RIGHT TO EXIST

It may seem strange to think that we don't all feel we have the right to exist, but the sad truth is that not all newborns are welcomed into the world with equal enthusiasm. Also, children who are constantly controlled or criticized may grow up with the sense that they have no right to be as they are. For instance, I remember one therapy client who told me that her mother would always criticize the way she smiled, and that she barely felt she had a right to her own life.

Even if you were not fully welcomed into the world or respected for your right to exist, you can still give this existential permission to yourself. During your day, take a moment to pause and go deep within yourself. Breathe and experience the reality of the following statements: I have the right to breathe. I have the right to exist.

Imagine yourself as a newborn baby, naked, vulnerable, and perfect. Greet yourself with love, welcoming your presence into the world.

I Am

One of the most basic and profound meditations simply uses the mantra "I am." A variation on this phase is "I am that I am." Either way, this mantra refers to the Divine Presence or the divine within us.

Step 1: *Entering into Retreat:* Sit with your back as straight as is comfortable, with support if needed. Use the first two minutes to acknowledge that you are giving yourself this gift of time.

Step 2: For the next fifteen minutes, float the mantra, *I am*, on your breath. As you inhale gently, breathe *I am*; as you exhale gently, breathe *I am*. Allow your breathing to become smooth and refined. Feel the subtle energy flow as you breathe. Let the *I am* mantra permeate your physical body. Breathe *I am* into and through your bones. Allow the *I am* mantra to radiate outward into your energy field.

FIVE-MINUTE RETREAT—YOUR NAME

Use this retreat only if your name conveys warm feelings of love and acceptance. If this is not the case, skip this exercise. Our names carry our whole personal history from childhood. Use your first name as a mantra, or you may prefer a nickname, name from childhood, or term of endearment. Be sure to use a name you were called in your early years in order to evoke a deep sense of your own identity. With every inhale and exhale, imagine that you can hear your name being called. Hear your name from all four corners of the space you're in. Hear your name whispered and called over a distance. Finally hear your name from deep within you.

Step 3: *Returning to the World:* For the final three minutes, stretch and gently allow your eyes to open. Notice the clarity and vibrancy of the world around you, as if seeing it for the first time. Maintain a connection to the *I am* mantra deep within you as you go about your day.

Life Story

We all have in our heads the story of our life, beginning with childhood and our family of origin, and moving through our teenage years and our adult lives. This retreat asks you to review your life story in three different ways. This repetition will help desensitize you to some of the pain you may have in your own story. This means you will gradually have less negative emotional reaction to the telling of your story. The repetition helps to flatten your reactiveness, creating space for greater self-acceptance and compassion. The third repetition, telling the story as if it were about someone else's life, is designed to awaken compassion for yourself, since we are generally more compassionate in our response to others than to ourselves.

This retreat extends over a three-day period, with a twenty-minute retreat spent on each version of your life story.

DAY 1

Step 1: *Entering into Retreat:* Arrange pillows and soft blankets for your comfort. Choose a private space so you don't have to worry about anyone hearing you talking to yourself. Sit or lie down according to your preference. You may want to light an aromatherapy candle as part of this retreat; try sandalwood or rose, which are emotionally soothing. Take two minutes to become present to yourself, feeling the movement of your breathing.

Step 2: Begin telling your story out loud. It's important that you say your story aloud so you experience telling it and listening to it at the same time. Use a full fifteen minutes to tell your story. You may want to refer to a clock so you can space out the telling. For instance, five minutes for birth through elementary school; five minutes for adolescence and young adulthood; and five minutes for adult life. Or you may want to spend the whole fifteen minutes on your childhood family experiences. Tell your story in whatever way you want.

Step 3: *Returning to the World:* Take the last three minutes to soothe yourself. Use any technique that you personally find calming. For example, you might sing or hum to yourself, rub your body vigorously, stretch, or get a cup of hot chamomile tea.

DAY 2

Step 1: *Entering into Retreat:* Again, I suggest that you light an aromatherapy candle for this retreat. Sit comfortably for writing. Take the first two minutes to simply tune in to yourself and to the story of your life as you told it in day 1 of this retreat.

Step 2: Use the full fifteen minutes to write out your story. Tell it in first person, repeating the same story you said aloud on day 1. As you write it all out, notice any themes that emerge through the story of your life. An example of a theme would be taking care of everyone else and neglecting yourself, or repeatedly sabotaging yourself when you get close to a goal. What meaning do specific events have for you? How does your path unfold over the years? Trust your writing hand to let your story flow over the paper. Don't stop to read or rewrite. Don't worry about spelling or grammar. Just keep writing.

FIVE-MINUTE RETREAT—DISIDENTIFICATION

This retreat is based on Psychosynthesis, a spiritual approach to psychotherapy that asserts that there is a larger Self beyond the psychological self with which most of us identify. We are far greater than who we think we are. This reminds me of the Hindu concept *neti, neti,* meaning "not this, not that." We are not this; we are not that. We can approach who we really are by realizing what we are not. Then self-acceptance means recognizing our divine nature. The following quote is by psychiatrist Roberto Assagioli, founder of Psychosynthesis. Let it sink deeply into your being.

I have a body, but I am not my body.

I have emotions, but I am not my emotions.

I have desires, but I am not my desires.

I have a mind, but I am not my mind.

I am a Center of pure Consciousness.

Step 3: *Returning to the World:* Don't read what you've written. Again, use the remaining three minutes to soothe yourself, finding comfort in having completed this stage of the retreat.

DAY 3

Step 1: *Entering into Retreat:* Once again, you may want to light an aromatherapy candle for this final day of the "Life Story" retreat. Sit so you can imagine someone sitting opposite you and telling you the story of their life. You can place a pillow across from you to represent this person. Put your written life story from day 2 of this retreat on the pillow. Use the first two minutes to center yourself, feeling your connection with the ground you're sitting on. Take a few breaths, expanding your chest to help your heart be receptive and compassionate.

Step 2: This step will take fifteen minutes. Pick up your written story. Using it as a reference, don't read it word for word, but tell the story as if you were describing someone else's experiences. Go through the whole life story as if you were hearing it for the first time. Decide consciously *not* to identify with it. Allow warmth and compassion to rise up within you, overflowing toward the soul who lived this life.

Step 3: *Returning to the World:* Sit quietly for the last three minutes, allowing your heart to remain open. Experience the compassion within and around you. Let this feeling of compassion extend to include yourself in childhood, your early adult years, and you as you are right now.

Fear

Fear is one of the most difficult emotions for us to accept or even talk about. The closest many of us come to it is laughing about horror movies or reading Stephen King. If you haven't thought about this, intentionally try to initiate a conversation about a real fear you have with someone else. Notice how uncomfortable the other person becomes, either ignoring the issue altogether or profusely reassuring you. Fear is clearly an unacceptable feeling and is commonly relegated to our shadow so we can deny it's a part of our lives. The more we can bring this portion of our shadow into the light of consciousness, the more accepting we can be of our whole self and all of our feelings.

Step 1: *Entering into Retreat:* Set yourself up with several sheets of drawing paper and oil pastels (see page 22). During the first five minutes, simply give yourself permission to feel fear. It could be fear of anything, internal or external, or just pure fear with no reference. It could be an old fear from childhood or one that makes no sense. The source doesn't matter; simply let fear come up from within you. Notice especially how you experience fear in your body.

Step 2: In the next five minutes, use the oil pastels to do an emotional drawing (see page 27) that illustrates your experience of fear. Don't try to depict an actual scene. Just let colors and shapes cover the paper. Trust what feels and looks right to you.

Step 3: For the next five minutes, write on a separate piece of paper all the words or phrases about fear that add to the expression of your drawing. Don't worry about making sense, just brainstorm and write down whatever comes up.

FIVE-MINUTE RETREAT—COSMIC PERSPECTIVE

There are times when working on self-acceptance that we just need to remind ourselves to get some perspective. Whenever we find ourselves immersed in or overwhelmed by our small lives, we need to step back to see a larger vision. NASA has given us the perfect photos to help us regain a cosmic perspective. You can get them from the NASA site on the Internet or from Pomegranate Art Books, which publishes two books of postcards called *Space* and *A View of the Universe.*

Simply sit quietly and look at these photos one right after the other. If you're curious, read the description of what each photo is. Let your view of life broaden to expand into the cosmos. From that perspective catch a glimpse of your life at this very moment and accept yourself as you are right now. Breathe.

Step 4: *Returning to the World:* During the final five minutes, write a sentence or statement using some of the words from your list. You don't have to use them all, and you can add other words to help express your message.

Place your drawing and statement where you, and only you, can see them every day. Remember to acknowledge your expression of fear at least once a day. You can consider this practice in accepting difficult-to-accept feelings. After about a week, put it away for a rest. If you want to do more, you can take it out at a later time. The idea is *not* to become so used to your expression of fear that you end up no longer seeing it, but to see the fear that is inside of you with greater objectivity and consciousness. The more we can face all of our feelings, the greater our acceptance of our whole being.

Remembering Success

Even though I prefer the concept of self-acceptance to self-esteem, there is no question that it's easier to accept ourselves if we feel good about ourselves. High self-esteem contributes enormously to self-acceptance. I want to clarify, however, that self-esteem is not primarily how we feel about how we look. The psychological research on self-esteem shows that it develops as a result of feeling competent. Thus the emphasis is on our behavior—when we accomplish something, especially if we have risen to meet a challenge, we feel more competent and our self-esteem grows. This is quite a different approach from simply repeating personal affirmations without any actual accomplishment. The same goes for developing self-esteem in children. Unfounded praise leads to personal ego inflation, while praise for specific behaviors and accomplishments builds solid self-esteem.

Step 1: *Entering into Retreat:* Use the first seven minutes to settle into a very comfortable position and relax. With every exhale, allow your body to relax even more. Let out an audible sigh with every exhale. Allow yourself to sink more deeply into yourself.

Step 2: For the next five minutes, remember a time in your life when you were successful in some way. It could be a big event or a small victory. Really re-create the details of the situation in your mind—what you did, how you felt, and the successful outcome.

Step 3: Now, take five minutes to clearly identify what the elements were that contributed to your success. Scan through all possibilities, including specific behavior on your part, timing, patience, luck, and others' contributions. When you have identified precisely what you did that contributed to the positive outcome, allow yourself to feel a deep inner sense of competency, a very strong internal, "I can do that. I have what it takes."

Step 4: *Returning to the World:* For the last three minutes, become more aware of your inhalation, feeling the temperature of the air as it enters your nose. Notice your sitting position and surroundings. As you return to your current time and place, remember that you bring these inner competencies with you into every situation you encounter in your everyday life. Remember also that the more competent you feel, the higher your self-esteem and the easier it will be to accept yourself.

Adopt Yourself

We all have unmet needs from childhood. It's a given that nobody's family was perfect. This retreat gives us the opportunity to accept the child we once were and give ourselves now what we needed then. One of the ways children feel that they are accepted is when we give them our undivided attention. The child's most frequent request is "Please listen to me. Really listen to me."

Our role as a grown-up listening to our inner child is to be a cross between a parent and a therapist. Our job is to really hear their emotional communications, understand their feelings, and empathize with their experience. In short, to accept and love them.

Please note that it's entirely possible to have more than one inner child who needs you, of more than one age. Start with whichever age expresses the greatest need.

Step 1: *Entering into Retreat:* Find a photo of yourself close to the age of the child you want to reach. Sit comfortably with this photo nearby. Close your eyes and, for the first five minutes, just tune in to your breathing. Imagine your breath lightly massaging your heart, warming and softening that energy center. Open up your heart so you can be attentive and responsive to your inner child.

Step 2: Gently let your eyes open and softly focus on the photo. For the next five minutes, simply let the being of this child enter your heart. See her in her life, playing, sleeping, living. Hear her voice. Sense her energy. Feel her emotional moods. Understand her problems. Allow her in to as great an extent as you possibly can, and be there for her with your full presence.

Step 3: For the next five minutes, imagine a connection between your heart and the heart of your child. It may be a golden thread, a light beam, a rainbow, or any variation on this theme. Imagine you can strengthen the vitality and magnetism of this heart connection with every breath you take.

Step 4: *Returning to the World:* During the final five minutes, make a commitment to respond to your inner child in some small way as part of your day-to-day life. Please don't promise too much. For example, you could light a candle to honor your inner child, imagine your golden thread connection as you drift off to sleep, or just think of your inner child at random times during your day. At this moment, feel the movement of your rib cage as you breathe. Sense the outline of your current grown-up body. You are now old enough to accept and love your inner child.

What is going on in your innermost being is worthy of your whole love.

—Rainer Maria Rilke

14

Self-Care

The first step in the curing process is taken when you begin caring for yourself.

—Gerald Epstein, psychologist

How many of us actually take good care of ourselves? Do we eat right, exercise regularly, spend quality time with friends and family, pursue our dreams, take time to retreat, choose our associates wisely, say no to overextending ourselves, get yearly medical and dental checkups, indulge in moderation, get the sleep we need, laugh often, save money for extended vacations, wear seat belts, use sunscreen, enjoy holiday celebrations, ask for help when needed, communicate our feelings appropriately, plan for retirement, give and receive love, have fun, learn new things, watch a sunset, *and* rotate the tires on the car? The list seems overwhelming.

Taking good care of ourselves involves all of the above plus a sensitive attending to how we need to grow and develop. This means being aware of how our spiritual life is unfolding, and how we can nurture that process in ourselves. For forty-eight-year-old Betsy, self-care is currently focused on learning about menopause. For thirty-year-old Ben, whose father has lung cancer, self-care is spending quality time with his dad. So self-care is far more than doing what feels good or makes us feel good about ourselves. Self-care is about developing our highest Self. Admittedly, this is not so easy to do, particularly given the large and growing demands on our time.

It seems that, as life moves faster and with greater complexity, it becomes more important, but increasingly difficult, to take good care of ourselves. Both men and women are torn between work responsibility and family needs, concerned with current living expenses and future planning. Yet many of us, women particularly, seem to have a more difficult time putting our own needs ahead of the needs of others. Jennifer Louden, author of *The Women's Retreat Book*, spoke to this issue when she asked women, "What would you most want to see in a book about retreating for women?" The most frequent response was that they needed the permission to take time for themselves.

This is the central issue in self-care: giving ourselves permission to make it a priority. Caring for ourselves is an inalienable right that many of us don't exercise. We may have been taught that spending the necessary time is selfish or, worse yet, narcissistic. We may feel guilty doing something for ourselves before everyone else's needs are met—and that generally never happens. We may have neglected ourselves for so long that we don't even know what type of care we need or how to start. This is especially true for those of us who have been taking care of others, whether a growing child or an aging parent.

Learning to Adjust

We can become so accustomed to postponing or sacrificing our own needs in order to respond to the needs of others—be it in family or business— that we forget how to care for ourselves. When we're no longer needed in the same way, we should take time for a transition period, first of all to get in touch with our needs, and then to figure out the best way to respond to them.

At long last, Mary's third child was ready to enter kindergarten. Now she would have whole blocks of free time. But free to do what? Suggestions were overwhelming: get a job, help out in her husband's business, go back to school, start her own furniture painting business. Mary had tried very hard to take care of herself throughout the last ten years, but she had not lost the weight she'd gained with each pregnancy and had stopped exercising

ONE-MINUTE RETREAT—WHAT DO I NEED RIGHT NOW?

Pause frequently throughout your day, no matter what you're doing. Take one full breath. Ask yourself, "What do I need right now?" and wait for an inclination, an inner response, any small glimmer of direction. If no answer emerges, don't worry. Go on about your day until you pause again to repeat this question. If you do receive a response to this question, please honor it—within reason, of course. If you regularly ignore your internal yearnings, getting in touch with your needs will become more difficult. This will help you begin to notice your inner messages and honor them as they appear.

altogether. She felt older than her thirty-eight years and bone tired. It seemed an obvious choice for her to begin a healthy eating and exercise program. But Mary was wise enough not to push herself into another schedule.

"I'm going to do *nothing*," she said.

What she really meant was, "I'm going to do whatever I want to do." Because she no longer had to respond to children's schedules all day, she was free for at least six solid hours. Mary began using the one-minute "What Do I Need Right Now?" retreat frequently during the day. This brief reflection allowed her to connect again with her own needs.

Asking the question "What do I need right now?" is quite different from the usual way we structure our time as caretakers: "What do you need? What *should* I do? What's next on my list?" This one-minute retreat, repeated at frequent intervals throughout the day, will free you from the pressure of caring for others and encourage you to focus on self-care.

I define self-nurturing as having the courage to pay attention to your needs.

—Jennifer Louden

Caring for All of Me

Some aspects of self-care will feel more natural to us than others. Each of us has personal preferences, inclinations, or strengths. For instance, one person may find it second nature to include an early morning jog in their schedule, while someone else might cherish their quiet reading time at night. As we learn to take better care of ourselves, it's important to pay attention to all aspects of our being and respond to the cravings that come from them.

Elizabeth was past fifty, had great friends and family, walked regularly, nourished her spiritual life, and was even learning French in preparation for a vacation. She thought she was taking great care of herself. But when Elizabeth completed the "Self-Evaluation for Self-Care" retreat, she quickly realized that she had seriously neglected an important aspect of her life. She had never focused on her financial planning and, to her surprise, discovered that her retirement funds were inadequate. The self-evaluation retreat helped Elizabeth to focus on the one area where she needs to take better care of herself.

It's likely that most of us neglect at least one area of our self-care. Realistically, we need to accept the strengths and weaknesses in our ability to care for ourselves. However, by using the structure of the "Self-Evaluation for Self-Care" retreat, we can objectively identify which areas we are overlooking, so we can develop a plan for taking care of ourselves more completely.

SIGNS THAT YOU NEED A SELF-CARE RETREAT

1. You tend to get sick frequently.
2. You're busy doing everything for others, but you don't easily get around to doing what you need or want to do for yourself.
3. You make self-care resolutions, but then break them.
4. You have trouble saying no.
5. It's difficult for you to ask others for help.
6. You're on too many committees or go to too many meetings.

7. You don't know how to end a telephone conversation politely and gracefully.
8. Your spouse, children, or friends take advantage of you.
9. You feel lost, empty, weary, disconnected from yourself, on automatic pilot most of the time.
10. You feel exhausted but continue to do everything by sheer willpower.
11. You don't celebrate your birthday.
12. You have no idea what you would do if you had a whole day just for yourself.

Sam's Story

Although we may assume that women need self-care retreats more than men, we all know at least one man who is doing too much. Sam was one of those men. A fireman by profession, he coached a local athletic team every season, was active in his church, and ran a small business doing home repairs for which he never charged enough money. Even though Sam's wife complained about his giving too much of himself away, every one else loved him for it.

When Sam's doctor warned him about his high blood pressure and threatened to put him on medical leave from the fire department, Sam finally got the message. He started with the five-minute "What Do I Want?" retreat. At first his answers were all about others: "I don't want my wife to worry. I want my kids to grow up safely and be happy. I want to be liked. I want to feel needed." As he continued using this retreat, Sam's answers gradually reflected more and more of what he needed to take care of himself. "I want more time to build furniture. I want to go on a yearly fishing trip. I want to live." Now Sam was down to basics. The retreat helped Sam to clarify what he *really* needed, and how essential it was for him to take care of himself.

At this point, Sam was ready to move on to the "Balancing Generosity" retreat. This twenty-minute retreat is designed for people like Sam who need to learn to care for themselves as much as they care for others.

FIVE-MINUTE RETREAT—WHAT DO I WANT?

Give yourself a full five minutes to continuously come up with answers to "What do I want?" Write them down if that appeals to you. Just keep responding to the question. If you get stuck, simply repeat the question and wait. You will find that your responses are layered and that, as you continue, you will gradually descend to the very depths of what you really want and what is most important to you.

Sam practiced this retreat for weeks. He learned to recognize when he was doing too much for others, and also how to redirect that energy toward himself. Gradually Sam was able to make a real decision when someone asked him for a favor, rather than automatically saying yes. He still wanted to please everyone, but he knew he also had to take care of himself, so Sam became quite adept at finding win/win solutions.

> When we say "yes" when we mean "no," we lose
> personal power and become victims or martyrs.
> When we say "no" to someone else when we know
> the situation calls for us to say "yes,"
> we become stingy or selfish.
>
> —Angeles Arrien, anthropologist

Retreats to Cultivate Care of the Self

Self-Evaluation for Self-Care

Self-care is an issue that is often dependent on our childhood experiences. Frequently we tend to treat ourselves similarly to how we were treated by our parents or siblings in childhood. That news may be good, bad, or, most likely, a confusing mixture of the two. Also, we naturally tend to favor certain areas of self-care and neglect others, depending upon our personal preferences. Because self-care is a complex emotional issue, you may want to take an analytical approach to discover which areas need more attention. Often in psychotherapy, I recommend to clients that it can be helpful to intentionally consider their emotional situation from an intellectual point of view. The following retreat provides the structure for you to do this.

Step 1: *Entering into Retreat:* Find a cozy spot where you can be comfortable reflecting upon yourself and your patterns of self-care. Spend two minutes settling in and committing yourself to the process of being very honest with yourself.

Step 2: During the next fifteen minutes, complete the following questions, using the chart below to give you an overview of the different areas of self-care. Remember your intention to be honest. Evaluate yourself in

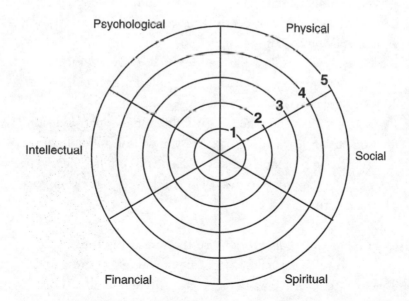

each area, giving yourself an overall rating from one to five, with one being very low self-care, three being the midpoint, and five being very high self-care. Fill in the pie chart up to your rating level for each section.

- *Physical*   Do you do some type of physical exercise four to five times a week? Do you include strength building, stretching, and aerobic activities? Do you work hard enough to break into a sweat?
- *Social*   Do you have fun with friends or family at least once a week? Do you contribute in some way, with time or money, to the larger community? Do you have people in your life whom you love and who love you?
- *Spiritual*   Do you commune regularly with your experience of the divine? Do you reflect on your spiritual values in daily living as you make decisions and set priorities? Do you have spiritual friends for sharing and support?
- *Financial*   Do you live within your budget? Do you know what debts you're carrying and at what interest rates? Do you have the necessary financial plans in place for the future, in areas such as unexpected disability or death, your retirement, the birth of a child, or paying for college education?
- *Intellectual*   Do you learn something new every week? Do you seek stimulating experiences through cultural events, lectures, books, or the media?
- *Psychological*   Do you take responsibility for your part in a conflict so you can learn and grow? Are you willing and able to see things through someone else's eyes? Can you communicate your feelings in an appropriate way? Do you have someone in your life you can turn to for help?

Step 3: *Returning to the World:* Use the remaining three minutes to begin to plan how you can take better care of yourself in those areas that require more attention. Reassert your commitment to be honest with yourself.

Permission to Retreat

This retreat takes two issues into account. First, as previously mentioned, many of us have great difficulty granting ourselves the time and priority required to retreat regularly. Second, it's far easier for us to give this permission to someone else than to ourselves. This retreat asks you to take care of yourself as well as you would take care of a friend. In this way, you practice having compassion for yourself.

Step 1: *Entering into Retreat:* Sit comfortably with writing materials at hand. For ten minutes, jot down all the things you do for others. Start by including all the little things you do automatically each day, like straightening the living room, grocery shopping, making coffee, picking up dry cleaning, and remembering phone calls. Then add to this list all the extra things you do during a full week.

Step 2: For the next three minutes, read over this list as if it described someone else's life. Imagine that a dear friend of yours wrote this list and was coming to you for advice on self-care. Really let yourself see the list objectively, with psychological distance. Imagine this person's day-to-day life.

Step 3: Take five minutes to think through what advice you would give your friend. How much time each day and each week should this person take for herself? What type of retreat does she need? How can she balance her life? Write down the advice just like a medical prescription.

Step 4: *Returning to the World:* For the final two minutes, read this prescription and take its advice to heart. Notice any objections or excuses that arise in you about how you can't possibly follow the instructions. Don't resist them, just notice them and let them go. Thank your wise friend for the advice. Think about one small step you could take today to begin carrying out this prescription.

Balancing Generosity

Some of us are too generous with our time and energy—we give away too much of ourselves. Someone asks us to do them a favor or accommodate their schedule, and our answer is always yes. Perhaps this isn't even generosity but our inability to set boundaries or say no. We overextend ourselves, bend over backward, and often end up feeling exhausted, unappreciated, and resentful. The "Balancing Generosity" retreat uses the feedback from our personal energy field so we can create a better balance between our giving and receiving.

Step 1: *Entering into Retreat:* Use the first five minutes to imagine your energy field. This is the personal space that surrounds your body. What is the shape of your energy field? How far does it extend from your physical body? Can you bring it in closer or move it out farther? Remember that this is your personal energy field; no one else can occupy it. People enter it upon your invitation or consent.

Step 2: From within your personal space, think back to the most recent time you said yes when you should have said no, when, looking back, you realize you gave too much. For the next five minutes, replay this episode, noticing specifically what happens to your energy field. For instance, does your energy field shrink or expand? Does the quality of your energy change?

Step 3: For the next five minutes, visualize the flow of energy from others toward you. You may actually imagine people giving their energy to you. How comfortable are you receiving from others? What happens to your energy field? Look for changes in color or temperature of your energy field. Also notice how far your personal space extends.

Step 4: *Returning to the World:* Use the last five minutes of the retreat to simply sit in the center of your energy field and visualize a balanced flow

---

FIVE-MINUTE RETREAT—DO NOTHING

 This is, of course, an impossible retreat. We are always doing something, if only breathing. But use this five minutes to do nothing you think you *should* be doing. In other words, just let yourself "be" for five minutes. And if your mind wants to flood you with shoulds, lists, or great ideas, just notice your mental tapes and then return to your experience of doing nothing. Just be. After all, it's only five minutes.

---

of energy from you to others and others to you. Remember that balance is not always exactly equal, but rather a harmonious ebb and flow over time.

***I**n prayer, do nothing.*

—St. John of the Cross, sixteenth-century Christian mystic

Nurture Yourself

Imagine the effort and care you take when you prepare a special dinner for guests. Now imagine taking that amount of care to nurture yourself, preparing a snack that looks beautiful, tastes enticing, and nurtures you.

So many of us are not quite sane when it comes to food. We simply eat too much of the wrong things and not enough of the right ones. We eat for many reasons other than to nurture our health and well-being. I have chosen to use a snack for this retreat rather than a meal, only partially out of time constraints. We are even more likely to be unconscious about our snack choices, and eat them on the run, than we are with our meals. This retreat asks us to be conscious for just one snack, and in the style of Zen tradition: when you eat, just eat.

Preparation for Retreat: Do this step a day ahead of time. Make sure you have all the food and equipment you will need to prepare a tasty, healthy snack for yourself, alone.

Step 1: *Entering into Retreat:* Take just a minute to stand in your kitchen and breathe. Remember that breathing is another way of nurturing yourself, giving yourself energy and discharging toxins.

Step 2: Take about seven minutes to prepare your snack. You can use your favorite music in the background, if you like. Don't answer the phone. Make sure you arrange your snack so it's pleasing to the eye, perhaps on a tray with your best dishes and a crystal flower vase.

Step 3: Use the next seven minutes to sit in a lovely spot and enjoy eating your snack. Give yourself permission to take pleasure in eating. Eat slowly, chewing your food longer than usual. This giving yourself permission to experience pleasure in such a common activity as snacking may seem mundane, but it's essential for taking care of ourselves in the midst of our busy lives. There are many nurturing moments during your day, if you would give yourself permission to enjoy them. Notice the phase of the moon, a kind word from a stranger, a shared laugh with a loved one. Give yourself permission to take pleasure in these moments.

Step 4: *Returning to the World:* In the remaining five minutes, complete this retreat by washing your dishes. Remember that cleaning up is also part of the whole ritual of preparing foods to nurture yourself. And of course it's an opportunity to be mindful: when you wash dishes, just wash dishes.

Each thought, each action in the sunlight of awareness becomes sacred. . . . I must confess it takes me a bit longer to do the dishes, but I live fully in every moment, and I am happy.

—Thich Nhat Hanh

ONE-MINUTE RETREAT—NEUROLOGICAL WAKE-UP

We all have deeply ingrained physical and neurological patterns that "feel right" to us merely because they are habitual. Moshe Feldenkrais developed an extraordinarily creative way of freeing the body from these old habits by using *Awareness through Movement.* He suggested that we experiment with consciously changing these physical and neurological patterns. For instance, when you lace your fingers to bring your palms together, one thumb is habitually placed closer to you—usually the one from your dominant hand. Lace your fingers the other way, so your other thumb ends up closer to you. You'll notice this takes thinking to change your pattern, and it will feel strange. By intentionally changing your physical patterns, you encourage your mind to wake up to new possibilities.

Create Beauty

This traditional Navaho prayer is a wonderful reminder to refine our aesthetic perception. The "Create Beauty" retreat extends our appreciation of beauty into another dimension, creating a mirror reflection between our inner beauty and the beauty in the world around us. This retreat sensitizes us to the impact of beauty on our inner world.

Preparation for Retreat: Create an arrangement of objects that symbolize beauty for you—flowers, shells, lace, crystals, artwork, jewelry, ribbons, glass, wood work, anything that speaks to you of beauty. This preparation may be a process in itself, extending over a few days as you collect and arrange the items in a way that suits you. Think of the way a designer creates a traditional Japanese garden, with loving, detailed attention to the arrangement of elements and a sensitive concern for the atmosphere created.

Step 1: *Entering into Retreat:* Use the first three minutes to settle into a comfortable seated position in front of the beautiful arrangement you created. Become sensitive to the refined atmosphere of beauty surrounding your arrangement, and allow that atmosphere to extend so that it includes you. Throughout this retreat, you can alternate between opening and closing your eyes in your own rhythm.

TRADITIONAL NAVAHO PRAYER

May it be beautiful before me.
May it be beautiful behind me.
May it be beautiful below me.
May it be beautiful above me.
May it be beautiful all around me.

I am restored in beauty.
I am restored in beauty.
I am restored in beauty.
I am restored in beauty.

Step 2: Spend five minutes breathing in this refined atmosphere, as if you could breathe in beauty with every inhalation.

Step 3: Experience the presence of beauty within you. Allow this experience to deepen over the next ten minutes, so you are both inhaling and exhaling beauty. Notice how your inner world reflects the outer world and the outer world reflects the inner. You create beauty within and without.

Step 4: *Returning to the World:* For the final two minutes, allow your eyes to stay open while you continue your breathing and experience beauty within. Stand and walk around your arrangement so you can see it from all angles. Maintain the connection to your inner experience of beauty as you go about your day. Remember, there is always something beautiful in your environment to remind you of your inner beauty.

Supported by Water

This retreat is for those of us who spend a considerable amount of time and energy taking care of other people. So often we're warm and supportive to others, while we're barely holding ourselves together. We can create an opportunity to take care of ourselves whenever we need it, simply by withdrawing into our bath. Candles, aromatherapy oil and bath salts, or

---

ONE-MINUTE RETREAT—BEDTIME WISH

The moment just before you fall asleep is an important threshold in consciousness. It's a good time to visualize your goals, review your day, plan your next day, or request a special dream. This hypnagogic state, as it's called, is a moment when the veil is thinner between the material world and the unseen world, between the day dream world and the night dream world. Use this moment to think of something you'd like to do for yourself the next day. Give yourself permission to be intentionally "selfish." Remember, there is such a thing as healthy selfishness. Think of one thing just for you.

FIVE-MINUTE RETREAT—COLD COMPRESSES

For those late afternoons when your head is overflowing with thoughts or your eyes are burning, you can use a cold compress to cool off and slow down. Keep a jar of herbal tea in your refrigerator so you can easily care for yourself in the following way: soak a washcloth in iced tea. Chamomile tea makes a soothing compress for burning eyes. Use peppermint tea for your forehead. A word of warning: don't let the peppermint compress drip into your eyes. Just lie down with the compress on and concentrate on the feeling of coldness on your skin.

music can all be added, but the essence of this retreat only requires a bathtub full of water and a lock on the bathroom door for privacy.

Step 1: *Entering into Retreat:* In a comfortably warm, very full bathtub, allow yourself to just stretch out for three minutes. Arrange a pillow or facecloth behind your neck for comfort.

Step 2: For a full fifteen minutes, allow yourself to be softened, cleansed, and held by the warm water. With every breath, imagine allowing the water to support you. Allow your arms to float on the surface of the water. Feel how their floating allows you to let go of them from deep inside your shoulder girdle. With every exhale imagine that your arms can float away. Use your exhale to similarly let go of your legs from deep within your hip joint. Even though your legs won't literally float on the surface of the water, imagine that they can just drift off. Allow the water to surround and support you.

Step 3: *Returning to the World:* In the final two minutes, gently begin to shift position in the tub, stretching and preparing to get out. Please move slowly and treat yourself gently as you dry yourself off and get dressed.

Inner Strength

We are constantly encouraged to exercise regularly as part of our self-care. Even though posture is not always emphasized, it's important in terms of how we look and how we feel. Ida Rolf's approach to postural alignment, called Structural Integration, focuses on the psoas muscle. This is the muscle that originates in front of the lumbar spine and crosses through the pelvis to attach at the top of the femur, or thighbone. It lies deep inside the body and is not usually included in exercise routines. However, Alvin Ailey emphasized the psoas muscle in his modern dance approach, and Joseph Pilates focused on it for his exercise routines. By consciously working with the psoas, you develop inner muscle strength, which naturally leads to improvements in your posture.

Step 1: *Entering into Retreat:* Lie on your back on a well-carpeted floor with your buttocks a few inches away from the wall. Extend your legs up in front of you, and rest your heels against the wall. Use the first five minutes to rest in this position. Try stretching the backs of your legs by extending your heels up while pointing your toes down toward the floor. You can also stretch your arms along the floor above your head, by reaching with your fingertips. This is a relaxing position at the end of a long day, when you have spent too much time standing on your feet. It's also wonderful for the circulation in your legs.

Step 2: Push your buttocks a little farther away from the wall so your knees can be at a right angle and your feet flat on the wall. There should also be a right angle in your hip joint. Spend ten minutes in this position, working with your psoas muscle in the following way:

Gently press your feet against the wall to give you leverage to press your lower back against the floor. Your stomach should be very flat or even concave. Hold this position for a few seconds and then relax completely and breathe normally. Work gently with your body, going in and out of this intense position.

During this step, add to the exercise by stretching your arms along the floor above your head while your lower back is pressed to the floor. Remember not to arch your neck, but tilt your chin slightly toward your chest. This will stretch the entire length of your spine and back. Hold this position for only a few seconds. Then allow your arms to relax, by bending your elbows or returning them to rest by your sides.

Step 3: *Returning to the World:* Begin the final five minutes by simply rolling over to one side and curling up in a comfortable position. After a few minutes, roll to the other side and curl up. Then rise slowly to an upright position. Feel yourself standing taller, with greater ease.

Harmonize Life Energy

Frequently we find ourselves in a situation where we can discreetly use part of our attention to tend to our own self-care. We may be at a lecture, movie, or concert, on a long drive, or even in a meeting. The following self-care technique is so simple, you can do a secret retreat right in the middle of your busy day.

Jin Shin Jyutsu is a technique using the energy meridians of traditional Chinese and Japanese medicine. By simply holding one finger with your other hand, it is possible to harmonize the entire circulation of life energy in the body. By holding your thumb you can help digestion; stress; tension in your head, shoulders, or lungs; worry, preoccupation, or depression; and the inclination to talk too much. By holding your index finger you can aid jaw, tooth, or gum problems; constipation or digestion; bursitis; backaches; self-criticism, shyness or fear, and backaches. Holding the middle finger aids nursing mothers and can help to overcome general fatigue, visual problems, headaches in the front of the head, indecision, irritability, or anger. Holding your ring finger can help respiratory problems, skin conditions, ringing in the ear, excessive mucus, a negative attitude, sadness, or grief. By holding your little finger, you can help heart conditions, bloating, anxiety or judgmental attitude, and the tendency to try too hard.

Step 1: *Entering into Retreat:* Start by deciding to focus some of your attention in an inward direction for an invisible twenty-minute retreat. Subtly shift your hand position so you can hold each finger of one hand with your other hand. Hold each finger for at least two minutes. Repeat for other hand.

Step 2: *Returning to the World:* Simply let your hands return to a neutral position and refocus your energy on your immediate situation.

Receiving Energy

To fully care for ourselves, we must tend to our spiritual well-being. Many of us need to connect with a source of spiritual energy to sustain ourselves throughout our worldly lives. This simple retreat is designed to help us receive the spiritual energy that is universally present and abundantly available.

Step 1: *Entering into Retreat:* Sit comfortably in a chair or on the floor, with back support if needed. Close your eyes and place your hands on your thighs with your palms facing up. Simply breathe for three minutes, adjusting your body as you need for comfort.

Step 2: For the next fifteen minutes, imagine that you are breathing in the energy of the universe. Feel it stream into your body. Imagine also that you are receiving energy through your open palms and the very top of your head. Visualize sitting under a shower of energy that is raining down all around you. Breathe that energy in with every inhale. As you exhale, let go of any tension or negativity.

Step 3: *Returning to the World:* Spend the last two minutes gently stretching. Then when you're ready, slowly stand up.

The intense energy of life is always there, night and day.

—J. Krishnamurti

15

In the World

The soul should always stand ajar
Ready to welcome the ecstatic experience.

—Emily Dickinson

We retreat so we can connect with the divine within ourselves and recognize the divine in the world. The moment in time when our inner world meets the outer world presents an opportunity for our spiritual lives to unfold. It is in these ordinary moments of daily living that our spiritual retreat practice can blossom. One of the Hasidic rabbis explained this emergence of the sacred within ordinary life: "I did not go to my master to learn his words of wisdom, but to see how he tied and untied his shoes."

How we tie and untie our shoes is our spiritual life. And sometimes we manage our daily life with more grace and ease than other times. When things are going smoothly, it's easier for us to remember to breathe, to open our hearts, and to practice our twenty-minute retreats. Other times, often when we need it the most, we lose our way on the spiritual path.

Too Busy

Sometimes we are just too busy with deadlines and workload to take even twenty minutes for ourselves to retreat. Even though I know those twenty minutes will be a great investment, allowing me to function more creatively and effectively in the rest of my day, I don't do it. When we're so stressed, it's very difficult to stop and switch gears. Yet that's exactly what's needed. Retreat time is slow time. The one-minute retreats are brief retreats, not fast retreats. I find they can be very helpful during busy times. Even a momentary respite or acknowledgment of our inner landscapes can help us perceive and approach the exterior challenges with greater calm and perspective.

This was certainly true for Carl, although he wouldn't express it that way. Carl came to me to learn how to reduce his stress, but there was no way he could do a twenty-minute retreat. He was legitimately too busy. At thirty-five, Carl was managing millions of dollars and a staff of twenty. He struggled daily to carve out a few minutes of personal time for his wife and young son. Of course, he did manage to get to the gym regularly and even catch a basketball game occasionally. I suggested Carl start with any retreat he could do lying in bed before falling asleep. This way, I pointed out, he didn't have to change his schedule.

Sometimes we have to outthink ourselves to get ourselves to do what's best. There was no way Carl could imagine finding even five minutes to devote to spiritual retreats. The time in bed before sleep was "found" time, time he hadn't thought of filling in any other way. So Carl ended up feeling that he gained time, rather than losing time to do a retreat. Then I asked him to take one more small step. I asked Carl to simply pause for a moment during his workday to remember how he felt during the retreat last night and perhaps even take a breath the way he did in the retreat. Finally, I suggested he take a few minutes at his desk to re-create his retreat experience. This describes one gradual approach to integrating retreats into a workday that is too busy. In fact, Carl found that pausing during his workday for these "breathers," as he teasingly called my retreat instructions, allowed him to clear his head so he could work more effectively. He didn't get home any earlier, but he was not quite as stressed after his busy day.

Emotional Quicksand

Do I have to explain what this means? Am I the only one in the world who falls into emotional quicksand? It's very hard to do a twenty-minute retreat when I feel as if I'm slowly sinking, mired in anything from self-pity, rejection, and insecurity, to guilt and self-blame. We each have a unique recipe for the particular quicksand to which we fall prey. Personally, I don't even want to hear about twenty-minute retreats at these times.

Needless to say, this is precisely the time when I most need a twenty-minute retreat to restore my psychological and spiritual equilibrium. What I have found is that I can only start with where I am. I can't do what sounds like it would be good for me. So I generally start with a journaling or emotional drawing retreat, one that gives me the opportunity to express what I'm feeling in the quicksand, so to speak.

What I found through this approach to my emotional quicksand is that once I'm able to express in the outer world what's going on inside of me, I begin to feel more objective. At least I stop sinking deeper into quicksand. After a few hours or a good night's sleep, I can read over my journaling and look at my drawing and recognize that I'm no longer in that exact same sinking place as I was. I gain some perspective and see that I've moved emotionally and spiritually. My view has shifted, sometimes ever so slightly, but enough to allow me to move on to another retreat, maybe one on healing or self-acceptance, maybe one on anger or dancing freely. Then I know that I've worked myself out of the lowest spot and can feel encouraged that I'm regaining my emotional equilibrium and my inner peace and calm.

*U*nder Attack

I think it's safe to say that we will all have the experience of being under attack at some time in our lives. Sometimes we will be able to understand the other person's ire, and sometimes we will be able to seek peace together. But there will likely be other times when we will have no clue what's behind the hostility being directed at us. We may simply be an unlucky bystander or an easy target. Either way, there will be nothing we can do to resolve it.

When we are under attack, this is an important time to use twenty-minute retreats, because continuing on our own spiritual path is the very best way to protect ourselves in these hostile situations. Our daily retreats will help us to tend our own gardens and not get caught up in someone else's battle. We'll be less likely to react defensively or in retaliation and more able to allow any negative energy to pass us by.

Sandra had a difficult neighbor in her apartment building. She had tried to be politely friendly and cooperative, but he regularly greeted her with a hostile stare. He was inconsiderate about noise in the very early morning, and he left his garbage out much longer than necessary. Polite requests were met with angry accusations.

Sandra was astonished by his vehemence, but she maintained an objective serenity that gave her an air of being extremely neutral and unflappable. Her retreat practice sustained her even in this hostile situation. She didn't react with anger or even impatience but instead chose to do retreats that cultivated peacefulness. Her neighbor eventually settled into a pattern of ignoring her, and this was as good an improvement as possible. Sandra continued with her retreats. You might think here about a strained situation in your life that may be relieved by a calm inner strength brought about by regular retreats.

At Work

We spend about a third of our adult lives working, and to the extent that we seek to integrate our retreat experience into our daily lives, we need to do so at work. Actually, *integrate* isn't quite the correct word. Work is an expression of our spiritual lives, if not the actual craft of what we do, then the way in which we handle ourselves in the workplace. How we behave during our workdays, including our attitudes; the way we treat other people; our decisions; and even the quality of our energy field—all reflect our retreat experiences.

The simplest, and one of the most accurate, descriptions of a spiritual life is how kind we are in our daily treatment of others. This is applicable no matter what type of work we do, no matter what the setting is. This doesn't mean we're not assertive, competitive, or ambitious. It just means we're kind.

If we could all just decide to be kind, there would be no need for spiritual retreats. Our ability to be consistently kind in our daily lives is a reflection of our progress along the inner spiritual path. And those moments when we're not kind or when we're reactive, are our teaching moments, our opportunities for a spiritual lesson. We just have to be aware and awake enough to get the message.

Paula is a good example of someone who would say she was on a spiritual path but hadn't yet made the connection that her everyday life *was* her spiritual path. Paula was a high-powered executive who had trouble keeping a secretary. She always expected too much, too soon, and no secretary was able to match her pace. Paula was just plain rude about her frustration at how her expectations were not being met. She'd say things like, "I gave you that yesterday! What is your problem? Why is it not on my desk?"

Paula's secretaries usually quit within six months and left a disorganized mess behind. It would take Paula a week to reorganize, catch up, and train another secretary, only to start the cycle all over again. Looking at someone else's life, the message seems startlingly clear: Paula's behavior was neither kind nor effective. Yet Paula didn't see her pattern, nor did she connect her spiritual life with her daily life at work. Paula didn't know how to use her emotional reactivity at work as grist for the mill, meaning as part of her spiritual practice. The peace retreats "Catch Yourself" and "Equanimity" would help her to do that.

Here's another example of how our behavior in the everyday work world not only reflects our spiritual life but actually *is* part of our spiritual path. Joseph was going for an interview for a teaching position at a well-respected high school. He parked his car in front of the school, and one of the teachers on duty outside asked him to park elsewhere. Now, of course Joseph would comply with this request. After all, he was seeking employment at the school. But it was the way Joseph responded to the request that made the difference. He approached the teacher and chatted at length about the school, the layout of the facilities, including the parking, and the community and kids the school served. Joseph was his usual self, warm and open. Then he went into the principal's office to wait for his job interview. The principal was the "teacher on duty outside." Joseph's handling of this situation helped him bond with the principal and start a good relationship with his new boss. He loves his new job teaching there.

Probably the most important retreat we can do while we're at work is simply to stop and take a breath. In that momentary pause we can reconnect with one of our twenty-minute retreats—we can open our heart, feel our feet on the ground, imagine we can breathe up through the top of our head, feel divine love, have compassion for our human condition, or shift perspective so we see the immediate situation completely differently. Giving ourselves that pause opens up a possibility for us, the possibility to reconnect to our deeper selves, our spiritual reality, and to respond from that greater source of wisdom.

I have heard this advice—to stop and breathe—from teachers representing each of the major religions of the world. It goes beyond the cultural belief systems of these different faiths and springs forth from the essence of spiritual teaching. Our retreat experiences are expressed in how we walk on the earth, how we see one another, and the kind and loving care we take with it all.

Traveling

One aspect of traveling is that there's plenty of opportunity for the unexpected to happen. We have so much less control traveling than when we're in our home territory. Weather, airplane and train schedules, traffic jams, lost reservations, logistical miscommunications—anything can happen. How you perceive such unexpected events will influence how you respond. If your judgment is that this delay is a disaster, then that's how you'll respond. If you see the same delay as a chance to make phone calls or finish a memo, then that's how you'll respond. With traveling, especially, we have the opportunity to see how we create our experience of the world and then react to it as if it's being imposed on us. Here is a retreat suggestion for relating to "The Unexpected."

Twenty-Minute Retreat—The Unexpected

When you're traveling, look forward to the unexpected as part of the adventure and mystery.

Step 1: *Entering into Retreat:* Whether you're stuck in an airplane on the runway or have just found out that your hotel no longer has room for you, stop and breathe. Use just three minutes to take a few deep breaths and feel the movement of your breath in your body. This will help calm down any worries, anxieties, and catastrophic thoughts.

Step 2: Then, look at the people you're dealing with or the people around you. For another three minutes, see them as spiritual beings, each on their own path. Block out the current context, if need be, to see them as sacred human beings.

Step 3: Now find a piece of paper for some quick journaling. Take about eight minutes to write down: What I can change in this situation; What I can't change in this situation. Include how you feel about the extent and limits of your influence. Also list one—two—three actions that are appropriate and realistic for you to do right now.

Step 4: For the next four minutes, breathe in *peace* and breathe out *calm*. Say and feel the words internally.

Step 5: *Returning to the World:* For the final two minutes, continue your peace/calm breathing and visualize yourself taking the actions listed in step 3. Imagine yourself behaving with loving-kindness toward all, including yourself.

Retreating in Hotel Rooms

Once you finally get to your destination, you'll find yourself in a hotel room crowded with the energy vibrations from previous guests. The problem is how to clear and cleanse this atmosphere so you can create a space for yourself. You have to be very careful of the risk of fire if you light a candle or incense. As an alternative, you can fill a glass of water and let it stand on a table. Water absorbs negative energy and will help purify the space. Just be careful you remember *not* to drink this water after it has sat and absorbed all the room's negative vibes.

The very best thing to do to prepare your hotel room for a retreat is pick up some fresh flowers. Often you can get them at the airport or a local grocery. If I'm traveling by car, I'll often stop to pick wildflowers along the way. Even just a few flowers will bring sparkling, fresh energy into a room.

Some people like to travel with small sacred objects like a crystal, a photograph, or an altar scarf. Unpacking a well-used retreat object and purposely placing it in the room immediately sets up a space for a personal retreat. Although you could use any of the twenty-minute retreats from the previous chapters, I would suggest you consider the following retreat on centering. It will help you feel present and prepared for whatever is the purpose of your traveling.

Centering

Step 1: *Entering into Retreat:* Start by standing up with eyes closed and no shoes on. Use the first five minutes to find your balanced center standing. Start by swaying front to back, gently leaning as far as you can in each direction, then gradually reduce the swaying until you come to a comfortable midpoint in the center. Then begin again, this time swaying side to side. Sway as far as you can in each direction, then gradually reduce the swaying until you come to a comfortable midpoint in the center. Find a compromise between these two midpoints (front-back and side-to-side) that you feel is a solid center for you right now.

Step 2: Sit down with as straight a back as is comfortable. Use the next five minutes to repeat step 1 in this new position. Notice if it's becoming easier for you to recognize the midpoint position. This physically centered position should be the easiest balance point for your sitting—where you feel you can sit up the straightest with the least effort.

Step 3: For the next five minutes, really keep focused on this inner center. Notice how you experience this inner center, what images describe it. Some people feel it as one centered point, while others describe an inner column. From this physical center, notice the flow of your breathing.

Step 4: *Returning to the World:* Stay centered. In other words, maintain your focus on this physical inner center. For the final five minutes, use your imagination to go through your planned schedule for the next day or so, as you maintain your center. Picture yourself in different situations and really staying centered.

𝒦indred Spirits

All of the retreats in this book can be practiced on your own or in a group setting. Well, maybe the nude dance retreat is a possible exception. But I have used most of these retreats in my workshops and lectures with intimate groups of ten to audiences of a few hundred people. The need to retreat, to experience the sacred, is universal.

I think we are, each of us, on a spiritual path. Some of us may not realize it or even care. Others of us may be temporarily lost or sidetracked, while the rest of us may be moving along, each at our own speed, in our own way. When a few of us get together for a spiritual retreat, something very magical happens. Retreating with a group can change the gifts we receive from retreats and alter our experience of them. For me, the atmosphere in the room changes, the silence is more still, and my experience deepens. I feel more personally whole and a greater part of a larger wholeness. The shared retreat experience supports and nourishes my daily individual retreat practice.

There are many privately organized retreat groups springing up all over the country. These are usually small, intimate groups of seven to ten people who come together to share their personal journeys and to support each other in their spiritual process. They may focus on dreams, creativity, prayer, or book discussions. Some meet weekly, others once a month, usually in members' homes. Leadership often rotates so everybody has a chance to create a retreat experience for the group. It's my hope that the retreats I've shared here will be a practical guide and source of inspiration for people joining together to enrich and expand their spiritual lives.

Extended retreats also enrich and inspire my practice of twenty-minute retreats. Extended retreats can last for a weekend, a week, forty days, or months. I find that these longer retreats are a totally different experience from a twenty-minute retreat and are usually done with a retreat director who focuses more deeply on one of the meditative traditions of the world's religions. I have emerged from these longer retreats with an interior spaciousness and silence—an inner sense of sacredness.

However, no matter how long the retreat, most of us return to the world, and go grocery shopping. To live in the world, while being continuously aware of the divine within me, within you, and within all, is my spiritual path. The twenty-minute retreats help me travel along that path.

What I've Learned

I reached a point in writing all of the retreat chapters where I said something like, "Real faith, forgiveness, gratitude, healing, intuition, joy, love, patience, peace, relaxation, self-acceptance, and self-care come from within and are independent of situational circumstances." Now, in my heart, I know this to be true. But most of the time in my life I am not that clear about it. How can I forgive, when she just did *xyz* again? How can I feel peace when there's fighting going on? How can I take care of myself in this toxic situation? I forget what I know to be true: I can choose to cultivate these qualities, no matter what the external circumstances are.

To keep this perspective requires a very broad capacity to embrace whatever is and open ourselves to accept those challenging situational circumstances. Jack Kornfield describes it this way in *A Path with Heart*: "To discover the capacity to bless whatever is in front of us, this is the enlightenment that is intimate with all things." To embrace what is without resistance, without judgment, without even hesitation, but solely because this is what is, *this* is the spiritual path. It's a path of transformation, and we are transformed as we journey. These retreats have continually renewed me as I've traveled along my path, and I hope they will do the same for you on your journey.

> *Our real journey in life is interior:*
> *it is a matter of growth, deepening,*
> *and of an ever greater surrender*
> *to the creative action of love*
> *and grace in our hearts.*
>
> —Thomas Merton

Bibliography

Albom, Mitch. *Tuesdays with Morrie*. New York: Doubleday, 1997.

Assagioli, Roberto. *Psychosynthesis*. New York: Viking, 1965.

Bacovcin, Helen, trans. *The Way of a Pilgrim*. New York: Image, 1977.

Bahá'u'lláh. *Tablets at Bahá'u'lláh Revealed after the Kitáb-i-Aqdas*. Wilmette: Bahá'í Publishing Trust, 1992.

Bair, Puran. *Living from the Heart*. New York: Three Rivers, 1998.

Barks, Coleman, and John Moyne, trans. *The Essential Rumi*. Edison, N.J.: Castle Books, 1995.

Benson, Herbert. *The Relaxation Response*. New York: Avon, 1975.

Bly, Robert. *The Kabir Book*. Boston: Beacon, 1971.

Boorstein, Sylvia. *Don't Just Do Something, Sit There*. San Francisco: HarperSanFrancisco, 1996.

Bradshaw, John. *Homecoming*. New York: Bantam, 1990.

Brennan, Barbara. *Hands of Light*. New York: Bantam, 1988.

Brooks, Charles V. W. *Sensory Awareness*. New York: Viking, 1974.

Bruyere, Rosalyn L. *Wheels of Light*. New York: Simon & Schuster, Fireside, 1989.

Burns, David D. *Feeling Good*. New York: Signet, 1980.

Cooper, David A. *Renewing Your Soul*. San Francisco: HarperSanFrancisco, 1995.

A Course in Miracles. New York: Foundation for Inner Peace, 1975.

Cousins, Norman. *Anatomy of an Illness*. New York: Bantam, 1979.

Dalai Lama. Foreword to *Peace in Every Step*, by Thich Nhat Hanh. New York: Bantam, 1991.

Das, Surya. *Awakening the Buddha Within*. New York: Broadway, 1997.

Dostoyevsky, Fyodor. *The Brothers Karamazov*. Chicago: Great Books, 1952.

Einstein, Patricia. *Intuition*. Rockport, Mass.: Element, 1997.

Feldenkrais, Moshe. *Awareness through Movement*. New York: Harper & Row, 1972.

Fischer, Louis. *Gandhi*. New York: Mentor, 1954.

Foster, Richard J. *Celebration of Discipline*. San Francisco: HarperSan Francisco, 1978.

Fowler, James W. *Stages of Faith*. San Francisco: HarperSanFrancisco, 1981.

Friedman, Philip, and Gail Eisen. *The Pilates Method*. New York: Doubleday, 1980.

George, Mike. *Learn to Relax*. San Francisco: Chronicle, 1998.

Goldberg, Philip. *The Intuitive Edge*. Los Angeles: Jeremy P. Tarcher, 1983.

Goleman, Daniel, ed. *Healing Emotions*. Boston: Shambhala, 1997.

Gray, Eden. *Mastering the Tarot*. New York: Signet, 1971.

Harvey, Andrew. *The Essential Mystics*. San Francisco: HarperSanFrancisco, 1996.

Hirshfield, Jane, and Mariko Aratami, trans. *The Ink Dark Moon*. New York: Vintage, 1986.

Hubbard, L. Ron. *Dianetics*. New York: Paperback Library, 1950.

Iyengar, B. K. S. *Light on Yoga*. New York: Schocken, 1965.

Jones, Alan. *SoulMaking*. San Francisco: HarperSanFrancisco, 1985.

Jung, C. G.*The Archetypes and the Collective Unconscious*. Princeton, N.J.: Princeton University Press, 1959.

———. *Mandala Symbolism*. Princeton, N.J.: Bollingen, 1959.

Keeney, Bradford. *Everyday Soul*. New York: Riverhead, 1996.

Kornfield, Jack. *A Path with Heart*. New York: Bantam, 1993.

Labowitz, Shoni. *Miraculous Living*. New York: Simon & Schuster, Fireside, 1996.

Lasater, Judith. *Relax and Renew*. Berkeley, Calif.: Rodmell, 1995.

Laubach, Frank C. *Learning the Vocabulary of God*. Nashville: Upper Room, 1956.

Lesser, Elizabeth. *The New American Spirituality*. New York: Random House, 1999.

Levine, Stephen. *Healing into Life and Death*. New York: Anchor, 1987.

Levy, Fran. *Dance Movement Therapy*. Reston, Va.: Alliance for Health, Physical Education, Recreation, and Dance, 1988.

Louden, Jennifer. *The Woman's Comfort Book*. San Francisco: HarperSanFrancisco, 1992.

———. *The Woman's Retreat Book*. San Francisco: HarperSanFrancisco, 1997.

McKay, Matthew, and Patrick Fanning. *Prisoners of Belief*. Oakland, Calif.: New Harbinger, 1991.

Merton, Thomas. *Contemplative Prayer*. New York: Image Books, 1969.

———. *Thoughts in Solitude*. New York: Farrar, Straus & Giroux, 1956.

Miller, Alice. *Pictures of a Childhood*. New York: Farrar, Straus & Giroux, 1986.

Mitchell, Edgar. In *The Home Planet,* edited by Kevin W. Keeley. New York: Addison-Wesley, 1988.

Mitchell, Stephen, ed. *Tao Te Ching*, by Lao-tzu. New York: HarperPerennial, 1988.

Moody, Harry R., and David Carroll. *The Five Stages of the Soul*. New York: Anchor, 1997.

Mookerjee, Ajit. *Kundalini*. New York: Destiny, 1982.

Nhat Hanh, Thich. *Peace in Every Step*. New York: Bantam, 1991.

Nouwen, Henri J. *Out of Solitude*. Notre Dame, Ind.: Ave Maria Press, 1983.

Novak, Philip. *The World's Wisdom*. San Francisco: HarperSanFrancisco, 1994.

Paramananda, Swami. *Silence as Yoga*. Boston, Mass.: The Vedanta Center, 1974.

Peck, M. Scott. *The Road Less Traveled*. New York: Touchstone, 1978.

Perls, Frederick S. *Gestalt Therapy Verbatim*. Lafayette, Calif.: Real People, 1969.

Pierrakos, John. *Core Energetics*. Mendocino, Calif.: Life Rhythms, 1987.

Pipher, Mary. *Reviving Ophelia*. New York: Ballantine, 1994.

Prager, Marcia. *The Path of Blessing*. New York: Bell Tower, 1998.

Progoff, Ira. *At a Journal Workshop*. New York: Jeremy P. Tarcher, 1975.

Reed, Henry. *Edgar Cayce*. New York: Time Warner, 1989.

Rogers, Carl. *On Becoming a Person*. Boston: Houghton Mifflin, 1961.

Rolf, Ida P. *Rolfing*. Santa Monica, Calif.: Dennis-Landman, 1977.

Salzberg, Sharon. *Lovingkindness*. Boston: Shambhala, 1997.

Smith, Robert Lawrence. *A Quaker Book of Wisdom*. New York: Eagle Brook, 1998.

Space. Rohnert Park, Calif.: Pomegranate Art Books, 1998.

Starhawk. *The Spiral Dance*. San Francisco: HarperSanFrancisco, 1979.

Stendle-Rast, David. *Gratefulness, the Heart of Prayer*. New York: Paulist Press, 1984.

Sufi Order of the West. *Toward the One*. New York: Harper, 1974.

Teish, Luisa. *Jambalaya*. San Francisco: HarperSanFrancisco, 1985.

Vaughan, Frances. *Awakening Intuition*. New York: Anchor, 1979.

A View of the Universe. Rohnert Park, Calif.: Pomegranate Art Books, 1997.

Waite, Arthur Edward. *The Pictorial Key to the Tarot*. New York: University Books, 1959.

Wiesenthal, Simon. *The Sunflower*. New York: Schocken, 1997.

Wilhelm, Richard, trans. *The I Ching*. Princeton, N.J.: Princeton University Press, 1950.

Yogananda, Paramahansa. *Whispers from Eternity*. Los Angeles: Self Realization Fellowship, 1975.

Index

Index

children
  gratitude in, 74–75
  joy in, 136–37, 141–42
  patience in, 174
Christianity, 162, 220
chronic pain, 217–18
clock, 23
Cloud of Unknowing, The, 24
cognitive therapy, 28, 39, 65, 79–80, 141, 160, 179, 182, 240, 245
cold compresses, 269
compassion
  toward oneself, 69–70
control, 46, 48, 175–76, 179–80
  letting go of, 44
Cooper, David, 204
Copland, Aaron, 140
core beliefs, 160
Core energetics, 29–30
Cousins, Norman, 142
creative expression, 24, 27, 41, 229
creative process, 190–92
  intuition in, 111–12, 116–17
crystals, 23
cultural values, 234, 242

daily retreats, 11–12, 13–14
  time for, 15–17
Dalai Lama, 16, 195, 207, 208, 234
dance therapy, 29, 143
dancing, 142–44, 236, 242
dark times, 33–34
death, 35, 49, 66, 82–83
depression, 135–36
desensitization, 241, 247
Dianetics (Hubbard), 143
divination tools, 23–24
divine (the), 6, 273
Don't Just Do Something, Sit There (Boorstein), 184
Dostoyevsky, Fyodor, 166
dream journal, 116–17
dreams, 26, 28

earth (element), 104
Edgar Cayce (Reed), 120
Einstein, Patricia, 124
emotional drawing, 7, 27, 41, 71, 79, 210–11, 230, 250, 275
emotional intuition, 112, 125
emotional quicksand, 274–75
emotional reactivity, 196–97, 198, 277

empathy
  emotional, 125
  intuitive, 112–13
energy field, 93, 145, 164, 215, 264, 276
  smoothing, 31, 93, 199, 200
Energy Healing, 30–31
equanimity, 6, 197, 200–1, 277
escape, 217–18
Everyday Soul (Keeney), 115
eyes, healing, 99

faith, 17, 33–51, 282
  in face of loss, 34–35
  retreats to cultivate, 8, 14, 23, 39–51
  tests of, 35–36
faith retreat
  signs one needs, 36–37
Fanning, Patrick, 160
fantasy, 28
Farmer's Almanac, 139
fear, 250–51
Feeling Good (Burns), 28
feet, focus on, 231
Feldenkrais, Moshe, 29, 266
Feldenkrais movement, 29
fire (element), 104
five-minute retreats, 15, 16
  faith, 32, 38, 40, 47
  forgiveness, 55, 59, 69
  gratitude, 80, 83, 85, 88
  healing, 97, 104, 107
  intuition, 116, 123, 127
  joy, 141, 146, 148
  love, 159, 166, 171
  patience, 184, 187, 191
  peace, 197, 200, 202
  relaxation, 216, 220, 222, 226, 231
  self-acceptance, 247, 249, 251
  self-care, 259, 260, 264, 269
food, 265–66
  pleasure in, 146–47
forgiveness, 52–72, 282
  resistance to, 55
  retreats to cultivate, 8, 14, 59–72
forgiveness retreat
  signs one needs, 57
forgiving others, 53–54
forgiving ourselves, 56–57
Four Elemental Breaths, 26, 65, 104
Fowler, Jim, 41
Freud, Sigmund, 28, 29

Index